CRAFTING
CRIME
FICTION

Manchester University Press

CRAFTING CRIME FICTION

Henry Sutton

Manchester University Press

Published by Manchester University Press
Oxford Road, Manchester M13 9PL
www.manchesteruniversitypress.co.uk

British Library Cataloguing-in-Publication Data
A catalogue record for this book is available from the British Library

ISBN 978 1 5261 6051 5 paperback

First published 2023

Typeset
by Cheshire Typesetting Ltd, Cuddington, Cheshire
Printed in Great Britain
by Bell & Bain Ltd, Glasgow

CONTENTS

INTRODUCTION: BEGINNINGS

What is crime fiction? Let's start here, with the biggest mystery of all. Or is it? This book will ask many questions and hopefully answer quite a few. Crime fiction is spectacularly dynamic. It's also, of all the genres, very much of the moment. As a writer you can't second-guess it, and there's no point jumping on a bandwagon if you want to be original, successful and true to yourself. The genre (and this term will be variously used and interrogated in due course) is far-reaching. It's inclusive, it's individual. Contrary to old beliefs, old habits, it loves busting boundaries and breaking rules. I like to think that it's the genre that got away, and kept running. *Catch me if you can …*

Pace is intrinsic to crime fiction: structurally, practically and theoretically. This book will also endeavour to shift with purpose and energy, and entertain. The novel was designed as a unit of new entertainment, let's not forget, and the crime novel perhaps even more so. And it is the novel, both long, and preferably short, on which this book will focus. One of the few commonalities of the genre is that crime writers tend to work at speed. Georges Simenon wrote the Maigret novels in days: on average, fourteen. Ed McBain spent nine days a pop on his early 87th Precinct novels. Patricia Highsmith usually took around three months' writing time on a novel. Such speed fits the dynamism of the genre as it forever and urgently breaks new ground. It also, arguably, cuts out a lot of waffle. Being succinct is another great commonality. Too much interiority, too much description, too much indecision will sink any plot; at least if you're looking for a plot that moves with purpose and strives to appeal to more than a very few. Crime fiction is not elitist. It needs an audience, and why not an audience as large and as international as possible?

This breadth of appeal lies at the heart of genre fiction, of popular fiction, as opposed to what some term 'literary fiction'. Literary fiction can seemingly exist on its own terms, with or without a large audience, because it's 'important': artistically, culturally, politically, academically. Yet genre fiction and crime fiction particularly can be just as 'important'. More so, you could argue, because the mass-market appeal means it invariably has a bigger reach, a bigger audience, a much bigger sphere of influence.

Raymond Chandler, who was forever troubled by literary insecurity, angrily nailed it in his landmark 1950 essay, 'The Simple Art of Murder'. Attacking Dorothy L. Sayers for daring to suggest that crime fiction, or in fact the detective novel, was a 'literature of escape' and not a 'literature of expression', Chandler declared that such labelling was 'critics' jargon, a use of abstract words as if they had absolute meanings'.[1] For Chandler, the most important thing was that 'everything written with vitality expresses that vitality', and that 'there are no dull subjects, only dull minds'. Recently, I realised that for years I had invented a Chandler quote, in relation to this essay, and often recalled it while teaching. As Chandler declared, I'd say in class: 'There is no such thing as literary writing, there is only good writing and bad writing.' I can no longer find this quote anywhere. But it is something I believe, passionately, whether Chandler ever said it or not.

Bad writing can be popular in spite of its shortcomings, though never as popular as good writing. The fact is that good popular writing is extremely hard, and quite rare. It's potentially far harder to pull off than good literary writing, because it's arguably determined by purpose, style and accessibility, as opposed to individuality of expression. Also to be contemplated is audience, and who we're writing for. Form and control, knowing what you are doing and who you are doing it for, can determine fiction that works with real intent.

Lee Child was particularly vocal on the literary/genre divide, well before he retired and judged the Booker Prize. 'We're doing our thing,' he said, when I interviewed him at the University of East Anglia (UEA) in 2013, 'and they are doing their thing – ours is very big and theirs is very small. They know that we could write their books but they can't write ours.'[2] Literary writers, he suggested, don't get what it takes to 'create suspense and evolve a story, with a non-stop, seamless narration'. In other words, I believe, he was talking about the importance of form and craft.

He used the analogy of manufacturing a Ferrari compared to a Ford. One of these is a no-expense-spared indulgence for a tiny few, and the other is a utilitarian tool of immense global use at a reasonable cost. Interestingly, Lee Child decided to retire from writing fiction and the Jack Reacher novels at the age of 65, and hand on the legacy – to his younger brother – just as if it were any other retirement from a family-run business. No pretension, no fuss. However, in practice hitting that universal

Crafting crime fiction

'utilitarian' sweet spot isn't just about approach, or even having an idea of an audience. It's much more about authenticity, being true to yourself, and believing in what you are doing. You need to bring to the table the right goods in the right order. Readers sniff out frauds with remarkable ease. Believing in and knowing what you are doing takes time and experience, and this book, like much of my teaching, is designed to speed up and enable that process. Creative writing courses, such as the ones I've run at UEA, can't make brilliant writers, but they can make good writers into better writers. They can spot potential and they can accelerate and focus the learning curve. Vitally, they can also create a constructive and supportive environment: a place where you'll find like-minded individuals; a place where advice and insight are readily given; a place to absorb and collaborate. Writing should not be lonely, nor should it be excruciatingly hard work. It should be fun, certainly if your aim is to entertain.

Graham Greene, as we know, divided his work into 'entertainments' and 'other novels'. It was a ruse to attract interest from the film industry and push up sales. Few critics can determine a difference in 'literary' quality from, say, novels such as *Brighton Rock*, *Our Man in Havana* and *A Gun For Sale*, to *The End of the Affair*, *The Heart of the Matter* and *The Power and Glory*. If anything, the former are more engaging. Is that a problem, and for who?

The 'literary' writer and Booker Prize winner John Banville took to writing crime fiction (including even a Philip Marlowe mystery, *The Black-Eyed Blonde*) under the pseudonym Benjamin Black. Ever outspoken, he created a furore among crime writing circles when he suggested at a crime writing festival that writing a Black novel was infinitely easier and more enjoyable

Introduction: beginnings

than writing a Banville novel. This was largely seen as dismissive of the skill and effort needed to write good crime fiction. I think this reaction was misconceived, as did Banville. He elaborated on this when I interviewed him some years later. It could take him twelve hours or so to write a paragraph for a Banville novel, where he would enter an almost a trancelike state. 'It's very painful,' he said, 'exhausting.' He didn't seem particularly proud of it. Whereas, writing a Black novel he'd whip out 3,000 words in a couple of hours and enjoy every minute. Writing crime fiction, just as reading it, should never be torture, least of all achingly slow torture. Provocatively, Banville went on to say: 'Most contemporary literary fiction is weak. The novel has to be about life, not just language.'[3] Similar to Lee Child's former practice and approach, he described 'Benjamin Black' as his day job. Vitally, he then explained: 'A crime novel has to have a crime in it, but just because a novel has a crime in it doesn't mean it's a crime novel. What it comes down to is craft. The essence of writing crime fiction is speed and fluency.'

According to Patricia Highsmith it's also individuality, while knowing how to develop a strong story idea; which is both practical and thematic. Highsmith did say, in her intriguing and non-prescriptive guide, *Plotting and Writing Suspense Fiction*, that 'good books write themselves'.[4] Sadly, I don't think this is true. Perhaps more importantly, she explained exactly what she thought was behind a good novel. 'It is the joy of writing, which cannot really be described, cannot be captured in words and handed to someone else to share or make use of.' I would like this book to be a joyful experience to read. I also hope it might make your journey into the next chapter of your crime writing and reading life as pleasurable and rewarding as possible. A good recent example of a writer having fun with the genre while being practically and thematically innovative is Oyinkan Braithwaite's *My Sister, The Serial Killer*. This mini-masterpiece was rightfully lauded across the literary genre divide for paying homage to old 'serial killer' tropes while showing heaps of humility, humanity and of course dark humour. It was fresh and funny, and knowing (and will be discussed further in Chapter 7).

The 'genre' has so much possibility still. Many writers and critics talk about how we're in a second golden age of crime writing. If we are, it's one that's far more open, enlightened, innovative and inspiring. This book will not be prescriptive, and it certainly won't abide by any rules. There won't be any limbering-up exercises, or what I think of as time-wasting automatic-writing prompts. Writing a good book requires control and persistence – albeit in as short a time-frame as possible. It also requires a good story idea, and that really is all up to you. Your book won't write itself, Patricia Highsmith won't write it for you, and neither, I'm sorry to say, will I. However, over the next nine chapters you'll find ways and ideas to make the process easier, more fulfilling and more knowing. There will be new approaches and new ways of looking at old concepts. There will be consolidation and simplification. It's the stuff I wish I'd known twenty-five years ago, though some of that stuff was not known back then, simply because the genre moves so damn fast. It's an amalgamation and a distillation of my reading, writing, teaching and interviewing experiences.

As a literary editor, critic and festival director, I have interviewed numerous international writers and crime writers. The range of news and review outlets I've worked for also allowed me to quiz both the key 'literary' and 'popular' writers around: everyone from Don DeLillo to Attica Locke, from Kazuo

Introduction: beginnings

Ishiguro to Yrsa Sigurðardóttir. Listening to writers (of all genres), to how they approach their craft, their themes, their audiences, has been invaluable for me. But I've also learnt a huge amount from less well-known and fledging writers, including creative writing students. Engaging in practical and thematic creative conversations with committed writers at all stages of their careers is always rewarding. New approaches largely come from new writers. Teaching is a constant wake-up call, while as a fiction writer you never stop trying to be better, trying to produce the best novel you can. The reason we continue is because we never get it just right, we never finally crack it, and so we never lose the compulsion to keep writing.

My own initial studies were not in creative writing: I studied journalism. I studied journalism because I wanted to be a writer, and thought this would be the best training – training on the job, if you like. Many writers I deeply admire trained and worked as journalists, including, notably, Val McDermid, Michael Connelly, Stieg Larsson, Maj Sjöwall and Per Wahlöö. Go back a bit further and there's Fred Vargas, Jim Thompson and James M. Cain. To this day, I write to a word count: daily targets, weekly targets, monthly targets. I know how long a novel will take before I start writing (though I'm nothing like as quick as I'd like to be). I aim for succinctness and clarity, and getting the 'story' in the right order – structure, in other words. Journalism helped greatly with this approach. But aiming for something and executing it are two different things. The word-count targets are perhaps more help in relation to persistence, consistency, continuity and commitment. They make it easier, more possible, more doable. Think in bite-size pieces and after a while you'll end up with a cake …

Crafting crime fiction

But fiction is not journalism, and crime fiction, as Banville/Black articulated, requires special attributes. I have come to think of the crime novel as the perfect form of the novel: a distillation of decades, of centuries of literary entertainment and enlightenment. That distillation, that dynamism continues naturally and vitally. It's for you as a crime writer to run with, to make your own. I began slowly, rudderless, low on resources, without experience. I knew only one thing – that I wanted to write fiction, I wanted to write a novel. It's what I'd always wanted to do. That compulsion is pretty important, because all the odds are stacked against a successful outcome. And this is where having the right approach as you begin is fundamental. You have to enjoy what you are doing. The actual process of writing has to be fulfilling, and as fulfilling and necessary as reading.

The subject matter of my first novel, like millions of others, was very much about what I knew and felt strongly about. In this case it was my despicable grandmother and her outrageous sisters. The result, *Gorleston*,[5] was a comedy of sorts, and billed as modern British fiction. It was not a crime novel in any sense. My next three novels were not crime novels. A generous description might be something like 'explorations of dysfunctional relationships, in contemporary settings'. I couldn't get beyond what I thought were meaningful observations and reflections, with some nice descriptions. There was too much interiority and not enough direction. I didn't then know the difference between plot and story, even what a plot was. Points of view drifted. Coincidence and character passivity dominated. I didn't know what my audience might be, or have much control over the register I was aiming for. I was lurching around in the swamp of indecision, overly relying on the writing to do the

Introduction: beginnings

thinking. You could say, my work was weak, in the doldrums, and I was very confused, if not deflated. Then I wrote a novel called *Kids' Stuff* and everything changed.

Increasingly, I'd been reading noir suspense and aspects of its more contemporary manifestation, the psychological thriller. The idea of writing a series had always appealed. Being a methodical writer I got the expansive consistency, and also the heightened productivity: the speed of production and the regularity of publication. But the idea of writing a detective novel didn't particularly appeal. I was not so interested in police procedure, or some peculiar private eye. It seemed too much like journalism, founded on research and factual accuracy, or worse, whimsy masquerading as originality. I had yet to encounter P. D. James' line on G. K. Chesterton (who was also a journalist of sorts), where she said: 'He was among the first writers to realise that it could be a vehicle for exploring and exposing the condition of society, and for saying something true about human nature.' Flash forward ninety years and writers such as Attica Locke and Sara Collins, both who employ strong detective fiction traits, are not just 'exposing the condition of society', but directly addressing contemporary and historical injustices. They are doing so with such verve and integrity it takes your breath away. As Attica Locke said in her 2021 Noirwich Crime Writing Festival lecture: 'I explore the crimes behind the crimes.'[6] These invariably are societal, state-induced.

It took me a while to begin to understand the nuances and dynamism of the 'Golden Age' writers, along with the vast reach of suspense writers, such as my favourite, James M. Cain, who in a *Paris Review* interview memorably said that he didn't care for detective fiction; he wrote love stories. Years later

Crafting crime fiction

I would devise a Master's module, The Writing of Crime/ Thriller Fiction, which began with a seminar on 1932, the year that Cain published *The Postman Always Rings Twice* and Agatha Christie published *Murder on the Orient Express* – two very different novels. As a fledgling novelist, however, I had yet to appreciate these ideas, or indeed the sheer practical and theoretical diversity available to the crime writer. I ploughed on writing what I thought was a 'straight novel', albeit one with a very dark ending. My then editor at Serpent's Tail, the legendary Pete Ayrton, surprised me when he said that *Kids' Stuff* was the most chilling depiction of a psychopath he'd ever read, and that the novel was pure noir. (I thought I'd been writing about another family member …)

Terms and categories such as noir (and one of its later incarnations, domestic noir), detective fiction, the police procedural, psychological suspense, sensation and hard-boiled will be explored from the perspective of the writer, shining a light on the writer's craft, or toolkit, and how I've approached such 'sub-genres' with my own writing. I'll be as candid and open as possible as to where I have gone badly astray and where others have certainly succeeded (if a writer can ever truly succeed). A strong story idea is one thing, but how to focus that story, how to people it, how to get the right register and effect, how to make it engaging and thrilling, with meaning and consistently strong syntactical composure, are others. The crime novel, as we know, needs more than just a crime in it. It needs more than a solution. The theory of literary detection has been variously explored by the likes of W. H. Auden, Gertrude Stein, Tzvetan Todorov, Heather Worthington and Lee Horsley, alongside the more common theoretical approaches to plot outlined by E. M. Forster, Boris Tomashevsky, David Lodge, James Wood

Introduction: beginnings

and Rita Felski. Screenwriters such as Robert McKee and John Yorke have huge currency in genre fiction writing worlds, primarily because of the idea that they know about 'plot' and 'structure'. I have shelves of this material. Just how useful such theory, literary critical and practical approaches are to crime writers and/or creative writers is arguable. In many ways you have to pick the bits that resonate. You'll find my picks in this book along with, perhaps more importantly, what many key writers have to say about their process.

At UEA I became known for being obsessive about plot and point of view. I even have *Plot* and *Point of View* posters in my office: a (part) satirical gift from a colleague. The two concepts are intrinsically linked, and determine the direction and success of any long-form fiction. You can't begin without them. Naturally they are the focus of Chapter 1. Before you dip in, I would like to leave this introduction by offering the two phrases that have come to define my approach to writing crime fiction and which determine my teaching. They are: pace and purpose; menace and motivation. I'd also like to reiterate how collaborative writing is. Imaginative writing stems from questions as well as conversations: conversations with others and yourself. It's a pleasure to have you here with us. Enjoy the ride.

1

PLOT AND POINT OF VIEW

What is plot?

Even titling this chapter 'Plot and point of view' feels a little controversial, not least because character plays such a crucial role. We can't discuss plot and point of view (POV) without character. To me and many others, plot and character are completely entwined. You can't have – or see, or hear, or smell, or taste or understand – character without POV, whether from the perspective of that character, or another character who's doing the observing, or from an authorial or omniscient stance. So why not start with character? Well, we're not starting with character because character involves more than the narrator(s) or protagonist(s) thinking their way into a story. It involves character depth and evolution. It involves subsidiary characters, and all manner of relationships. Character builds on and develops plot. Character enhances and complicates POV. Character takes time: arguably, a whole novel.

We're beginning with plot and POV because, to me, these are the foundations from which character and characterisation spring. Of course, we could begin with character and see where he/she/they might take us. However, because crime fiction needs to move with purpose, with pace, with, as you already know, menace and motivation, a character will not be able to do that on their own, or at least without some 'authorial' design. We want to begin with energy, focus, drama. Allowing a character to dictate from the beginning can lead to all sorts of problems, especially if you haven't thought enough about that character. Even if you have, it's extremely common to ditch the first few paragraphs, pages or chapters, and for good reason. They'll be slow, emotionally hesitant, ill-considered. And please don't contemplate a prologue until you have finished the first full draft. Or if you can't resist and feel it'll help you get into the flow, write it, then put it away until you have finished that first draft. I bet you it'll then seem either irrelevant or inappropriate. (I'll talk more about prologues in Chapter 5.)

John le Carré offered the best advice I've ever heard as to where to begin a novel. 'As near to the end as possible', he said.[1] (Except le Carré had in fact borrowed this line from Kurt Vonnegut's '8 Basics of Creative Writing'.)[2] The only problem with this concept is that you'll need to have a pretty good idea about what that ending will be in order to have any chance of being able to start a novel 'near' it. John le Carré had plenty of wonderful advice for writers, some more original than others, in fact, and came up with this pithy idea: '"The cat sat on the mat is not the beginning of a plot, but "the cat sat on the dog's mat" is.'[3] This is of course a riff on famous advice from E. M. Forster about just what plot is, as opposed to story. I never get bored of reciting these lines, first aired in his series of lectures for Cambridge University in 1927, which became *Aspects of the Novel*. Forster's chapter on plot is essential reading for any fiction writer. Within it you'll find his simple explanation:

Crafting crime fiction

'The king died and then the queen died' is a story. 'The King died, and then the queen died of grief' is a plot.

Forster's point was one of 'causality'. Or put it another way, the why and the because. He went on to elaborate:

'The queen died, no one knew why, until it was discovered that it was through grief at the death of the king.' This is a plot with a mystery in it, a form capable of high development.[4]

P. D. James put a further twist on this in her non-fiction work *Talking about Detective Fiction*, saying:

To that I would add, 'Everyone thought that the queen had died of grief until they discovered the puncture mark in the throat.' That is a murder mystery …[5]

Forster's theories on plot, while groundbreaking in English literature at the time, coincided with a Russian Formalist's. Boris Tomashevsky's essay 'Thematics' actually came out two years before Forster's lectures, but it was not translated into English until the 1960s. Tomashevsky took an effectively mathematical approach when analysing key situations or developments in a host of novels. His work is full of diagrams and equations concerned with chronology and causation.

His premise was that plot was an entirely artistic creation of 'story', stating: 'The development of story may generally be understood as a progress from one situation to another, so that each situation is characterised by a *conflict* of interest, by discord and struggle among the characters.'

It's perhaps worth emphasising here what story is (because numerous writers, including Margaret Atwood in her short story *Happy Endings*, get it wrong, or at least the wrong way round – check it out once you've read this chapter).[6] The term

14

is also further complicated, if not confused, by its appropriation
by screenwriters. My understanding, and the premise of my
writing and teaching, is that it is this:

> Story is a sequence of events, while plot is how the events in a
> story relate to one another through cause and effect. The term
> 'narrative' technically relates to story and time.

Plot, as defined above, is really the engine of a novel. It drives
the fiction forward, is intrinsic to character, and is quite distinct
from what is variously termed the 'puzzle plot', or 'clue plotting', as most obviously found in traditional, Golden Age detective fiction. Such 'puzzle plots', as executed by the likes of
Agatha Christie and Dorothy L. Sayers, are reliant on events,
clues, ingenuity and aspects of investigation and deduction, and
are conceivably devoid of character development or insight.
P. D. James described them as often 'ingenious but lifeless sub-
literary puzzles'.[7] Some works, such as, famously, Sayers' *Gaudy
Nights*, stretched to reflections on 'society's conscience',[8] tackling
aspects of social realism, but the overriding conception was one
of escapism and contrivance, rather than literary expression,
or anything more freewheeling and natural. Such sub-genres
and their contemporary global manifestations will be discussed
in Chapter 9, because for now we need to concentrate on the
engine: on getting that plot, and a plot in its truest theoretical
form, into gear.

Before we do wield our spanners, it might be worth spend-
ing a brief moment with Aristotle. Aristotle's *Poetics*[9] established
the dramatic framework around a beginning, middle and end.
He was quite clear all those centuries ago that 'incidents' are the
raw material of drama (or story), while 'plot' is the abstract concept referring to the organisation of the incidents. Interestingly,

the same incidents can be organised in different sequences, with each different arrangement resulting in different 'plots'. Story, to summarise Aristotle, is the natural chronological order of events before the storyteller turns them into a plot.

While theory can be a pretty dry concept, and frankly off-putting to a creative writer, my point in including a little here is to allow a greater understanding of the mechanics of what we are doing when planning and writing our crime novels. Being in control of the material, from both a thematic and craft perspective, I've found to be crucial. Planning is part of the plotting process. Stephen King has some stern things to say about plot in his classic *On Writing*. 'I won't try to convince you that I've never plotted any more than I'd try to convince you that I've never told a lie,' he wrote, 'but I do both as infrequently as possible. I distrust plot for two reasons: first because our lives are largely plotless, even when you add in all our reasonable precautions and careful planning; and second, because I believe plotting and the spontaneity of real creation aren't compatible.' He went to echo Patricia Highsmith, declaring: 'I want you to understand that my basic belief about the making of stories is that they pretty much make themselves.'[10]

In *Plotting and Writing Suspense Fiction* Highsmith elaborated: 'A plot should never be a rigid thing in the writer's mind, when he starts to work. A plot should not even be completed. I have to think of my own entertainment, and I like surprises.'[11] Nevertheless, Highsmith thought deeply and consistently about her work-in-progress, which in my mind is akin to 'plotting'. It might not be writing it down in bullet points, or sketching scenes and chapters, but thinking ahead first does not lead to writing blind. 'I make a habit to think about the next day's work at the end of a day's stint',[12] she wrote in *Plotting*. She also suggested that she spent many weeks and sometimes months thinking about a new work before putting pen to paper.

Interestingly, King thinks his way into a story before writing, and tellingly, he uses an Aristotelian premise. 'The situation comes first', he states in *On Writing*. 'The characters – always flat and unfeatured, to begin with – come next. Once things are fixed in my mind, I begin to narrate.' He goes on to reveal: 'I often have an idea of what the outcome may be, but I have never demanded of a set of characters that they do things my way.'[13] But he often has an idea … What crime writer doesn't before beginning? Professor Leslie Epstein, the former Director of Boston University's Creative Writing Department,[14] is known for his forthright and somewhat strict views on writing approaches. Apocryphally, he believes that a fiction writer needs to know 'between 68 and 72 per cent of the ending' before writing. Know any less and you are 'swaying around in the swamp of indecision'. Know any more and you are 'strait-jacketed'. There does seem to be something almost too 'cool' about implying you don't plot. It's like homework and school. All the really bright, cool kids don't do homework, but always somehow get the top marks. Top writers don't need to plot because their stories write themselves and there's an inherent authenticity to this. Too much work beforehand will kill the freshness, the originality, not least the spontaneity, the argument continues.

That approach, like the kids who supposedly never do homework, will never get most writers very far. Crime fiction, that is fiction that moves with pace and purpose, relies on planning, on plotting, on craft. King actually reveals quite a bit about his approach in *On Writing*, perhaps more than he'd intended. While he declared that he leaned 'more heavily on intuition', he said he was able to do this because 'my books are based on situation rather than story'. He continued: 'I want to put a group of characters (perhaps a pair; perhaps even just one) in some sort of predicament and then watch them try to work themselves free.'[15]

Situation doesn't appear out of nowhere. It is part of plot. It's where story becomes rearranged. Or as Aristotle put it and as we already know, plot is the abstract concept of referring to the organisation of the incidents of drama. For Aristotle incidents, or for that matter situations, represent the 'raw material'. The same incidents, or situations, can be organised in different sequences with each different arrangement resulting in different 'plots'. Strikingly, Ruth Rendell began her novel *A Judgement in Stone* by completely shuffling the pack and starting with not only the ending, but the full reveal.

> Eunice Parchman killed the Coverdale family because she could not read or write.

Having immediately been told who did it, the second paragraph begins the explanation, the 'why', with the 'how' coming much later.

> There was no real motive and no premeditation. No money was gained and no security. As a result of her crime, Eunice Parchman's disability was made known not to a mere family or a handful of villagers but to the whole country. She accomplished by it nothing but disaster for herself, and all along, somewhere in her strange mind, she knew she would accomplish nothing. And yet, although her companion and partner was mad, Eunice was not. She had the awful practical sanity of the atavistic ape disguised as twentieth-century woman.[16]

This was Rendell subverting known crime fiction, or in reality detective fiction, traits, by reversing the order of information and information reveals, and what the reader might have been expecting from such a crime fiction novel, to give us the answer first. Except that answer was just fact. It was what was behind the fact that was the real story, the real mystery. She shifted the terrain from the whodunnit to the whydunnit, moving from the basic elements of deduction and reveal to a place that explored psychological disturbance, and an old woman pushed to her limits. This was partly because Eunice Parchman could not read or write, but also partly because why she could not read or write. Society, and numerous failings and prejudices, as Rendell depicts, were as much to blame as a fractured mind.

Aristotle

Aristotle deemed that tragedy comprised six elements: plot, character, reasoning, diction, song and spectacle. The order is specific, with character subservient to plot. Effectively, the plot is the source and the soul of tragedy, while character comes second. As I've implied, plot and character are intrinsically linked. Nevertheless, and with the notion that writers (and certainly writers of crime fiction) have to begin somewhere, this is why plot is edging character in the chapter sequence of this book. For the sake of my clarity, and to cut the theory to a minimum, I work on the premise that while characters determine the overall destiny (and success) of a fiction, the author envisages, if not contrives, early situations, incidents and complexities that have defining impacts. While Kurt Vonnegut might have said in his eight rules of writing that 'every character should want something, even if it is only a glass of water',[17] a character just wanting something is not enough to drive a novel, and certainly not a crime novel, forward with any

Crafting crime fiction

real momentum. It's the stuff that gets in the way of a character's want, or desire, which compels and complicates – whether
it's external, or even internal. Devising that stuff, that conflict if
you like, is very much part of the plot. Let's not forget: Story +
Conflict = Plot.

But here's the thing with this vast genre: there's still an
expectation, or very compelling pressure to incorporate twists
and turns, mystery, surprise, suspense and often aspects of
investigation and deduction Mystery and suspense will be discussed at length in Chapter 7, as will structure in Chapter 5.
However, in relation to 'plot' and crime fiction I have come to
the understanding that we're really dealing with two types of
plot, and both are derivatives of classical Greek drama.

There's the pure plot; that is, plot driven by character and
conflict; and there is plot contrived by the author to thicken
the entertainment by loading up the mystery and surprises,
and the investigative aspect. Arguably, the former is where
the most interesting, insightful and engaging writing lies, and
from where the genre continues to develop and expand into
what was once deemed 'literary' terrain. Golden Age detective fiction relied on mystery and deduction, the puzzle, and
is where the genre has always been curtailed by expectation,
limitation and often repetition. Here characters remained
static and observations beyond the four walls of the 'puzzle
plot' itself were minimal. Or at least that's a very general view,
because there's increasingly been much merging and blurring,
with both 'paths' – if you like – enabling and enhancing each
other. From James M. Cain's *The Postman Always Rings Twice*,
to Paula Hawkins' *The Girl on the Train*, elements of psychological acuity meet puzzling and murderous clues, surprises and
trails.

Plot and point of view

For me, plotting, in all senses, is the hardest aspect of writing crime fiction. It's taken me 25 years and 15 novels to feel less daunted and even to enjoy some of it. I don't believe in writer's block. Anyone can sit there and write away, even if it is meaningless rubbish. Automatic writing, as championed by numerous creative writing professionals to get you into the swing, is an example. You can even do this a third or three-quarters of the way into a novel, if you are stuck, though you'll invariably have to ditch those words. Novels without enough planning will come unstuck eventually and probably very quickly.

That initial spark of inspiration, or that idea that has been bubbling away for a while, if not properly considered and planned, will run out of energy. I always used to find the 20,000–30,000-word mark, or a third or so of the way in, to be the point when things started to collapse. I'd written so much but the interest was beginning to wane. What had seemed like such a good idea and what had begun in such a writing flourish was becoming boring and trite. I couldn't see where to go next. Other novel ideas would be popping into my head – ideas that seemed fresher, better, more pertinent, more sellable. I'd only written so much; why not cut my losses? I have a few abandoned first thirds of novels. Looking back I know I could have stuck with them, those original ideas and sparks of inspiration. Yet the planning, the plotting, hadn't been there to continue with conviction. The reality was that I was suffering not from writer's block, but 'plot block'. I didn't come up with this phrase. Indeed, I'm not sure who did, but all credit to them. It's the greatest affliction that a crime writer can encounter. And yet it's largely avoidable. Apart from everything else, in my case those first thirds of novels were not necessarily crime novels. I didn't know what they were.

Crafting crime fiction

This is perhaps where story and plot become even more nuanced and complicated, if not confusing. I encounter academic colleagues who invariably champion writing over storytelling. Indeed 'Against Storytelling' was the title of one such colleague's symposium.[18] For them storytelling is very much the lesser art, and not essentially literature at all. What determines a story – a journey, or the events, say, of getting from A to B – might not be expressive of anything more conditional on consciousness or the 'state of being'. For them literary writing is much more about unravelling a mind (whether in flux or not) than the events leading up to a course of action. In fact action, particularly thrilling or highly dramatic action, is usually frowned upon. Yet storytelling would appear to be a primal, or instinctive urge. Lee Child believes this urge comes from the premise of survival, where hunter-gatherers would be warned of the possible dangers outside the cave. Child has often likened such narratives to be the beginnings of the 'thriller', and how the 'thriller' is the first and truest form of storytelling.

'Are you a writer or a storyteller?' I've been asked. 'Both', I've hopefully replied. This academic literary division is not remotely new and was railed against by E. M. Forster in *Aspects of the Novel* as such: 'Yes – oh dear yes – the novel tells a story. That is the fundamental aspect without which it could not exist.' He went on to describe one of the key appeals of the novel, which is particularly pertinent to crime fiction. We all want to know what happens next, he explained. 'That is universal and that is why the backbone of a novel has to be story.'[19] The detective story has this down to a T. We not only want to know what happens next, or where an investigation may lead us; we want to know what happened before the novel begins – that is, who murdered who. However, mystery alone is not the overriding factor in a novel's appeal and engagement, nor for that matter is it the posing of key questions. The strength of the writing itself – for instance the descriptive powers on display, or the crispness of dialogue – plays a strong part. This is where we need to do a little more unravelling of the story/plot dynamic, and to a degree the storyteller/writer dichotomy.

Unless you know what you're doing, where you're coming from and where you're aiming to go, it's extremely hard to settle on a 'story' (commonly regarded as a basic sequence of events), let alone a plot (in its purest form: being character-driven and usually conflictual; Story + Conflict = Plot). Literary register comes into this decision – you need to have an understanding of the genre and sub-genre you're aiming for in terms of what readers have already seen and what they might expect your story to look like. Only then can you really begin to exploit the terrain and start to map out some new territory. If you aim to bring a new angle to the genre, be it syntactical or thematic, it's worth knowing the existing ones. Sure, trial and error and lucky experimenting along with a good degree of literary foraging can come into it, but the fact that you are reading these words, this book, would imply you have an interest in understanding what you are writing (and reading), why and for whom. Obviously it's my job to keep that interest going – we're only on Chapter 1! And of course in this initial planning process, this should be a writer's chief concern: hooking the reader in, increasing the engagement, and delivering a fulfilling, insightful, exciting narrative.

Being aware of an audience, being aware of the effect and impact your work might have, is very important. On the Creative Writing MA Crime Fiction course at UEA we have a marking criterion which specifically addresses the reader.

Crafting crime fiction

'We expect you to demonstrate a sophisticated awareness of the reader, the reader's relationship to your narrative, and control of the process through which the reader engages with the text.' Writing fiction is a partnership as much as a collaboration. An invested reader does plenty of the work, in enhancing description and characterisation, in identifying key themes, while perhaps trying to second-guess where the story might be heading – also, and crucially, in making the story their own. Everyone has a different experience of reading a particular work and it's just that personal connection that is so powerful.

So what am I, a writer or a storyteller? A crime writer? Where does my own fiction writing story begin? However prescient, fiction is a product of time and place. The so-called Golden Age of crime writing spanned the First and Second World Wars. Many believe it was an attempt at literary escapism, a distraction from reality. However, running alongside such 'locked-room', or in my mind 'locked-in', outputs such as Agatha Christie's *Murder on the Orient Express* were the expansive apocalyptic noir works by James M. Cain, Jim Thompson and Dorothy B. Hughes. There was nothing cosy or escapist about their work.

This is maybe another way of saying a writer constantly takes from reality as much as, say, reading. Yet, as contemporary as the fiction might be (with or without a historical setting) the real world is still interpreted and filtered by the author, that author's experience, resource and talent. There's no way Agatha Christie could ever have written *The Killer Inside Me*, nor could James M. Cain have written *Murder on the Orient Express*. Of course they weren't just creating fiction, but expressing aspects of themselves in the thematic and practical approaches they deployed. This brings us back to Highsmith's line in *Plotting*: 'There is no secret of success in writing except individuality, or call it personality.'[20] Interestingly those noir writers all had early aspirations to write 'literary' fiction. Success for them in that area was not forthcoming, but in one way or another they were not curtailed by old-school genre conventions and created some of the most arresting crime fiction of the twentieth century. Other more recent writers, such as John Banville, Kate Atkinson or Louise Doughty, have very successfully (if not always quite deliberately) ploughed both 'literary' and 'crime thriller fiction' furrows. Though how much these distinctions are a product of time, place and the publishing industry is something to which this book will inevitably return.

Purpose and register are largely determined by what you can bring to the table. You will also need a fair amount of drive to write. This might be a desire or an almost inexplicable compulsion to put pen to paper, or fingers to keyboard. However, the act of deciding upon the sort of work you want to create and for whom can be spectacularly hard, especially at the beginning. Most highly acclaimed non-genre authors I've interviewed have admitted to having little idea of the type of fiction they first wanted to write, while admitting to relying more on instinct than design. My colleague and 'literary' novelist Professor Andrew Cowan, who's also a champion of automatic writing, loves to illustrate his struggle with the form and how his achievements on the page fall short of his ambitions by using a line from Samuel Beckett's *Worstward Ho*: 'No matter. Try again. Fail again. Fail better.'[21] Walter Mosley in his recent monograph *Elements of Fiction* elaborates further:

> Luckily for us and our work, failure is an essential raw material from which our stories arise. Failure encompasses the negative spaces of our tales; it guides us, teaches us, it loves our intentions

better than any ambition. Failure makes our stories stronger while allowing humility to flow in our hearts.[22]

Determining point of view

The premise of this book, however, is to cut back on the trial and error, the failures, save time and progress with purpose (and pace). There is a strong correlation between knowing what you are doing beyond the sentence, that moment of literary reflection for some, and plotting. Plotting, even in its purest sense, is ordered, knowing, contrived, controlling, persuasive. Walter Mosley calls it 'the structure revelation'. This all might seem counter to where great writing and freedom of literary expression spring from. However, the crime novel and even more so the crime short story are carefully arranged forms that do spark from the very first word. Consider these first lines:

They threw me off the hay truck about noon.
I bet you didn't know that bleach masks the smell of blood.
Tom glanced behind him and saw the man coming out of the Green Cage, heading his way.
The silence startled Sarah from a hundred fathom sleep.
You always remember the first time.

The authors and titles here, in order – James M. Cain (*The Postman Always Rings Twice*),[23] Oyinkan Braithwaite (*My Sister, The Serial Killer*),[24] Patricia Highsmith (*The Talented Mr Ripley*),[25] Denise Mina (*The End of the Wasp Season*)[26] and Val McDermid (*The Mermaids Singing*)[27] – have used the first-person, third-person and a version of the second-person points of view to get their stories going, to immediately intrigue the reader. Here's the first line from my novel *Kids' Stuff*:

Plot and point of view

Words don't come easily to Mark when he's in shock.

And here are the next few sentences:

They don't come easily to him at the best of times. He can read,
but doesn't. He's into practical things.[28]

The echo of the opening of Ruth Rendell's *A Judgement in
Stone* quoted earlier in this chapter was at the time uninten-
tional, as I hadn't then read the Rendell, or anything like as
much crime fiction as I should have read, and in fact I wasn't
at all sure I knew what sort of novel I wanted *Kids' Stuff* to be.
Perhaps that's often the way, and finding a register, a genre is
part design, part stumble, certainly for the fledgling writer.

My previous novels were thematically and stylistically dispa-
rate. I had little sense of a collective readership. The necessity of
having a sophisticated awareness of the reader and the reader's
relationship to my work, and, crucially as I see it now, control of
the process through which the reader engages with the text, was
beyond my comprehension then. Having studied and trained
as a journalist, I'd then taken to writing fiction without much
formal creative writing support. Mark was an extreme version
of people I grew up with and who didn't, for whatever reason,
pursue a legitimate career. I felt compelled to write a novel
about this badly educated, early middle-aged man, who'd long
been misunderstood and all but written off, who had little confidence in his abilities, though had yet somehow managed to
pull his life together; albeit with the help of a generous, hard-
working and loving partner. However, it wasn't that sense of
stability and solidity triumphing over adversity I wanted to
explore, but another fall – a fall so steep and dark there'd be no
possible escape. The very precariousness of family life seemed
the more dramatic, engaging and possibility realistic scenario

to explore. While my previous novels were centred on relationships, on the domestic, I hadn't pushed the material in the way I did with *Kids' Stuff*. I wanted things to happen, explosively.

After a long period of stability Mark's life spirals out of control when his past hits him in the form of his estranged, wild teenage daughter Lily, from a previous relationship. We're alerted to this sudden dilemma on the first page, in the first paragraph. Immediately, and appropriately for him, Mark is rendered speechless. Over the next few pages and chapters we seen how incapable Mark is of handling Lily and the new dynamic. We see how incapable he is of articulating his feelings to his partner, or his daughter. He's barely capable of articulating anything except road rage. Certainly, Mark feels things, is sensitive, but a world of understanding and articulating such emotion is largely beyond him. It seemed to me at the time a likely premise for such a character from such a moment and place. Besides knowing people like Mark and his extended family I set the novel in a small, provincial city and part of the country I was very familiar with. Though not explicitly named, the setting was as accurate as I could make it. In many ways it was small-town, small-minded stuff. However, this seemed to be the perfect place to amplify personal issues and very fractured dysfunctional relationships. While the domestic had always interested me, previously I'd shied away from extremes and pushing situations to their logical outcomes. My own upbringing was somewhat dysfunctional, though not violent. Could I even describe violence on the page? Why would I need or want to?

As the story progressed and the conflict increased – or to put it another way, as the stakes were raised – the novel did turn darker and more violent. The ending still chills me.

However, mostly the violence is off-page, with only the after-math being described. (This is a recurring position of my work and one I explicitly and metafictionally explored in my novel *My Criminal World*, and which I expand on in Chapter 4. Imaginary violence needs to be treated incredibly carefully in realist crime fiction.) At the time of writing I didn't know what sort of novel I wanted *Kids' Stuff* to be, or that it might be a psychological suspense, a work of crime fiction. I was stumbling, but with more urgency and intent than before. The writing felt strangely powerful. It was also angry and sad, or rather the voice of the novel, like the voice of the protagonist – and the two things can be different – was angry and sad. I couldn't help the novel from becoming so dark, or frankly murderous. It was like I was rushing down a tunnel. I hadn't seen the very ending coming and when it did it shocked me, as it still does.

However, and as contradictory to my stance now as this might sound, I had done little planning or 'plotting'. There was no detailed outline; only a sense of the situation or key conflict, and that the novel would be around 75,000–80,000 words long. This was 20,000 words or so shorter than *Flying*, the novel that preceded it, and which, arguably, was my most 'literary' or consciously 'writerly' novel. It was also my most peopled and researched novel, being entirely set on an aeroplane and told from the perspective of seven members of the flight deck and cabin crew. Maybe *Kids' Stuff* was something of a short, hard, sharp reaction to *Flying*, where nothing out of the ordinary happens, except a slow realisation of lost opportunities and the loneliness of life, even on a packed jumbo jet.

Kids' Stuff is told entirely from Mark's perspective, in the third-person subjective. That is, we never really leave his eyes and ears, his consciousness, yet we use 'he', 'him' and not 'I', which allows a tiny bit more distance from straight first-person, or the 'I', 'me' mode; it also allows for more syntactical or descriptive leeway and perspective slippage, as there's a 'voice'/ narrator behind the voice of the character. I wanted to enhance the third-person subjective for two reasons: to simplify the story and approach following my previous fictional foray (which had seven third-person subjective POVs, a lot of dialogue without speech marks and great chunks of italicised description), and firmly to anchor the story to one character. Importantly it always felt like Mark's story, as both perpetrator and, to a degree, victim of circumstance and background. That's not to say Lily, Lily's mother Kim and Mark's wife Nicole weren't also victims, and variously survivors, but Mark was also the most active of the key characters within the narrative timeline.

'Whose story is it?' is a question I always ask my students. And then, especially if the answer's not wholly revealing: 'Why is it that person's story?' Through the writing of *Kids' Stuff* and my then reading and swift immersion into the world of popular contemporary crime fiction – thanks largely to my reviewing work – I was at last beginning to see the appeal and importance of key characters that actually did things as opposed to characters to whom things happened – or worse, characters who reflect on not a lot happening to either themselves or anyone else. In retrospect, I wanted to write a novel in which stuff happened, where the drama was properly dramatic, where characters were in extremis. The active versus inactive or passive character position is especially significant for crime fiction (and crime fiction that moves with pace and purpose, menace and motivation).

Stephen King elaborates on this in *On Writing*, advising writers always to avoid using passive verbs and the passive tense, and just letting things happen to the 'subject' or character. He advocates for the use of active verbs and having the subject determine the action and the course of the plot. He states:

> I think writers like them for the same reason timid lovers like passive partners. The passive voice is safe. There is no troublesome action to contend with; the subject just has to close its eyes and think of England ... I think unsure writers also feel the passive voice somehow lends their work authority, perhaps even a quality of majesty.[29]

I've always found King's analogy somewhat troubling; maybe that's because I'm English, even if the point he's trying to make is clear and strong. In *Kids' Stuff* Mark's inability to articulate himself clearly, thoughtfully and rationally ultimately translates into physical action, with chilling consequences. He doesn't use passive verbs so much as very few verbs at all. How many men are like this? While he's not the most verbally gifted of people, or the most emotionally intelligent, we do begin to understand him and his rage, through his interiority and observations. Empathy was the intention, along with a highly dramatic – for me – story. Mark and Mark's situation drove the story, or rather controlled and determined the narrative drive. Through the close third person we see his world and how he sees it. He is our window and our interpreter. While this might not necessarily be a very pleasant place to be, and certainly not a learned or wise world, it has a fictional and dramatic legitimacy. When asked in a *Paris Review* interview why he never wrote detective fiction, James M. Cain said that invariably such a detective protagonist was coming to a crime or a situation as an outsider. What interested Cain was telling the story from the perspective of those closest to it – be they perpetrator or victim, lover or family member.

Crafting crime fiction

> I take no interest in violence. There's more violence in Macbeth and Hamlet than in my books. I don't write whodunits. You can't end a story with the cops getting the killer. I don't think the law is a very interesting nemesis. I write love stories.[30]

There is a challenge in creating and enabling a perpetrator like Mark to carry a narrative. Why would a reader want to spend time and energy in such badly educated, angry company? Shouldn't the reader want to 'fall in love' with the main character? That was a phrase gaining increasing currency at the time of writing *Kids' Stuff*; and one that was being relentlessly propagated on TV and radio book-club programmes. Popular fiction was fast becoming a love-in. Even the crime fiction featured on such programmes had its soft edges, because the protagonists and narrators (very often cops or quirky private eyes) were ultimately good, sympathetic people, defying overly bureaucratic protocol and almost unimaginable evil.

Wasn't this always the case, good triumphing over evil, order from chaos? Not at all and most definitely not with noir, which was and is premised on the darkness behind the curtains and truly apocalyptic outcomes. *Kids' Stuff* was my first novel to sell internationally and be translated, and my first novel to be adapted for the stage. Amazingly it became a long-running play at the Latvian national theatre in Riga, under the title *Psiho*, which is Latvian for 'psycho'. Without doubt it was my darkest novel to date and my first that could be considered crime, in the broadest sense. One review (in the *Times Literary Supplement*) suggested my greatest achievement was to keep the reader interested in 'the fate of a profoundly unpleasant man' and why some people might do 'unspeakable' things to each other.[31]

Noir

What I didn't quite acknowledge at the time was that *Kids'*
Stuff was pure noir. That review should have been in the crime
fiction round-up. Or perhaps the fact it wasn't, and it didn't
appear in any other crime fiction review space, only on the
straight-fiction pages, is illustrative of the ever-flexible and
dynamic parameters of crime and genre fiction, and a possible literary critical ignorance of crime fiction sub-genres and
the very concept of 'noir'. Just what is noir? Charles Ardai,
the legendary publisher of Hard Case Crime, gave the best
explanation and definition of what literary noir is in a blogpost.
Originally used to describe a series of French paperbacks, then
a category of black-and-white films, noir, he stated, referred to
a story steeped in emotional darkness.

> There is a feeling of dread and doom that suffuses the action; the
> story typically features a protagonist who's in trouble, who often
> doesn't deserve the trouble he's in, and whose trouble just gets
> worse as the narrative grinds inexorably toward an unhappy –
> often tragic – ending.[32]

In the same blog, Ardai defines 'hard-boiled' and the distinct
difference between hard-boiled and noir. '"Hard-boiled" refers
as much to style as content – it describes a story in which the
characters and the dialogue are tough and colloquial, where
there's usually plenty of action, plenty of sex and plenty of
atmosphere.' Most significantly, he states that a noir novel can
be written in a hard-boiled style, or equally, told in a delicate
or refined or purple prose. 'Not all noir is hard-boiled and
not all hard-boiled is noir.' The easiest way to think of this is
as 'noir' being thematic and 'hard-boiled' being stylistic. Both
concepts are intrinsic to plot and point of view. Managing noir

stories, making them readable, appealing, engaging and even entertaining depends largely on voice. The benefits and pitfalls of creating and strategically deploying nice and nasty protagonists and narrators (and I've used my fair share of both) will be explored further in the next chapter. For now we need to think about voice and how this is also controlled by point of view, prose style and theme. Novels individually, distinctly have 'voices'. Crime series can have 'voices'. Some critics describe authors as having voices, and that might be the case, especially with muscular 'literary' work. Yet, for me, an individual novel, or series of novels, have 'voices'. Voice and register are also intrinsically linked. How do you want your novel to 'sound'? What literary register are you aiming for, or how are you pitching it? What sort of novel does it feel like to you and how might a possible audience perceive it? Where within the vast crime genre spectrum might it sit? What boundaries might it be breaking and what fusions might it be creating?

Readers inevitably begin their connection to a novel via characters, via the protagonist(s), or narrator(s). This is where engagement and identification begin. Walter Mosley talks about 'Voice' as having an 'identifiable personality', which provides the reader with an opportunity to bond with the novel 'through empathy with this linguistic personality'.[33] Usually, the reader identifies with a character or a situation. The reader goes on a journey with the writer, not least filling in the gaps that the writer might purposefully be leaving out. The reader brings their own insight, resource and experience to the table too – hence the pact fiction writers make with readers. However, and vitally, that connection to character, to story, to plot, is made through point of view, and point of view is orchestrated through control of voice, which is in effect a control of the

Plot and point of view

prose, a control of syntax – language, in other words. The words have to do what writers want them to do. POV is the key building block to fiction. It's how we are drawn into a story. It's the way into character.

Take these two examples:

> I am a police. That may sound like an unusual statement construction. But it's a parlance we have. Among ourselves, we would never say I am a policeman or I am a policewoman or I am a police officer. We would just say I am a police. I am a police. I am a police and my name is Detective Mike Hoolihan. And I am a woman, also.[34]

> The shutter outside the wide-open window slammed so hard against the wall that it sounded like a gunshot. Montalbano, who at that moment was dreaming he was in a shoot-out, suddenly woke up, sweaty and at the same time freezing cold.[35]

The first paragraph comes from *Night Train* by Martin Amis, the second from *The Scent of the Night* by Andrea Camilleri. We are introduced to Inspector Salvo Montalbano and Detective Mike Hoolihan, respectively. We have the first person and the third person, and two openings that could not be more different stylistically. Yet, we are drawn in immediately. We know who the protagonists are, who we will be following and intimately connected to, and we also have some idea of the sort of novel we are embarking upon: a high parody, or homage of the hard-boiled American detective novel, and a characterful, colourful and quietly humorous and rebellious southern European police procedural.

Deciding who will 'tell' a story is a key choice a writer makes. Asking the question: 'Whose story is it?' can help. It might be more than one person's story. If so a number of POVs could be considered: first person, third person (usually subjective) or second person (that is, using 'you'; however this in turn has two applications: 'you' as in an address to someone else, the reader perhaps; or as in 'you' belonging to the subject or effectively narrator). These three key approaches each have their own stylistic and subjective nuances, to be further determined by tense, commonly: present, past, pluperfect. There is also a fully omniscient approach to point of view, where the 'author' is all-seeing and all-dancing and very much the storyteller – think Jane Austen and a writer who knows everything about their subjects, dips in and out of perspectives and adds plenty of wry authorial comment. Even without the authorial commentary the omniscient perspective has become deeply unfashionable, possibly because we don't want to hear from a godlike 'author', or master of the characters' universe. Instead, we want to hear directly from the characters themselves, the people whose story it is.

Some writers like getting in the way of the 'story', or fiction, of course, showing what they are capable of syntactically, observationally and invariably intellectually. Others are on a mission to remove themselves, any trace of the writer, from the story, and allow the characters to speak for themselves. Obviously, all fiction is a contrivance of one sort or another. That said, there is often an instinctual, organic approach to POV. We often begin writing, even considerable planning and plot consideration, and the POV naturally determines itself, be that first-person, third-person subjective, or less commonly second-person (where the author uses 'you'). Writing from additional POV might usefully add a different perspective and tone. This second POV could also be in different perspective – say, a switch from first to third. It might also be in a different tense, from present to past perhaps. As such, it might signal a different timeline and narrative thread. We will look at structure in depth in Chapter 5, and mystery and suspense in Chapter 7, but for now it's worth considering how using different perspectives can alter suspense and mystery. You have a character walking down a street – we're in the first-person POV with them. They might be anxious, nervous, fearful, expecting to be attacked. Or they might be blithely unaware that someone, whose POV we might jump to next, is waiting silently for them behind a dark corner ...

Important early decisions need to be made about the number of POVs you'll deploy and who the key characters are, not least because of structural balance and tonal consistency (which is closely related to voice). The two decisions are also closely bound. There has been quite a trend to sprinkle a novel with snippets of a perpetrator's first-person POV, usually in breathless italics, while they close in on a victim. Do we need any more? I would also say such an approach, such a use of POV, is part of the story and not the plot. In other words, we are seeing plot in action, as opposed to character development and progression; we are seeing the building blocks of story, one dramatic event after another, and not necessarily the dynamics of characterisation. Meaningful characterisation is of course determined by motivation, or if you like desire, and conflict. Further, and tangentially, your most important POVs are determined by who the key and active characters are and so they form an integral part of plot, and for that matter, the voice and/or register of the novel. Individual characters' POVs don't necessarily determine the 'voice' of a novel, especially if we have several contrasting characters and styles, but they contribute a lot to it. Indeed, every word in a novel contributes to that novel's voice.

Naturally, a novel requires stylistic coherence and consistency if it is to feel whole and satisfying. How do you do that if you are switching POVs from wildly different characters, and especially if you are using multiple first-person POVs? Characters need to be distinctive, but what if everyone sounds so different? How can dialogue, if colloquial and rendered with some ear and skill, add to the overall coherence and consistency? Dialogue is not necessarily the preserve of the key characters and POVs – others can speak too. In many ways these additional voices can enrich the depth and pace of a novel by breaking up dominating voices and POVs. They can add to the sense of place and time. We live in a busy, loud world. Contemporary fiction needs to reflect this. Snippets of dialogue from subsidiary characters can also be very useful to reveal clues, facts and surprises, aside from acute observations.

Nevertheless, crime fiction – novels that move with pace and purpose – hinges on key or dominating characters. This is why it's so essential to determine whose story it is, while also deciding upon the best POV or POVs to capture that story with. By doing this an overriding 'voice' will establish itself. This might be as much to do with the key characters' personalities as the prose style – though both concepts can often be linked. I'm thinking here of the highly distinctive 'voice' novels by Elmore Leonard and Kate Atkinson. Interestingly Leonard believed that you should be able to tell what a character was wearing from the way they spoke.[36] Leonard used multiple POVs in most of his novels, as did Atkinson in her Jackson Brody series, though slightly less so. Leonard's technical point on this was that he used the character best placed to narrate/describe a scene, often switching POVs from scene to scene (though rarely within the scene). Atkinson, on occasion, switches POV within a scene. This is unusual and hard to pull off, which she mostly does because she's an extremely skilful writer. I'm a firm believer in simplicity and consistency, and making life easier and more accessible for the reader. Too much POV switching around can be both jarring and disconnecting, and rarely contributes to a satisfying and appealing overall 'voice' (unless you are Elmore Leonard).

Why not stick to one, two or three POVs? How many characters' stories are we trying to relay within a fast-paced crime novel of no more than average length (which I take to be 90,000 words tops, though frankly I love the crime novella, and think 35,000–40,000 words can work brilliantly)? We want to engage with and be fully invested in those characters, even if we don't necessarily like them – even if we are horrified by them.

Are we having a protagonist, or a narrator? Technically, the term 'protagonist' describes the key character (or characters), and is usually rendered through the third-person subjective (he/she/they), while the term 'narrator' describes the teller of the story, and uses the first person (I). There is often some confusion, or blurring of the terms protagonist and narrator; not least because a narrator could be a protagonist and vice versa. It's worth bearing in mind the semantics here. Commonly a protagonist is the leading character or one of the major characters in the novel, film, play, and so on. A protagonist is also (Oxford Languages online definition) 'an advocate or champion of a particular cause or idea'.[37] There we have an inherent sense of someone being active, or doing something, of moving the agenda, the story forward. A narrator, meanwhile, is a person who narrates something, 'especially a character who recounts the events of a novel'.

Crafting crime fiction

The first-person POV is hard and risky, unless you find a fantastically captivating voice (which is largely determined by writerly skill way beyond character choice), while the third-person subjective is more forgiving and accommodating (and can include snippets of first-person narration snuck in as extensions to a character's third-person thoughts). One of the most successful crime series in the world, Lee Child's twenty-five Jack Reacher novels, saw two-thirds of the books told from the third-person POV (with a number of characters, including of course Reacher, giving their perspectives), and one-third from Reacher's first-person POV. That ratio is pretty much what you will find among contemporary crime fiction. In a way, do you want to hear a story, or be told a story? Either way, we are effectively dealing with a contrivance. But as a writer, where do you want to place yourself? Centre stage, or to the side?

The writer (and quite possibly a writer of numerous stories) is not appropriating the exact voice and persona of someone else, but articulating that person's very being from a highly privileged position of knowledge, insight and empathy. Besides, a switch in POV if we are in the third-person subjective is arguably less jarring and easier to accommodate for both the reader and writer. A reader is more willing to go along with the contrivance of fiction if they are not continually questioning every word choice, along with the very construct of fiction, which is why would someone be narrating a story in such a way and for whom, anyway? Fiction, and the crime novel especially, is a work of extreme design. We are meant to believe in the characters and the story, but that is something of a leap of faith. It is also something that is entirely in the hands and skill of the author. Good writers make us believe and forget the contrivance. They take us on that journey by making us think the characters are taking us on a journey: whether Martin Amis, with all his authorial audacity, or Andrea Camilleri, with his great empathy and gentle humour.

Authors, of course, have to be comfortable with their POV choices. It's part of your writer DNA. You have to enjoy, as well as feel confident in, writing from a particular perspective. Such enjoyment and confidence will be greatly enhanced if plot and character are pulling in the right direction. Given that they are practically the same thing, it shouldn't be too hard …

CHARACTER AND PURPOSE

Building on character

We began with plot and point of view, and how to devise and appropriate these elements. However, and as we know, we can't have plot or point of view without character. Ask a crime writer what comes first and they'll likely either say a situation, or they'll say a particular character. (They might also say a place, a setting, but we'll get to that in Chapter 4.) For now there are two ways of looking at how to get a novel into gear: we either have the situation that we drop the characters into; or we have the character(s) already in the situation (and rarely do you have a character in a situation without other characters somewhere close by). Another way of looking at the second version of this is to think that the situation arose from the character or characters. There would be no situation without such a character.

Initial inspiration hits us in different ways. I've always been struck by writers who think of a story and then people it, as if they are plucking them from thin air. These might be writers who talk about theme and what the fiction is really about, loading it with significance, or some fantastically complicated

Character and purpose

'plot' (or in the old detective fiction parlance, 'puzzle'). But themes (or worse, polemics) alone don't engage the reader, at least not in fast-paced crime fiction. I would suggest that highly complicated plots, reliant on systems, procedures and forensics, along with extraordinary cunning and sleight of hand (invariably from the author), don't engage either – or not me. A reader's way most satisfactorily and commonly into a fiction is via character and, by extension, point of view. We are then beholden to that character, or those characters, to take us to the end of the story (and hopefully as quickly as possible). Walter Mosley describes the novel as 'a journey of character'.[1] Yet we also know that a crime novel needs plenty of stumbling blocks to be put in the way, whether internal or external. That journey needs to be rocky, uncertain, surprising, with added equations of menace. We also need a character with agency. Passivity from a protagonist, or narrator protagonist, is not very attractive or engaging. This is why consideration of plot alongside consideration of character is essential.

Characters need to change, just as they need to surprise. One of the key tenets of fiction is change and development. One of the key complaints about Golden Age detective fiction is that the characters are wooden or flat and never change. To consider an idea for a novel without an idea of a character (or how that character might fit in if a series is being drawn up), as if the two concepts are distinct, seems inconceivable. I can't separate them. However, once an idea begins to form, combining plot and character, and following early decisions about POV, further character work is invariably needed. Yet characters on the page should not appear to be works in progress. A wooden character on page 1 can't then develop into an amazingly complex person on page 91. Characters need to

Crafting crime fiction

be complex from the get-go. They start life fully formed; at least adult characters do. How best then to get to know them, as a reader and writer, and in what context? A quick introduction or a lengthy description? Pacing will help determine this, and it's always worth remembering the eighth of Elmore Leonard's *10 Rules of Writing*: 'Avoid detailed descriptions of characters.'[2]

Patricia Highsmith, as is so often the case with landmark writers, had her own way, which seemingly runs counter to the idea of pacy crime fiction. In *Plotting and Writing Suspense Fiction* she explains:

> I am inclined to write books with slow, even tranquil beginnings, in which the reader becomes thoroughly acquainted with the hero-criminal and the people around him.[3]

While we perhaps don't get the full measure of Tom Ripley until page 91 of *The Talented Mr Ripley*, when he hits Dickie Greenleaf on the head with the oar,[4] the novel begins with Tom sensing that he's being followed. He's worried, behaving shiftily. There's a hint of menace. We soon get a strong idea of Tom's duplicitous and untrustworthy nature. Was Highsmith writing her way into Tom's head, or did she know him from the first page? She does elaborate on her choice of POV:

> Perhaps because it is all round easier for me, I prefer the point of view of the main character, written in the third-person singular, and I might add masculine, as I have a feeling which I suppose is quite unfounded that women are not so active as men, and not so daring. I realize that their activities need not be physical ones and that as motivating forces they may well be ahead of men, but I tend to think of women as being pushed by people and circumstances instead of pushing, and more apt to say, "I can't" than "I will" or "I'm going to".[5]

Character and purpose

While it is interesting to hear Highsmith's allegiance to active characters and agency, the world of crime fiction has certainly moved on in relation to her gender analysis. Writers from Oyinkan Braithwaite to Gillian Flynn have more than displaced such dated views with their fictions fully invested in female agency. However, Highsmith, like most writers, is wildly contradictory. She follows her passage about slow beginnings with this:

> But there is no law about this, and in *The Blunderer* I started out with a sharp bang, a brief chapter with considerable action – Kimmel's murder of his wife.[6]

In true Highsmith fashion nevertheless we then rather slowly follow Walter, the blunderer himself, learning all about him and why he might be capable of such violence.

Gender, ethnicity and age

Highsmith's fascination with, as she puts it, 'hero-criminals' is of course gendered. Choosing a character's gender and their sexuality, whether binary or non-binary, monogamous or polyamorous and everything in between, can have a significant impact on the fiction, and is entirely the choice of the writer. Like POV and the use of tense, deciding upon a character's mental and physical make-up largely comes down to what you are comfortable with and feel confident to explore and deploy. This should take precedence over a desire to include a different gendered perspective for the sake of, say, balance or representation; a notion that a certain stance would be more 'inclusive'. Just whose head and body can you really and convincingly get into? In many ways I've found age a harder aspect to encapsulate than gender or sexual orientation. Trying to capture much older or younger generations can be especially difficult. How people speak, what they wear, what they are interested in, how they relate to their friends and family, their sense of the world, are so determined by the contemporary and peer group.

Race and ethnicity are vital considerations too, and again usually rely on what a writer feels best able to create and convey, and how appropriate for the particular fiction. Cultural appropriation by definition is inappropriate. Imaginatively, insightfully and convincingly portraying someone other than yourself is not. Fiction largely resides in the imagination and imaginary characters and situations. This especially goes for crime fiction – it's part of the package. It's a crime writer's job, for instance, to create all manner of devious and murderous characters – many of whose heads we get right inside of. That doesn't mean only murderers and criminals can create such characters. Writing from experience and writing what you know are highly common approaches to creative writing. Such approaches are increasingly being seen as the only approaches. How dare we go into someone else's mind, body, life, society, culture. But let's not forget crime fiction is imaginative. We are practising imaginative writing. It doesn't need to be sympathetic in tone, theme or character specifics, though empathy is something I've always strived for with all my characters. We want to understand why someone might do such a thing, just as we want to understand the impact that action might have on others, however abhorrent.

Character sketches

There are numerous exercises and ideas for character sketches that can enable and enhance characterisation. Andrew Cowan's

Character and purpose

The Art of Writing Fiction suggests beginning with writing a portrait of yourself, with emphases on appearance, temperament and virtues.[7] A further exercise in *The Art of Writing Fiction*, and one often posed by creative writing tutors, revolves around ten or twenty questions to be answered about a photograph of an anonymous person (extracted from a newspaper or magazine for example), but in the first person. Such questions include: *How old are you? What do you do for a living? What's your most treasured possession? What keeps you awake at night? What do you most fear?*[8] To this I would add probably the most important question of all: What do you most desire? Then: What's in your way? Other knock-on questions I've also asked students to consider include: When did you last break the law? What's the most important thing you own? Whom do you love the most in the world? Whom do you loathe, and, crucially, why?

Some writers, notably beginning writers, go to extraordinary lengths building biographies of key characters. I've seen pages of material, with family trees going back generations, with all manner of likes and dislikes, habits, phobias and peculiarities neatly noted. Then there are the comprehensive education and work CVs, all current and past relationships fully charted, along with the details of every home ever lived in. Often photographs and pictorial assets are included. A lot of this material is aided and abetted by writing platforms such as Scrivener, which to me only encourage compartmentalisation and the creation of endless folders, pinboards and *aides-mémoire*. I really don't know how useful all this stuff is. It can become too concerned with unnecessary facts and signposting, and take an inordinate amount of time away from the actual writing. I do not want to be hindered by such biographies, such backstories. Besides, I don't want to spend forever looking up a character's particular details while I'm in the thick of writing a scene. I should know, and know by heart, most of these things already.

Their very essence needs to be palpable, which is also largely premised on plot, which is largely premised on purpose. What is the point of this character, what does this character want and who or what is in the way? Character is largely synonymous, in this context, with purpose. Biography is background. The factual stuff of a character's life is just that – facts. Too many 'life' facts, like too much research (discussed in Chapter 8), can get in the way of purpose, can slacken pace and weaken engagement (and, of course, distract from the writing itself). We're not aiming for *À La recherche du temps perdu* (*In Search of Lost Time*), or *Mein Kampf* (*My Struggle*). Don't overload a character with history and meaning. Stick to the present, which is wholly bound up in a character's past anyway. We are the sum of our parts. The very appeal of 'people', meeting new people and being surprised by old friends and acquaintances, is that you never really know someone – even those closest to you. This aspect, if handled well, can greatly add to the narrative drive and 'mystery' of a novel. As Elizabeth Bowen put it in her essay Notes on Writing a Novel:

> Characters pre-exist. They are *found*. They reveal themselves slowly – as might fellow-travellers seated opposite one in a very dimly lit railway carriage.[9]

However, you don't want to get their 'stories' wrong, or misremember exactly where they come from as your novel progresses. It could well become a redrafting and editing nightmare, especially if your plot is not properly considered, or is weak (editing and revising are addressed in Chapter 9). Yet as Bowen and Highsmith, and many others, have articulated, you don't want to know everything about your characters in the same way you don't want to know everything about your partner, say, or yourself for that matter. Do we really know who we are, and just what we are capable of, especially in extremis? Besides, such characters might be relaying their backgrounds inaccurately on purpose. There is a distinction to be made between exteriority and interiority, persona and personality, or characteristics and 'character': the front a character presents and who that character really is. E. M. Forster in *Aspects of the Novel* made a further distinction; that between 'flat' and 'round' characters:

> Flat characters were sometimes called 'humours' in the seventeenth century, and are sometimes called types, and sometimes caricatures. In their purest form, they are constructed round a single idea or quality: when there is more than one factor in them, we get the beginning of the curve towards the round.[10]

Andrew Cowan in the *Art of Writing Fiction* expressed the idea that genre fiction 'has a much higher tolerance of stereotypes and standard scenarios and tends to be far more plot-driven than character-driven. Genre fiction, we might say, is the natural home of the flat character.'[11] This charge might have had some currency levelled towards Golden Age detective fiction, but aimed at 'genre' fiction today? To contemporary crime fiction?

First, we need to deconstruct Cowan's idea of what a plot-driven, as opposed to character-driven, fiction is. Actually, I think we have done that in the previous chapter where plot – fundamental plot as opposed to a 'puzzle' plot – was explored as an intrinsic element of character. Second, I'd suggest, that any character worthy of appearing in your fiction, however briefly they might appear, needs to be credible, convincing and very probably compelling. Though an editor of mine did once say that unless a character appears more than once don't bother giving them a name. Well, who can remember names? And of course, too many characters can quickly crowd a scene, even a novel.

Significantly, and more usefully to the 'genre' writer, Cowan further explains:

> Character is associated not just with outward behaviour, but with the inner, moral choices and hidden psychological forces that govern it. Those choices may be complex; the forces may be contradictory. Character is never fixed or complete but always 'in process', and it is this dynamic aspect that most allows a person to come alive on the page and in the reader's imagination. A character's character, so to speak, is only fully revealed in response to events, but the nature of that response should never be obvious or predictable: it should never be 'calculable'. In this sense, the most compelling form of 'what next?' in fiction is perhaps not related to the events – to the story as such – but to a character's moral and emotional response to those events.[12]

To that I'd add, the most compelling form of fiction is that which finds a character not just responding to events but determining and sometimes executing those events. This is where the active versus passive concept of character and plot comes into play. This is where we have character and purpose combined. The 'moral' driver is interesting especially in the realm of the 'hero-criminal', as Highsmith put it. Being bold, being extreme with your character choices and developments, is all part of the drama and raising the stakes. Though let's not forget the imaginative element of fiction, and how we can portray despicable things. Highsmith took this point further in *Plotting*, stating: 'Creative people do not pass moral judgements – at least not at once – on what meets their eye … art essentially has nothing to do with morality, convention or moralising.'[13] This could be construed as being provocative, something Highsmith was pretty good at. It could also be taken too literally, and as an excuse to let your characters run bloodily amok.

Violent characters

Violence needs to be earned, and while it may surprise, it does still need to be, like your characters themselves, 'compelling, convincing, credible'. Chandler was wise to this, writing in *The Simple Art of Murder*: 'It is easy to fake; brutality is not strength, flipness is not wit, edge of the chair writing can be as boring as flat writing ...' He continued: 'murder is an act of infinite cruelty, even if the perpetrators sometimes look like playboys or college professors or nice motherly women with softly graying hair'.[14]

Understanding violence from all perspectives is a necessity of crime writing, especially the impact your writing might have on an audience. This is thematic as well as syntactical. Val McDermid has long been very vocal on the subject. In an interview with Mystery Readers Inc she said:

> When women write about violence against women, it will almost inevitably be more terrifying because women grow up knowing that to be female is to be at risk of attack. We write about violence from the inside, from the perspective of the victim. Men on the other hand do not grow up with the notion of themselves as potential victims, so when they write about it, it's from the outside.[15]

Writing from what you know has always been the foundation of fiction and character creation. However, it is where your imagination, and skill, takes you next that will determine originality and success as a crime writer.

Crafting crime fiction

McDermid's *The Mermaids Singing* (1995), featuring the series characters psychological profiler Tony Hill and DCI Carol Jordan, also introduced us to a particularly brutal serial killer, and serious questions about upbringing and gender (which might well raise many eyebrows now). As already noted, the prologue features the murderer's first-person italicised POV: 'You always remember the first time.'[16] The title of the novel comes from T. S. Eliot's 'The Love Song of J. Alfred Prufrock'. Eliot was in fact a lifelong fan of crime fiction, and especially Wilkie Collins' work. 'Prufrock' notably contains the line: 'There will be time to murder and create.' This in turn was influenced by Thomas De Quincey's essay 'On Murder Considered as One of the Fine Arts',[17] which also provides all the chapter epigraphs for *The Mermaids Singing*.

McDermid's novel was also heavily influenced by Thomas Harris' *The Silence of the Lambs*. While making gender one of the key themes (his approach might also seem dated now), Harris created probably the world's best known and most outrageously terrifying fictional serial killer in the form of Hannibal Lecter; who, interestingly, is not the serial killer being tracked down in the novel, but a twisted source of psychological resource. Hannibal went on to star in two further, though less successful novels (*Hannibal* and *Hannibal Rising*), having first appeared in *Red Dragon*. Lecter the character is more myth than reality. The novels, and especially *The Silence of the Lambs*, succeed because of the imaginative and (in a scholarly sense) instructive leaps Harris made. Hannibal has more in common with Dracula than any real-life serial killer. Our fascination with him and (arguably) attraction to him come from the fact that we know he's not real. He's gothic, fantastical. He's also incredibly learned. Any identification and realistic connection we as

Character and purpose

readers make in *The Silence of the Lambs* is with FBI trainee Clarice Starling.

There is a compelling train of critical thought that puts Lecter as a teacher, a 'lecturer', who ultimately guides Clarice towards the finer things in life, not just clues to unearthing the identity of the killer of the novel. The novel is sprinkled with Lecter's 'words of wisdom', such as this aside to Clarice:

> Dumas tells us that the addition of a crow to bouillon in the fall, when the crow has fattened on juniper berries, greatly improves the color [*sic*] and flavor [*sic*] of stock. How do *you* like it in the soup, Clarice?"[18]

The whole novel could be viewed as a metafictional text addressing teaching, learning and creativity. Harris was a trained journalist, who later developed a serious interest in cordon bleu cooking! There's no question in my mind that *The Silence of the Lambs* is as funny as it is terrifying, as erudite (it also contains a few references to T. S. Eliot) as it is absurd. It's immensely entertaining. Harris has spoken (though rarely) about his struggle to write creatively, how hard, even tortuous he finds it. This I find surprising, given the exuberance and enjoyment on offer. Perhaps the struggle had something to do with creating such an outlandish character, and keeping that character interesting, surprising and captivating, and not to become a cliché, or a parody of himself.

Because of the success and originality of Hannibal Lecter, *The Mermaids Singing* protagonist Handy Andy/Angelica, and on to and through *American Psycho*'s Patrick Bateman, Jeff Lindsay's Dexter, Luke Jennings' Villanelle and Oyinkan Braithwaite's Ayoola, the serial killer as hero-criminal is awash with cliché and imitation. In many ways, Hannibal Lecter is now the ultimate cliché. Avoiding cliché and stereotypes can be hard, likewise creating original characters. Yet that is what we crime writers must do; drawing from the well of our own resource, experience, individuality and imagination.

Originality

In *How Fiction Works* James Woods states, starkly: 'There is nothing harder than the creation of fictional character.'[19] How much were Harris or McDermid writing from what they knew? Where do such landmark characters, indeed where do any compelling characters come from? Such an imaginative leap can seem just that, a giant leap. But the rush to originality, the urge to avoid cliché, stereotype and perhaps even the sort of characters you have created before, might be closer to hand than you think.

The specific is invariably more attractive and engaging than the general, or obvious. Characters, like people, should be full of contradictions and be capable of change. They are complex individuals, and in a crime narrative they are individuals with a purpose; and quite possibly on a mission. Purpose and character, as we know, are so intrinsically linked that one can't exist without the other. Background, setting, along with aspects of backstory, are also intrinsic. A tip passed on by Kazuo Ishiguro when he came to our campus to conduct a special class, just after he was awarded the Nobel Prize, revolves around relationships. Ishiguro revealed that when he thinks of characters he thinks first of the relationships they have with others and what those dynamics are. Relationships, as we all know, are liable to change, if they are not in something of a permanent state of flux.

Character and purpose

Obviously and within crime fiction, those relationships can be heightened, dramatic, even traumatic. Before you know it key characters will emerge, and quickly make themselves vital – in your head anyway. They come in and out of focus depending on where you are with the plot. Having established a semblance of character, almost inevitably characteristics will begin to arise. Think about how much you can reveal of a character's inner life by describing their outer life; how exterior can signify and suggest interior, even the way someone talks, their intonation, their use of colloquialisms. But beware of overdoing it. As the Elmore Leonard aphorism goes: 'avoid detailed descriptions of characters'. He has another way of building character:

> I like a lot of talk in a book and I don't like to have nobody tell me what the guy that's talking looks like. I want to figure out what he looks like from the way he talks ... figure what the guy's thinking from what he says. I like description but not too much of that.[20]

My character notes, or sketches, amount to little more than name, age, names of children and siblings if they have any, perhaps place of birth, nominal nationality, and that's about it. They then reveal more of themselves as the novel progresses. But, and as already implied, the essence of them, the point of them, does need to be more considered and 'sensed' from the beginning. Their very being, their purpose, their established POV, are all crucial to plot, and taking the narrative forward. Do we want to be introduced to the character or immediately immersed in the story? Effectively we want to be pulled into the plot, which, hopefully, is already rolling at pace. As such, we want to be immersed in the character's dilemma or predicament. We also immediately need to be engaged by, if not 'attracted' to the character; however loveable or loathsome.

Crafting crime fiction

I struggled with those big Harris or McDermid leaps of violent imagination, and that tipping into the gothic, the fantastical, the mythic. The idea of adding satirical and humorous notes and tones to stories of murder and mayhem *à la* Lindsay, Jennings, Leonard or Braithwaite was also somewhat alien. That was until I understood I was actually writing imaginative crime fiction. Dirty realism or domestic dysfunction had seemed more logical to me as a writer, because those concepts seemed more 'real'. At least this was until I wrote *Kids' Stuff* and elements of high drama and character purpose, along with heaps of menace and pace, came rushing in.

Finding purpose, conviction and authenticity

The fictional world is a place of great licence. Is anything really beyond imagination? 'Write what you know' might be the old adage, especially directed towards beginning writers. 'Write about who you know' is possibly more interesting, especially if you consider the idea that characters don't have to be overly moral, likeable or sympathetic. Why not give us some monsters? We're writing crime fiction after all. On top of this, as illustrated by Harris – and actually we can go all the way back to Christie and Chandler, and Conan Doyle – characters don't need to be realistic to be compelling. How many private eyes have the literary skills of Philip Marlowe? Who thinks in such similes and metaphors? Characters just need to be convincing, and from that comes engagement. Specifically they need to be convincing in the world they are operating in, which might well be a different world to yours or mine, or any that we've ever encountered before. Setting those fictional parameters, building your world, is far more intrinsic and complex than simply

Character and purpose

deciding on a setting. What comes first, the plot or the person? The person or the place? The plot or the place?

Setting will be discussed in Chapter 4, but for now we need to build that person, warts and all, and by doing so we will enhance the plot. Indeed, effectively we will be making the plot. Yet, we will also be making the world the person operates in, so they can behave the way they do without us questioning the reality of such behaviour. Or rather, we might question their behaviour, and be surprised and variously shocked by it, but we should not be allowed to question our belief, our conviction in that person's reality or central place within a story, a fictional world. It should simply feel natural. We're all making this imaginative leap – the writer and the reader.

Yet, however much you rely on 'reality', on what you and others perceive to be factually correct and completely accurate, someone will know something else, and know it probably better. This particularly goes for police procedure and forensics, as well as the intricacies of law. Nevertheless, the writer needs to remind themselves that it is the characters' world. This is the world for the writer to develop, via character, and for the reader to interpret and expand. You write what you know up to a point, and then you adapt and embellish and fictionalise to fit your purpose, which shouldn't be too divorced from your characters' purpose. We're seeing the world from our characters' perspectives after all. They respond, explore, make assumptions, sometimes get things wrong. Authenticity, and by that I mean being authentic to the character, to the plot, to their world, to the fiction, is more important than being factually accurate to the real world, which is elsewhere anyway (and frankly quite often open to interpretation). This is not science, it's art: art striving for a different sort of truth.

Crafting crime fiction

Write who you know? We all know lovely people, and a few who aren't so nice. Numerous writers, myself included, take people we know as starting points. I also believe that all of my characters have traces of my DNA in them. They are the best of me and the worst of me, and aspects of me I'd never consider were part of me at all. When you shift from realism to high drama, when you accept the licence, the freedom fiction allows, when you push and embellish characters and worlds, might well be the moment you finally discover what sort of writer you were destined to be.

Whereas *Kids' Stuff* began on an exploration of a certain type of ill-educated masculinity, and a community on the fringes, with all intentions to keep it 'real', my next novel, *Get Me Out Of Here*, set out to shock, amuse and thrill from the very beginning. Hey, I thought, having had unexpected success with *Kids' Stuff*, having found that I was a crime writer, let's move it up a gear. While perhaps even more attuned to a time and place, *Get Me Out Of Here* pushed concepts of reality and fiction, or certainly delusion, to the core. To enhance the connection to character, to further enable a feeling of being stuck inside someone's head, I also deployed the first person, which was a first for me. The novel is as angry as it's funny, it's as serious as it's jovial, it's as literary as it's 'genre' – or so I like to think. One author endorsement declared: 'A very funny book for seriously unfunny times.'[21] Another review said: 'A dark comedy that will have you laughing and flinching at the same time.'[22] Job done!

Laughter in the dark

Val McDermid told *CrimeTime* in 2010: 'The contemporary crime novel has become the place where you can explore the unpredictable. Crime fiction has always been an area where writers have explored the edges of things.'[23] My idea for *Get Me Out Of Here* (the title having been taken from the *I'm A Celebrity … Get Me Out Of Here* TV show, which was widely popular at the time) was to bring those edges inside. I wanted to chart delusion, determined either by personality or circumstance. In many ways it was for the reader to decide which. Certainly delusion at the time – the financial crash of 2007/8 – seemed apposite. I always wanted to suggest something of the monster inside us all, and of someone pushed to the edge and then let loose. Just what are we really capable of? Such actions or outbursts of violence can create strong, dramatic effects. Ruth Rendell's fiction is often premised on spur-of-the-moment acts of violence, with devasting consequences. Lives and narratives are reshaped. She was deeply interested in exploring sudden events, often set off by something quite minor, that led people to commit appalling crimes; the inevitability of such a tragedy was what intrigued her. Asked by the *Guardian* how she came up with such characters and scenarios, she replied:

> I've never met a murderer as far as I know. I would hate to. It's not necessary … I just wait until I've got a character and I think why would anybody do that, what is it in their background, what is it in their lives that makes them do it. Usually these things are just accident or impulse, or because people are drunk or on something. The old detective story that's got a really complicated tortuous motive doesn't apply to mine. It's that people do these things almost by accident, or because of anger, their rage, their madness – and then probably regret it.[24]

Like Highsmith, Rendell was keen to explore a hero-criminal's path and psychology. Unlike Highsmith, Rendell's approach was conceivably less for exploitation, than explanation. In the same interview Rendell stated:

> I do empathise with people who are driven by dreadful impulses. I think to be driven to want to kill must be such a terrible burden. I try, and I think I succeed, in making my readers feel pity for my psychopaths, because I do.

Highsmith meanwhile was more concerned making her hero-criminal 'likeable', and having something of a laugh. In *Plotting* she wrote: 'It depends on the writer's skill, whether he can have a frolic with the evil in his hero-psychopath.' She also then slightly contradicted herself by adding: 'If he can, then the book is entertaining, and in that case there is no reason why the reader should have to "like" the hero.'[25] She suggested reader-identification could come from subsidiary characters.

With *Get Me Out Of Here* readers were firmly lodged in my hero-criminal's mind from the first word to the last. I initially set out to entertain, albeit with an already enraged and extreme narrator. My hero-criminal was called Matt Freeman, who was anything but 'free'. He was trapped by a consumer society and a world of high-finance work and expectation, which had brutally left him behind, along with everyone else. He pretends to others – those few who'll listen to him – and himself that he's still important, relevant and employed. The novel begins in Canary Wharf, where he (like me) was once employed. He's in an opticians, complaining about a pair of glasses he purchased a while back and which have broken. He wants a refund. But they're way beyond the guarantee period. However, when a very accommodating and attractive sales-woman offers to replace the glasses and lenses free of charge, he's stumped. The fact is he broke his glasses on purpose because he realised he didn't like them any more, if he'd ever liked them. He has plenty of old designer glasses at home. He has no use for another pair any more than he has any business being in Canary Wharf. In a world defined by paper money, fickle fashion and deplorable politics, Matt Freeman hasn't just lost traction, he's lost the plot. And then his day really spirals out of control: someone has slashed his tyre, there's a body on the line so he can't get the Tube and it's pouring with rain. By the time he eventually makes it to his long-suffering girl-friend's flat, he's met with warm Chardonnay and cold pump-kin ravioli. By now Bobbie is too engrossed with watching *I'm A Celebrity ... Get Me Out of Here* to pay him any attention. Who could blame her?

He goes on the rampage, imagining Bobbie's hiding some-thing from him – tokens from a new lover, perhaps. She accuses him of being a child, and a middle-aged loser. He's both of course, as well as an appalling snob. But all he can think about is betrayal, and the broken world he lives in. They fight. She sends his glasses flying. 'Now look what you've done. You've broken my glasses!', he shouts, not that he can tell whether she's broken them or not.

'I can't breathe', she says next. We return to Matt:

> I couldn't breathe. I was the one who was gasping for breath. I was the one who had the air knocked out of me. I was the one who was choking and puce and bulgy-eyed, with everything drifting in and out of focus. It was all too much. I hadn't been expecting this. Not after the day I'd had.[26]

The chapter ends shortly after the above passage with Matt's lines: 'Nothing ever worked properly. Nothing lasted. Everything broke.'

Crafting crime fiction

The reader doesn't know exactly what Matt might have broken. Bobbie's neck is the implication. We don't see Bobbie again in the novel, though neither do we see any police on Matt's trail. The closest we get to Matt being 'questioned' is when two inspectors turn up at his door because he doesn't have a TV licence. This, perhaps unsurprisingly, sets him off on a particularly vicious rant about the state of contemporary culture. Matt targets others he feels have contributed to his busted world, but again we never explicitly see any significant violence on the page. This of course doesn't mean that the abuse, the suggested violence is not serious. Matt is a despicable character.

By design

Is *Get Me Out Of Here* a thriller? Is it a crime novel? It's more of a thriller than *Kids' Stuff*, but less of a true noir. The apocalypse is really all inside Matt's head, and how he views the world, while the satire, the humour, and indeed something of a hopeful ending (for Matt anyway) is there to add lightness. Indeed, the ending was inspired by *The Talented Mr Ripley*, and in the next chapter of this book we'll address issues of influence and imitation and what you might be able to learn from others, including 'pinching' ideas. All writers do it in one way or another. *Get Me Out of Here* has been described as an English *American Psycho*. The theme of a fictional character railing against an inherently corrupt, consumerist world is by no means limited to *American Psycho* (which in fact concerned itself with a different, earlier financial boom and bust), or my novel. Themes have a habit of going round and round in fiction, however much writers think they might be doing something new. We're all plugging away at the same basic ideas of identity and place, belonging, love and

Character and purpose

betrayal; or as the saying goes: sex, death, money. And, invariably using the narrative structures and concepts of storytelling we're most familiar, or at least comfortable, with.

I was not attempting particularly to address any weighty socially or politically conscious theme with *Get Me Out of Here*, nor was I looking over my shoulder at Bret Easton Ellis' work. I was concentrating on the voice of Matt Freeman, and the voice of the novel. I was allowing Matt to fall freely, if you like, through the fictional space, and the metaphoric edifice that was and is Canary Wharf. Matt emerged absurdly, though logically for the fiction, in that Canary Wharf opticians, and then became more of himself.

As we know much is made of the necessity for 'literary' characters to change, as if somehow the novel, along with the human condition, insists on such a thing. It's worth coming back to this point. If Matt Freeman changed, it was to become more comfortable in the skin of a possibly murderous, scamming crook. We don't know whether he actually killed a number of people in the course of the novel – and neither still do I. It's up to the reader to decide, once the writer has got them on board. It's all about interpretation, and to an extent expectation. What do we expect from this sort of novel? Where's it leading us? Is it a thriller, a crime novel, or a satire, a play on tropes, on desires and devices (which is in fact the title of an excellent P. D. James novel)? Register and sub-genre are further explored in Chapters 3 and 8 particularly.

The one thing you won't find in *Get Me Out of Here* is any on-page violence. Describing violent acts is the genre's most troubling and complex issue, and wholly bound to character, and by extension reader engagement. Just what are your characters capable of, and what might such violence add to a novel? Is it insightful, appropriate, truthful? Can it ever be 'entertaining'? I think we all know when such a scene is gratuitous, and when it might be warranted. It depends on the world of the novel that has been created, and who is inhabiting it. Yes, a reader might initially be surprised by a sudden moment of extreme violence. But on reflection, does it feel necessary, relevant, justified? The same thoughts often go through the mind of the author. Judge carefully. Ultimately you are in control of the character, the situation, the scene, the fictional world, the overall effect. Control is the one sure thing a fiction writer should command. Otherwise, who else is in charge? Your imagination?

Graphic depictions of violence were certainly something I avoided with my first two 'crime' novels, along with any sense of police procedure or 'detective fiction'. Plot, true plot, is concerned with other things: primarily character motivation or purpose. The menace, largely suggested in *Get Me Out of Here*, is important in relation to the genre, and my aim to hit the thriller end of the spectrum. Interestingly, classic detective fiction mostly avoided any suggestion of ongoing menace by having the murder committed in the past, before the novel began. There was of course little character change or development, and almost total authorial control. The investigation, the puzzle, was everything, and effectively replaced 'plot'. The why became the who.

Except we've moved on a long way. The two branches of 'crime' fiction – the thriller (basically, where action moves forward from one menacing, threatening or murderous situation to the next) and the detective novel (where the investigation moves backwards to uncover the crime and who did it) – have variously merged and morphed, each contributing to

Character and purpose

the other. I didn't know quite how much until I tried my hand at old-school detective fiction. I also didn't know how satisfying aspects of detective fiction, or 'puzzle plotting', could be to devise and write – once, of course, the questions of character have been determined.

3

IMITATION AND LIMITATION

In the previous chapter we came across Val McDermid riffing off Thomas Harris' outlandish serial-killer creation Hannibal Lecter, with her own deeply disturbing version of hell in the form of Handy Andy. We came across my spins on the triumphant ending of Highsmith's *The Talented Mr Ripley* and the delusional nature of Bret Easton Ellis' *American Psycho* and its protagonist/narrator Patrick Bateman. A more recent reinterpretation of a landmark crime novel is Nikki May's *Wahala*, which insightfully and amusingly moves the mantle on from Oyinkan Braithwaite's *My Sister the Serial Killer* (where a loving and caring sister attempts to cover up, and justify to herself, her sister's wicked deeds). *Wahala* also focuses on identity and female friendship and kinship in Lagos; however here the main threat, or interloper, comes from the outside. With *My Sister the Serial Killer*, the threat is internal, far closer to home. Yet, both play with contemporary concepts of the thriller – that menacing, forward action – taking it to new darkly humorous, insightful and convincing cross-genre places.

On publication in 2022 *Wahala* was variously labelled the 'hottest debut of the year', following in the footsteps of *My Sister the Serial Killer,* which was also a debut. That both novels should have emerged so confidently is testament to two sparkling talents and new global voices hitting the ground running. But just how much of a debt does *Wahala* pay to *My Sister the Serial Killer?* Is debt the right word even? Writers have always been influenced by other writers. It's how we learn. Meanwhile, readers like to be given pointers as to where a new writer, a new novel might be taking them. Numerous reviews of *Wahala,* and significantly, even the publisher's own marketing material, suggest links to *My Sister the Serial Killer.*

Publishers do this all the time, especially with genre fiction. You only have to read the blurb and see the review quotes and endorsements they choose, to see a new novel being compared to a recent bestseller, or a global icon. 'Henning Mankell meets *The Wire* in the first book of a major new Scandinavian crime series.'[1] 'Beady-eyed yet tender, it resembles a collaboration between Agatha Christie and Muriel Spark.'[2] Or how about this other Christie comparison? 'Atmospheric and eerie with Agatha Christie vibes.'[3] However, consider it the other way. What are the writers pulling from, say, Mankell, or Spark or Christie? In the previous chapter, we touched on certain character and thematic debts (my own included), specifically in relation to serial killers and endings. These are clearly related to content. Perhaps there are not so many truly universal stories and themes for crime fiction writers to utilise. Or rather we can all recognise key story tensions and ideas. That identification can lead to easy engagement. 'The cat sat on the dog's mat, etc.' It's then how a writer makes such an idea specific and personal that will move the 'story' on. After all, as Jim Thompson said: 'There are thirty-two ways to write a story, and I've used every one, but there is only one plot – things are not what they seem.'[4] Even the centuries-old Aristotelian conception of plot – exposition, inciting incident, rising action, climax, falling action, resolution, denouement – is still adhered to.

Finding difference

Yet old constructs and mechanisms, old dynamics, can be elaborated on or masked by vernacular, colloquialisms, contemporary situations (cultural and political); by being specific as well as observant. Old stories can seem new, certainly refreshed. Simply, it can come down to saying, and seeing, the same things in different ways. Where does originality lie and what is its relationship to authenticity? These are the big questions; however, they are also questions that might best be pushed to one side while trying to work out your own approach, story and voice(s). Don't be afraid to imitate, copy, steal!

Writing is incremental, in the sense that writers' key resources are the books that they grew up on, the books that they were and are most influenced by. Influences change as you continue to read and develop as a practising writer. I used to panic that I'd never read enough. I still panic about it. However, we are reading writers who have read and been influenced by other writers. The chain goes on and on, across endless borders and canons and down through the decades and centuries. Invariably, it's only by coming across a writer that really speaks to you that an urge to write yourself first lodges in your mind. That moment of connection, of identification, of excitement, hopefully continues throughout your reading and writing life. It's the very air that writers breathe. It's why we first try to write, and write like someone else. As with musicians, as with all artists, we learn through playing (or painting) like others;

we learn through copying. Call it the conservatoire method. Practising 'artists' begin by practising what others have done before. It's how we learn to speak, after all.

Of course we steal. Or as the famous T. S. Eliot quote goes: 'Good writers borrow, great writers steal.'[5] Yet Eliot appears to have stolen and adapted that line from another American poet, W. H. Davenport Adams, who said in 1892: 'Great poets imitate and improve, whereas small ones steal and spoil.' Picasso said pretty much the same thing, which was much later picked up by Steve Jobs. Attributing this quote to the great painter, Jobs said: 'Good artists copy, great artists steal.' The internet is awash with posts and blogs discussing the matter: the merits, the licence, the pitfalls, who really said what, and various copyright issues.[6] Plagiarism is of course one of the most serious offences a writer, a student can commit, which is why most academic institutions, mine included, have plagiarism officers. Yet imitation, copying, borrowing, 'stealing', are fundamental to a writer's journey. We tend to imitate and copy prose style and syntax, and sometimes structure, and then borrow or reinterpret plot and character ideas. Another way of thinking about this might be to consider our reading as source material, those books we are most influenced by, and how we then endeavour to improve on them, or at least make them contemporary and in a way our own. On the one hand we might have the sentence, or someone else's arrangement of words and syntax, and then we might have the idea, or someone else's plot. We then move forward with this material, seeking difference and 'originality'.

While preparing to write this chapter I came across, and hurriedly devoured, Jean Hanff Korelitz's clever 'thriller' *The Plot*. The premise is painfully sharp: a busted literary novelist turned creative writing tutor comes across a very difficult student, who nevertheless has a brilliant idea, or 'plot' for a story. He shows the tutor the first few pages. However, a few years later the tutor, Jake, is surprised to discover that his promising student's work has still not been published. He can't understand why, nor can he forget the premise. Internet trawling reveals that in fact the student had died some time ago. By now Jake is beyond desperate for just a little financial security and literary acknowledgement, while his late student's idea won't go away. Indeed, Jake begins to feel that it's his duty, his destiny, to take up the mantle and complete the story. The T. S Eliot quote comes to Jake's mind, with the thought:

> Besides, Jake knew, as Eliot had known, as all artists ought to know, that every story, like every single work of art – from the cave paintings to whatever was playing at the Park Theatre in Colbeskill to his own puny books – was *in conversation with* every other work of art: bouncing against its predecessors, drawing from its contemporaries, harmonizing with the pattern. All of it, paintings and choreography and poetry and photography and performance art and the ever-fluctuating novel, was whirling away in an unstoppable spin art machine of its own. And that was a beautiful, thrilling thing.[7]

Needless to say it all goes spectacularly right then horribly wrong for Jake, as his 'novel', *Crib*, becomes a global bestseller, before old ghosts begin to stalk him. The ending is hard and brutal, but not before Jake has time further to ruminate on the nature of plot, storytelling and originality. Did it matter that Jake's own writerly skill rendered his former student's exceptional 'plot' into shape? Certainly, the student, Evan, as Jake sees it, had some 'moderate talent at making sentences'. Though he considers further:

Imitation and limitation

But creating narrative tension? Understanding what made a story track and grab and hold? Forging characters a reader felt inclined to care about and invest their time in? ... Any novelist would understand what he'd done. Any novelist would have done exactly the same![8]

Well, yes and no! As stated, plagiarism is a very serious issue that no one wants to be accused of. However, copying or imitating other writers to help find your own voice is a long-standing approach. Creativity develops by understanding how others did things. At my institution, the teaching and tutoring of creative writing runs hand in hand with the critical study of literature. The discourses inform and feed each other. The more you read and the more closely you read, the better. However, reading as a critic is different to reading as a writer. The more you write, the more you look at other texts, landmark texts, with different eyes; indeed, with practical considerations in mind. How did a writer do that? What effect were they aiming for?

Reading as a writer

When reading as writers, we consider the thematic and character approaches, we look at the overall structure and narrative devices in play: such things as POV, timelines, story arc, those Aristotelian markers, even chapter and paragraph lengths. Then (or maybe at the same time), we pay attention to the words, the rhythm of the prose, the syntax. Of course, for many writers, the very words themselves are what initially appeal and engage. The literary critic Derek Attridge proposes, in *The Singularity of Literature*, that what distinguishes a 'literary' work is 'otherness and singularity', which may 'arise from the encounter with the words themselves, their sequence, their suggestiveness, their patterning, their interrelations, their sounds and rhythms'.[9]

Attridge's position is interesting in that it distinguishes between the 'production' of a literary work, and its 'creation', as if the two concepts are somehow separated. He attests that 'intention' is one thing while another state of 'non-knowing', 'surprise' and 'discovery' come into play and are necessary to elevate a piece of writing into a piece of 'literary' writing or literature. This abstract, academic idea and approach might well help enable a work of extreme originality and delicacy. But try imitating any such 'literary' work from such 'literary' giants. You might sound a little pretentious. Moreover, scholarly study of what makes a work of genre fiction sing, and also be original, particularly from the level of the sentence, is rare. Yet, genre writers, crime writers of note, don't just care deeply about those words, rhythms and syntax, they invariably do amazingly complex things to make sentences accessible, surprising and arresting.

Is it easy to judge how successful your approach as a reader then writer might be? As Andrew Cowan states *In the Art of Writing Fiction*: 'In the act of writing we are also, constantly, engaged in the act of reading, and it is this continuous alertness to how we are sounding and what we are saying that allows us to gauge the likely effect of our words on our eventual readers; it's what allows us to depict the mysterious without becoming confusing (or the obvious without becoming *too* obvious).'[10]

Judging those words, your words, particularly for aspects of originality is hard. Can you ever truly gauge the likely effect you might have on a reader? This begins to address the idea of who you are writing for (a theme which will explored in depth in Chapter 8). As a writer, a crime writer, I could only hope

Imitation and limitation

to be writing for as many people as possible; as well as immediately to engage and arrest them with the prose. This then comes down to the importance of word choice, of punctuation and grammar, of syntax. The legendary American novelist and creative writing tutor John Gardner in his seminal work *On becoming a Novelist* nailed what effect writing can immediately have.

> We read five words on the first page of a really good novel and we begin to forget that we are reading printed words on a page; we begin to see images … We slip into a dream, forgetting the room we are sitting in … If the dream is to be *vivid*, the writer's 'language signals' – his words, rhythms, metaphors, and so on – must be sharp and sufficient; if they're vague, careless, blurry, or if there aren't enough of them to let us see clearly what is being presented, then the dream as we dream it will be cloudy, confusing, ultimately annoying and boring.[11]

If this is not a call to arms for sharpness, succinctness, intent and unambiguity, I'm not sure what is. We are drawn into the 'dream', by the greats who have gone before, and sometimes by our peers and new voices. It's a key feature of this amazing genre, and for many readers the reason we were initially pulled in and excited. Just a few words can do it, and indeed did it for me. As reader-writers it is especially powerful first coming across such lines – the piercingly sharp, uncluttered, invariably rhythmic prose that acts like a hook, before any situation, setting or character can begin to appeal. It's why we read and want to write, and read on and write on. No wonder there's an urge to copy and imitate. How could anyone come up with such a way of putting things? And no wonder so many of us begin by trying to sound like others: those words, those voices that connect and ring so true in your mind.

First lines

I used to run a seminar centred on first lines, with the aim of asking students to identify the authors and the books. Below are a few notables from the twentieth century in no particular order (in part to mask further the title and author and to allow you to concentrate on the words, and not who wrote them, or the particular novel):

1. They threw me off the hay truck about noon.[12]
2. Tom glanced behind him and saw the man coming out of the Green Cage, heading his way.[13]
3. They found the corpse on the eighth of July just after three o'clock in the afternoon.[14]
4. Hank counted the stack of money.[15]
5. You always remember the first time.[16]
6. It was about eleven o'clock in the morning, mid October, with the sun not shining and a look of hard wet rain in the clearness of the foothills.[17]
7. Eunice Parchman killed the Coverdale family because she could not read or write.[18]
8. It was good standing there on the promontory overlooking the evening sea, the fog lifting itself like gauzy veils to touch his face.[19]
9. I was surprised to see a white man walk into Joppy's bar.[20]
10. The rain rained.[21]

And here are ten from the twenty-first century:

11. The silence startled Sarah from a hundred-fathom sleep.[22]
12. But that spring she was fourteen and would do anything.[23]

13. It wasn't as though the farm hadn't seen death before, and the blowflies didn't discriminate.[24]

14. The October sun is as hot as the blood of the angry mob.[25]

15. Ayoola summons me with these words – Korede, I killed him.[26]

16. 'Have you ever been on a private jet?'[27]

17. The boat is smaller than he imagined.[28]

18. Whenever I meet a man, I catch myself wondering what our child would look like if we were to make a baby.[29]

19. Am I strong enough?[30]

20. They reached the canal along the track leading up from the river, their slingshots drawn for battle and their eyes squinting, almost stitched together, in the midday glare.[31]

The above first sentences come from twenty novels published over the last hundred years, and from authors from five continents – the international reach expanding greatly over the last two decades. A few of the novels are in translation, while not all the works were initially regarded as crime novels. Most of the first sentences run for over five words, perhaps stretching the John Gardner idea of a practically instant dream-state. However, all are suggestive, atmospheric, active and enticing. A few are menacing, already revealing the genre, while others manage to combine sparkling description with firm narrative drive. One says nothing and everything in just three words. 'The rain rained.' The next sentence, which begins a new paragraph runs to five words: 'It hadn't stopped since Euston.' The paragraph continues:

> Inside the train it was close, the kind of closeness that makes your fingernails dirty even when all you're doing is sitting there looking out of the blurring windows. Watching the dirty backs

75

of houses scudding along under the half-light clouds. Just sitting and looking and not even fidgeting.[32]

Note the repetition of 'dirty', of 'sitting', while we have 'close' and 'closeness' in the same sentence, which also includes 'Inside', and a description of the view out of the windows as 'blurring'. This is in fact from the first-person perspective of the narrator – one Jack Carter. He considers himself to be 'Just sitting and looking and not even fidgeting.' Yet, the prose also suggests something else, in a sharply, rhythmically, menacingly passive-aggressive way. That the narrator is a lethally coiled spring, barely able to contain his rage within a world that is dirty, blurred, sodden, half-lit. The first three words did it for me, and still do it. The novel, *Get Carter*, was originally titled *Jack's Return Home*, until the successful big-screen adaptation starring Michael Caine changed all that. In fact the film came out only a few months after the novel was published in 1970. The novel was nothing like as successful as the film; however, it cemented the author Ted Lewis' reputation and enabled the noir school of British crime writing, which went on to include authors such as Derek Raymond, Russell James and Cathi Unsworth.

Get Carter is as brutal as it is bleak, set contemporaneously around the east coast of England's Humber estuary (though the film was relocated a bit further north to Newcastle) in winter. The prose is equally hard-hitting and to the point. Its description is built around short sentences, each adding to the weight of the previous sentence and the atmosphere. Like this, for instance, from the beginning of the second chapter:

I could tell it was windy out before I could hear the wind. It was the daylight, what bit that was getting through the cracks

of the curtains. I knew it was windy because of the kind of
daylight it was.[33]

The narrative, told only from Jack's perspective, takes
place over just a few days: Thursday to Sunday. The action
becomes more violent and disturbing as Jack seeks revenge for
his brother's death. Despite his success, Lewis was a troubled,
self-educated writer who died prematurely. His life was almost
as 'noir' as his fiction, as often seemed to be the way with key
American noir writers such as Jim Thompson. Technically,
syntactically, however, Lewis was writing noir in a hard-boiled
British way. He brought a vernacular and an idiom to British
English literary prose that I found hugely exciting, because
here was a style and an approach that I could not only engage
with, but try to imitate. The rhythms were that much closer
to home. It was as if he'd taken on board what Hammett and
Chandler had done to the language of crime fiction in the US,
and created a British-English reply.

Brit noir

It might have taken quite a few decades for someone to rise
to the challenge, and do the only thing that really mattered
in relation to story, which was as Chandler said, 'magic with
words'. However, literary Britain of the 1950s, 1960s and 1970s,
or rather the crime fiction end of it, had still been under the
cosy and cloying shackles of the Golden Age detective writers,
as perpetrated by Christie, Sayers et al. It seemed to be a pecu-
liarly traditional form, with its Edwardian rules and wooden
characters sporting ludicrous moustaches and monocles. British
playwrights, poets and the kitchen-sink novelists of that time

moved more quickly to unshackle themselves from such stifling syntax and wooden clichés. Yet, Lewis' 'school' and reputation as a prose writer was not widely recognised at the time. That didn't come until the next century when such writers and critics as Cathi Unsworth (novelist and editor of *London Noir*),[34] Barry Forshaw (*Brit Noir*)[35] and Nick Triplow (*Getting Carter: Ted Lewis and the Birth of Brit Noir*)[36] set about rewriting British literary history, and putting credit where it was due.

Interestingly, Graham Greene's overlooked novel *A Gun for Sale* hinted at the syntactical possibilities of a British school of hardboiled noir, back in 1936, two years before *Brighton Rock* was published. It begins, arrestingly, with the lines:

> Murder didn't mean much to Raven. It was just a new job. You had to be careful. You had to use your brains. It was not a question of hatred.

The first sentence of the second paragraph reads:

> The cold wind cut Raven's face in the wide continental street.[37]

The novel concerns itself with an assassin, Raven, and a plot that eventually suggests the total destabilisation of the European continent and raises the spectre of war. The personal becomes deeply political. Along the way the novel is studded with cold-ness, alienation and an unambiguous detachment. Even the most tender and emotional moment, from the perspective of the relentlessly betrayed Anna, describes her inability to cry real tears: 'it was as if those ducts were frozen'. Another line describes Raven as carrying 'a chip of ice in his breast'.

The nature writer and academic Robert Macfarlane pointed out, in his introduction to the 2005 Vintage edition, that this line had reverberations all the way to Greene's autobiography,

Imitation and limitation

A Sort of Life (1971), where he wrote that 'there's a splinter of ice in the heart of a writer'.[38] *A Gun for Sale* is a curiously bleak Greene 'entertainment', but a novel that suggests the author's awareness and understanding of literary noir, and the hard-boiled style, in the American tradition. (While Hammett's *The Maltese Falcon* was published in 1929, and Cain's *The Postman Always Rings Twice* in 1934, Chandler's first novel, *The Big Sleep*, didn't come out until 1939.) Greene's 'entertainments' meanwhile seemed to become increasingly lighter and comic; the pinnacle, in my mind, being the gloriously absurd and pithily observed *Our Man in Havana* (1958). To mistake a vacuum cleaner for a blueprint of an atomic bomb? Who'd ever have thought up such idea? But an author with an extraordinary imagination and a deep interest in playing with perceptions, as well as tropes and the prose itself? Greene, you feel, could do almost anything and in a style (largely of his choosing) that masked layers of understanding. It was perhaps no surprise that as the novels continued to be published at an extraordinary rate of productivity and excellence, he quietly dropped the 'entertainment' side of things, letting the works speak for themselves without labelling.

Chandler

Raymond Chandler's last attempt at a novel, *Playback*, was also published in 1958. Here, however, we see an author who has run out of steam. It was his seventh novel, all of which had featured Philip Marlowe, and all written in the first person. That's nearly a twenty-year reign of the quintessential private eye, with all the hard-drinking, wisecracking baggage to hand. However, the drinking took its toll, and the wisecracks began to sound like tired clichés. The danger of eventually imitating yourself is one that crime writers, especially of series, all face. *The Long Goodbye*, published in 1953, and with its metafictional overtones sadly relaying a busted creativity, was the real swansong Chandler knew and designed it to be. Yet, how glorious the beginning to the series, with *The Big Sleep*:

> It was about eleven o'clock in the morning, mid October, with the sun not shining and a look of hard wet rain in the clearness of the foothills.[39]

This is what I read before I had much idea of what crime fiction was. This is what I read before Collins and Poe, Cain and Hammett, Thompson and Highsmith; well before I immersed myself in Christie, Sayers and Tey, before I entertained any idea there was such an extensive and wide-ranging Anglophone canon, let alone the point where I ventured much further afield. Chandler was also the first series author I read. The words, the syntax, the metaphors and similes, and Marlowe's louche and laconic stance, gripped and excited me at once. I hadn't realised what fun such reading (and significantly, writing) could be. That was what I wanted to do, to write with such prose, before I'd ever considered the full complexity of a 'detective' plot.

It's interesting to note that with *The Big Sleep*, Chandler was in fact copying, or plagiarising himself as he mined from and pulled together two earlier short stories, 'The Curtain' and 'The Killer in the Rain'.[40] Maybe there was already a hint of low productivity, and the creative struggle to come. After all, Chandler was nearing the age of 50 when writing *The Big Sleep*. The other highly significant, to me, aspect of his writing, is the fact that it's neither especially noir, nor hardboiled, despite the associations and endless labelling. The writer and my UEA

Imitation and limitation

colleague Tom Benn memorably describes Chandler's style as 'poetic realism'. For a number of years Chandler attended an English private school, Dulwich College in south London, where he was classically educated and wrote Edwardian-style poetry, and read voraciously the work of P. G. Wodehouse.

It was not until much later, when he mixed this traditional reading and writing background with the very untraditional, dark-alley and backstreet-facing approach of Dashiell Hammett, and other American writers making their mark in blue-collar pulp publications such as *Black Mask*, that his true style and 'voice' began to appear. In part it was because of his more 'traditional' writing roots that he became to be seen as a 'literary' crime writer, lauded by the critical and academic establishment. He was more than just the crime writer's 'writer'. He was a writer's writer. No matter that Hammett's truly hardboiled prose and unambiguously objective narration, featuring an unnamed narrator with no interiority at all, was the real stylistic landmark. No genre writer had taken such an approach before, even if Hammett was heavily influenced by Hemingway. Chandler fully acknowledged Hammett's influence on the genre. Nevertheless, Chandler fought for his own 'literary' recognition as hard as he fought for a 'realistic' concept of crime fiction for the rest of his writing life.

Self-acceptance of who you are, of what you write, does not always come readily to authors. Perhaps this is why we continue to write, to try to write better, to move things forward – as we're always aware (as that old Samuel Beckett line from *Worstward Ho* goes) of failure, of the intrinsic failure of never being able to write the perfect story, the perfect novel.

Acceptance generally, along with proper critical acknowledgement, often comes too late to writers. Besides, fashions and reinterpretations of key and undiscovered gems is a very common literary occurrence. Dead in the water one moment, revived and shining the next. As Margaret Atwood suggests in *Negotiating With The Dead: A Writer on Writing*:

> A book may outlive its author, and it moves too, and it too can be said to change – but not in the manner of the telling. It changes in the manner of the reading. As many commentators have remarked, works of literature are recreated by each generation of readers, who make them new by finding fresh meanings in them. The printed text of a book is thus like a musical score, which is not itself music, but becomes music when played by musicians, or 'interpretated' by them, as we say. The act of reading a text is like playing music and listening to it at the same time, and the reader becomes his own interpreter.[41]

The same could be said for a writer, like a musician, who learns to write by 'playing' other people's 'scores,' or texts. Yet, through that interpretation comes innovation, and individuality. For the writer, the fledgling writer, aspects of posterity are far better left in a dark, undisturbed part of your mind. Don't worry about consciously doing anything particularly new or innovative. You can't think about reputation before you can walk, though what you can do is look at the all too often transient and fickle nature of literary criticism and the publishing industry at the time and try to ignore it. Think of the texts. How someone did something, and try to emulate and reinterpret that. You are reading as a writer, then perhaps writing in the vein of so and so: rewriting what others have written, but in your way, with your own resource and talent. Concentrate on the writing that excites you – the syntax and approaches that turn you on the most, and which naturally you want to, or indeed can't help but emulate.

Imitation and limitation

Faulkner

Writers always seem to gravitate towards other writers that do things brilliantly and differently. Take the Nobel laureate William Faulkner. Struggling to make a living, he ended up in Hollywood working on scripts. One such script was an adaptation of *The Big Sleep* – the film of which, starring Humphrey Bogart and Lauren Bacall, premiered in 1946. Here was a writer, you can almost hear Faulkner thinking of Chandler, who knew 'how to do magic with words'. So what does Faulkner do? He sets about writing his own series of detective stories, featuring a crime-busting attorney called Gavin Stevens. These were then published under the title *Knight's Gambit*, possibly in reference to Philip Marlowe as the quintessential, twentieth-century knight errant, in 1949. They weren't so successful as far as the reading public went. However, their genesis is illuminating.

Faulkner, a university drop-out and a largely self-taught writer, had a not wholly dissimilar literary education to Chandler. He began writing in a high, late Victorian style, only to shift into a far more innovative and modernist form. The stylistic and thematic darkness on display in such novels as *Intruder in the Dust*, *As I Lay Dying* and *Absalom, Absalom* suggest metaphoric and metaphysical connections to the most dramatic and emotional of 'crime' dramas, too. Murder and death stalk the work, even if those novels are not specially regarded as crime novels.

Debt

So just who was or is copying who, how exactly, and does it matter? Descriptive similarities and echoes also crop up with surprising and unsurprising regularity. We have of course the beginning of *The Big Sleep*: 'It was about eleven o'clock in the morning, mid October, with the sun not shining and a look of hard wet rain in the clearness of the foothills.' Taking some licence, or perhaps it was simply a coincidence (though perhaps one borne out of reading and resource), we then have, some thirty years later, the start of *Get Carter*: 'The rain rained.'

What is it with the weather? What is it, behind the arrangement of words, that pulled me in to those two beginnings? The weather? The types of rain? There'll be plenty more about weather in Chapter 4, on setting and description. For now, I'd like to draw this chapter to a close by returning to an aspect of imitation, or emulation, if you like, which is more concerned with plot and character – as opposed to syntax – and my direct experiences of 'borrowing', albeit officially, someone else's structural devices, along with their key creation, character!

First, for moral permission for such 'borrowing', how's this from Atwood's *Negotiating with the Dead*:

> Chaucer and Shakespeare thought nothing of using other people's plots – in fact, to say that a story was not made up but came from an older authority, and/or had really happened, meant that it was not a frivolous lie and lent it vitality.[42]

Atwood goes on quite rightly and humorously to blame the writers of the 'Romantic' period for then appropriating a sense of 'genius', just because they actually wrote something down, and were utilising 'self-expression': 'the expression of the self, of a man's whole being – and if a man wrote works of genius, then he had to be a genius himself, all the time'. Before we get to ideas of artistic 'self-expression', which is perhaps where more

Imitation and limitation

'literary' minded writers overly occupy themselves, it might be worth reminding ourselves of what the early twentieth-century American critic and 'creative writing' tutor Carolyn Wells had to say. Wells was an Edgar Allan Poe scholar, who wrote arguably the first manual for detective fiction writers, *The Technique of the Mystery Story*, first published in 1913. Her premise throughout is that the mystery story is about 'technique rather than art'. Take this often quoted passage from Wells' opus:

> There will be less 'beautiful' passages, fewer lofty flights, and the flow of English will not be so charming; but these qualities aside, all the remaining points go to the mystery as a genre. For ingenious plot, logical movement, relentless subordination of means to ends, suppression of the irrelevant and unimportant character contrasts, sustained and climactic interests, and all the qualities that go to make up absorbing narration, the mystery yarn is unsurpassed. It is like a fictive game of chess, a story-telling fox-chase, a promising literary bass strike – combined.[43]

That game, or those detective plots, are according to Dorothy Sayers, Aristotelian; perhaps the source of our largest debt. In her landmark essay, 'Aristotle on Detective Fiction', also often quoted, she writes:

> Now to anyone who reads the Poetics with an unbiased mind, it is evident that Aristotle was not so much a student of his own literature as a prophet of the future ... what, in his heart of hearts, he desired was a Good Detective Story.[44]

She believed that the detective story followed the Aristotelian prescription of tragedy, where fear and pity led on to catharsis. Also, that the detective story adheres to the three-act structure of peripety, discovery and suffering. Others, of course, describe this as beginning, middle and end. Aristotle's concept of tragedy had the components as such: plot, character, reasoning, diction, song and spectacle. We looked at aspects of what 'plot' is earlier; however, the Aristotelian structural premise of those three acts became fundamental to western fiction, whether it's further broken into sequences or stages or not, such as, notably: situation, complication, crisis, climax, resolution. For a very long while, the Anglophone mystery canon, along with much other fiction, was one interpretation and exploitation of this or another. Were all these writers, generations of them, borrowing or stealing fundamental causal structures?

The structural 'copying' went deep. This is why contemporary writers can do better at looking further afield – to narrative concepts, from China, from Japan, for instance, which follow other modes of storytelling, often from previous centuries and dynasties. Digital and new media possibilities of, for example, branching and ever-folding storylines, of artificial intelligence in relation to syntax and 'plot', are also adding exciting elements of disruption. Things do not have to look the same. As we move further into the twenty-first century, I firmly believe the novel form will look increasingly different. There are more plots, both puzzle- and character-driven, and certainly more than '32 ways to write a story'. It's just that we are not familiar with all of them yet. They are yet to be discovered.

However, and obviously, it is easier to stick to common ground, especially if you are just setting out on your writing journey. It is no accident that detective fiction, particularly from the Golden Age, is often referred to as 'cosy'. To return to Jean Hanff Korelitz and *The Plot*, here's Jake towards the end of the novel looking for further justification for what he's done:

Imitation and limitation

In my world, the migration of a story is something we recognize, and we respect. Works of art can overlap, or they can sort of chime with one another. Right now, with some of the anxieties we have around appropriation, it's become downright combustible, but I've always thought there was a kind of beauty to it, the way narratives get told and retold. It's how stories survive through the ages. You can follow an idea from one author's work to another, and to me that's something I find powerful and exciting.[45]

Continuation fiction and co-writing

With my novel *First Frost*, co-written with the editor James Gurbutt and published under the pseudonym James Henry, we effectively continued someone else's series: same setting, concept and most notably lead character/protagonist. This was DCI Jack Frost, a grumpy cop who oversaw some bizarre crimes in a made-up English town called Denton. Denton was a cross between Swindon and Chelmsford, and firmly stuck in grey, 1980s British cultural and political impoverishment. Frost was the creation of radio scriptwriter R. D. Wingfield, and radio was where he first surfaced in the 1970s. Wingfield's novel, *Frost At Christmas*, was initially rejected, before finally being published in the UK (following successful publication in Canada) in 1989. However, it was the TV adaptation, starring the very popular actor David Jason, that really set the series alight.

While Wingfield went on to write a further five Jack Frost novels, the TV series ran and ran, with the adaptations quickly giving way to original scripts. Yet the novels remained very popular until Wingfield died in 2007. It's hard to put their success down to anything other than the strength of character, and the format of a quite traditional, albeit misanthropic cosy crime drama. British comedy drama is studded with misanthropes, and Jack Frost outdid most of them with his often blunt comments. I was aware of the TV series, as most of my generation in the UK would have been. Yet I had not read one of Wingfield's novels when I was informed that Wingfield's estate and his publisher were looking for someone to write a continuation of the series.

Continuation series are everywhere now. We have Sophie Hannah taking on Poirot, of course, and Lee Child's brother Andrew taking on Reacher. Two writers have continued Robert Ludlum's Bourne thrillers (Eric Van Lustbader, and then Brian Freeman), and David Lagercrantz continued Stieg Larsson's Lisbeth Salander journey. Innovatively expanding on the concept, we also have Nicola Upson's take on Josephine Tey's legacy, by creating a whole series based on the pseudonymous author of an actual 1930s crime series; and then there's Jill Dawson's thriller, *The Crime Writer*, which captures and murderously reinterprets a troubled period in Patricia Highsmith's life.

We also have James Patterson and his army of 'co-writers'. The phrase 'co-writer' is interesting in Patterson's case, as Patterson doesn't actually write the novels. What he does is direct and edit them. He explained the process when I interviewed him for the *Independent On Sunday* at his home in upstate New York in 2008. There, in his large office overlooking the Hudson River, were at least thirteen manuscripts – all printed paper copies – on a long shelf, currently in 'production'. They were from his various series, all being written by different authors. Patterson takes great care in choosing his authors – latterly Bill Clinton – and then enables their process, so the end result, depending on the series, sounds very much like the

Imitation and limitation

previous works in that series, be it, say, Alex Cross, Maximum Ride, Women's Murder Club or Michael Bennett. All, however, are similar, in that they are fixated on 'pace', and as Patterson says, 'being in the scene'.[46]

Sentences and paragraphs are short. Word count is strictly determined beforehand. Patterson provides extremely detailed notes and edits on the initial drafts as they come flooding in, to quickly go back out. It's an incredible creative 'factory', or 'studio', justly deserving Patterson's global success. Like many other genre writers, Patterson had originally hoped for success as a writer of more 'literary' thrillers, akin to his first novel, *The Thomas Berryman Number*. That he was a top advertising executive opened his mind to building and 'maximising' his brand instead. He couldn't write the novels (or create the product) quickly enough, so he began enlisting others to work on the project with him.

R. D. Wingfield had little literary aspiration and was not particularly prolific. Yet, he had created a very memorable character and a clear format for his novels. Each took place over a week, with every day determined by a number of chapters, or scenes. Each novel had a short prologue in italics, a central investigation, and four or so loosely connected sub-plots. There were the recurring subsidiary characters, scant domestic life, and an endless stream of wry comments and quirky observations. I jumped at the chance to engage with a continuation of a well-known and solidly conventional series, not least because my own writing and teaching journey was taking me ever deeper into the world of crime narratives. Practically, I wanted to see how to plot, and puzzle plot, a piece of classically structured, period detective fiction. I also wanted to pull apart someone else's work and put it back together.

Crafting crime fiction

The fact that Wingfield had only written six novels – all to the same format – helped immeasurably. Of help also was the fact that Wingfield didn't innovate and didn't change his process from one book to the next. Working with James Gurbutt, our process began to seem like plotting and writing by numbers. The timing of the plot twists and the 'beats' of the investigations, the discovery of clues and reveals, the red herrings and sidetracks, the surprises and cliffhangers, and what even constituted character development and momentum, were all there. Wingfield had created, for us anyway, a crystal-clear blueprint. We even got the prose to sound similar, with plenty of adverbs and a lot of stating the obvious. Here are the beginnings of Wingfield's series, and the James Henry attempt, respectively:

> The 999 call came through just before midnight. An elderly man, voice trembling, barely audible. He sounded terrified.[47]

> He followed them up the escalator to the third floor – children's clothes and lingerie. The woman was in no hurry. He was, but he knew he had to be careful.[48]

Like the originals, in *First Frost* the POV endlessly shifted from character to character, yet the investigations did gather pace, along with aspects of personal jeopardy. What we did differently, or the licence we took, was to create a young Frost, a detective sergeant, who was at the beginning of his career. So our continuation was in fact a prequel to Wingfield's series.

First Frost was a bestseller. However, I decided that working so intimately on someone else's idea and creation, someone else's voice, style, format and setting, was a one-off for me. It was a very useful thematic and practical education. But that's just what it was – an education into someone else's thinking and way of doing things. I'd taken everything I could from the process.

Imitation and limitation

The main thing I learnt, and stick to even now, is that your own voice, ahead of a voice for a particular work, is a summation, a distillation and an exploration of a great many influences. There's only so much that you can pull, copy and try to emulate from others. Regardless of cash, there will always be an urge to prove what you can do on your own, a necessity to develop your own creation – character and plot, syntax and story. Besides, setting a novel in someone else's idea of place and period is really hard and disorientating. Denton was a damp, middle-England dump, even if it was fiction. Perfectly apt for Jack Frost – no wonder he was so catty and grumpy – but it was not such a pleasant place to inhabit as a visitor. The fact that it was invented by Wingfield created issues for me of identity, belonging and feeling. I've always felt that the places and settings that I want to use in my fiction should truly resonate and mean something, and this makes them strangely personal. You have to feel strongly enough about somewhere to set your fiction, otherwise you can't see it, smell it, taste it or properly inhabit it. My next novel, in contrast to *First Frost*, was set very close to home. And there is a story or two.

SETTING AND DESCRIPTION

It was raining at the beginning of *Get Carter*, as we know. A little further on in the first chapter, we get to this:

> I was the only one in the compartment. My slip-ons were off. My feet were up. *Penthouse* was dead. I'd killed the *Standard* twice. I had three nails left. Doncaster was forty minutes off.
>
> I looked along the black mohair to my socks. I flexed a toe. The toenail made a sharp ridge in the wool. I'd have to cut them when I got in. I might be doing a lot of footwork over the weekend.[1]

We have a sense of what Jack Carter is wearing aside from his quality socks. We also know that he's on a mission. Effectively, we have description – place and person – working perfectly with plot, or if you like, purpose. Another way of thinking about purpose is as momentum. If we go back a few decades, and from the second sentence of *The Big Sleep*, we get this:

> I was wearing my powder-blue suit, with dark blue shirt, tie and display handkerchief, black brogues, black wool socks, with dark blue clocks on them. I was neat, clean, shaved and sober, and I didn't care who knew it. I was everything the well-dressed private detective ought to be. I was calling on four million dollars.[2]

Setting and description

Clearly Philip Marlowe is also a snappy dresser, who cares a lot about his appearance. We can also see how Chandler uses carefully considered repetition. (Look how many times the word 'blue' is used.) Here Chandler seamlessly integrates description, a sense of place and character, and purpose – the calling on that four million dollars. Ian Rankin, in a 2005 introduction to an edition of *The Big Sleep*, says the opening is his 'favourite paragraph in all crime fiction'. Rankin himself is a dab hand at a good opening. This is from one of his finest Rebus novels, *Let It Bleed*:

> A winter night, screaming out of Edinburgh.
> The front car was being chased by three others. In the chasing cars were police officers. Sleet was falling through the darkness, blowing horizontally. In the second of the police cars, Inspector John Rebus had his teeth bared. He gripped the doorhandle with one hand, and the front edge of his passenger seat with the other.[3]

The chase continues, along with Rebus' growing sense of fear that the icy weather will cause a terrible accident. The brief section ends with this: 'Rebus thought: I don't want to die in the dark.' From chase to coward, a lot of ground is covered in just a few sentences. We get a sense of Edinburgh in winter, the thrill and momentum of a chase, and Rebus' sense of mortality. We can see him in that car, gripping the seat in fear. Setting and description in all three examples are expansively working together; we get a sense of the place and the person, along with plot.

Weather

What is also fascinating, as we travel down the decades with these extracts – 1995, 1970, 1939 – is the arresting inclusion of

93

weather. If we shift forward nearly twenty years, we can find
this from Steph Cha's neo-noir debut *Follow Her Home* (2013):

> It was about ten o'clock on a Friday in mid-July, the Los Angeles
> night warm and dry, the only wind rising from the whoosh and
> zoom of traffic on Rossmore. I was wearing a slinky black dress,
> black patent leather platform pumps, silver cascade earrings,
> and a black lambskin clutch. I was perfumed, manicured, and
> impeccably coiffed. I was everything a half-employed twenty-
> something should be on the sober end of a Friday night. I was
> calling on an open bar at Luke's new apartment, ready to spend
> a little time and respectability on a blurry and colorful evening.[4]

Yes, the Chandler, and specifically *The Big Sleep*, echoes
are loud and clear. (Look how many times the word 'black'
is used, yet we end the paragraph on a 'colorful' note.) Steph
Cha is one of the most inventive and interesting crime writers publishing now, and more than acknowledges her debt to
Chandler. Indeed, the beginning of *Follow Her Home* could well
have featured in the last chapter on imitation and limitation.
However, Cha makes the private-eye trope her own in a very
twenty-first-century way, with her series narrator protagonist
Korean American Juniper Song. Like Philip Marlow and his
brogues, Juniper Song also has a thing about fancy footwear.
However, the similarities soon take on key differences, while the
LA background is brought firmly up to digital and brand-savvy
speed. What hasn't changed so much is the weather, or at least
sharp descriptions of it.

At the beginning of *Follow Her Home*, it's actually 'warm and
dry', as opposed to looking like the 'hard wet rain' of *The Big
Sleep*. Nevertheless, Cha, like Chandler, and Lewis and Rankin
quoted above, along with numerous other writers, calls on the
weather to bring a place and a character within that place

Setting and description

firmly and vividly to life. We all spend an inordinate amount of time thinking about and experiencing the weather, so why shouldn't it feature prominently in fiction? Why shouldn't it help us identify with a setting, to enhance that sense of place, and a character's mood within that world?

The novel I wrote after *First Frost*, *My Criminal World*, features a successful crime writer struggling to write his next novel. This is from, as labelled, 'Part One, The Wrong Beginning':

> As ever, I'm probably staring out of the window, at flowers, at foliage anyway – a few straggly roses, clematis possibly, ferns perhaps, a vine maybe, and plenty of other stuff, weeds notably. Or I'm looking at the sky through the long, slim, slightly grimy panes above the French windows – watching clouds build and threaten, while urging my mind to race off elsewhere.[5]

Of course the weather crept in, despite Elmore Leonard's first rule of writing (from his *10 Rules of Writing*) being notoriously: 'Never open a book with weather.'[6] Perhaps never one to obey rules, let alone his own, Leonard in fact often opened a book with the weather, most notably in *Get Shorty*.

> When Chili first came to Miami Beach twelve years ago they were having one of their off-and-on cold winters: thirty-four degrees the day he met Tommy Carlo for lunch at Vesuvio's on South Collins and had his leather jacket ripped off. One his wife had given him for Christmas a year ago, before they moved down here.[7]

Leonard did quantify that statement with the following: 'If it's only to create atmosphere, and not a character's reaction to the weather, you don't want to go on too long.'[8] This is a key point in relation to all description, and one that I touched upon in Chapter 1. It's the character's observations of the weather, the character's reactions to weather, that matter.

Crafting crime fiction

This is how we actually see and sense a place in fiction, if properly controlled and narrated. The weather doesn't just exist for its own sake, in the same way that a place doesn't exist for its own sake. Weather provides both active and reactive opportunities for a point-of-view character. Weather can also help with atmosphere and tension – think of all those frozen Nordic noir tales, or mysteries that go bump in the night. Think of the effect that a dense fog can have, or a burning sun. Though in reality, it's the effect it has, or had or will have on the character(s) that matters – otherwise we wouldn't know it was even happening.

Metafiction

My nod to weather and Leonard in *My Criminal World* was all part of the metafictional nature of the novel: a crime writer writing, or in fact struggling to write his next novel. (Even the name of the protagonist, David Slavitt, was a play. The real David Slavitt was in fact a US academic who wrote a series of lurid genre novels, with titles such as *The Exhibitionist*, *The Voyeur* and *The Sacrifice*, under the pseudonym Henry Sutton ... He'd borrowed my name, so I thought I'd borrow his. He got the joke all right, and was very gracious about it. At the time he'd recently published a metafictional novel under his own name, intriguingly titled *Aspects of the Novel: A Novel*.[9] Largely it's about ideas and inspiration, and how these can be incorporated, both successfully and unsuccessfully, in fiction.)

Leonard's *Get Shorty* is in many ways a masterclass on fictional approaches and writing. I used to run a seminar on *Get Shorty* as a writing manual. There are so many insightfully instructive lines. Take this for instance: 'I like the coat story, too, you mentioned. It plays, but would work better if it wasn't a flashback.'[10] Or: 'You know why it doesn't work. I mean even before I find out you don't know how it ends. There's nobody to sympathise with. Who's the good guy? You don't have one ... You have a first act, you're partway into the second.'[11] And: 'Once I have the authentic sounds of speech, the rhythms, man, the patois, I can actually begin to think the way those guys do, get inside their heads.'[12] While the above quotes are in reference to screenwriting, as *Get Shorty* is in part a comic deconstruction of Hollywood, the advice on how to get inside the head of a character is illuminating and useful.

It also reminds me of Jim Thompson's best and most shocking novel *The Killer Inside Me*, published some forty years earlier in 1952. There is a moment of unusual and knowing literary reflection from the brutal narrator Lou Ford:

> In lots of books I read, the writer seems to go haywire every time he reaches a high point. He'll start leaving out punctuation and running his words together and babble about stars flashing and sinking into a deep dreamless sea. And you can't figure out whether the hero's laying his girl or a cornerstone. I guess that kind of crap is supposed to be pretty deep stuff – a lot of the book reviewers eat it up, I notice. But the way I see it is, the writer is just too goddam lazy to do his job. And I'm not lazy, whatever else I am.[13]

While both texts address concepts of writing and the writer, they are also full of voice, of tone, of atmosphere: *Get Shorty* from the use of dialogue, while in *The Killer Inside Me* Thompson utilises interiority, or thought. We get such a strong sense of character from these 'voices', we can picture who's speaking, who's thinking.

Crafting crime fiction

Voice, tone and dialogue

Description doesn't actually have to look like 'description'. As with the senses, and using all of them, place and character become clear; the mood of the character especially. Dialogue is another way of looking at description, as is interiority, or that internal voice. It's also another way of looking at setting; voice and dialogue add to a sense of place, and time. Leonard believed that you should be able to 'see' a character from how they spoke, and what they said, the 'tone' of their voice. He also stated, in his rules, that you should not 'go into great detail describing places and things'. 'Unless you're Margaret Atwood and can paint scenes with language …'[14] Atwood is actually a great fan of crime fiction; her acknowledgement of Leonard being just one example. She also wrote the poem 'In Love with Raymond Chandler'. Read it, and you'll understand why and just what Atwood thought Chandler could do with words, with description. Here's the very beginning:

> An affair with Raymond Chandler, what a joy! Not because of the mangled bodies and the marinated cops and hints of eccentric sex, but because of his interest in furniture.[15]

Atwood thought that Chandler would have made a fantastic editor of *House & Garden* magazine, not just because of his interest in furnishings, but his eye for detail. Or was that really Philip Marlowe's eye for detail? Unlike Leonard, Chandler was certainly not shy of lengthy, simile- and metaphor-ridden description. That Edwardian education premised on the classics, then put through the Californian street-smart wringer, clearly created Marlowe's eye for detail and 'voice', or the voice of those Marlowe novels. This is where metafictional elements come into the scene, because as much as we like to think our characters are doing the seeing and describing, they are extensions of the writer's resource and equipment.

The reason I chose to illustrate this chapter with my and others' forays into 'metafictional' territory – a chapter on setting and description, after all! – is in part to highlight the personal nature of observation and how you go about capturing a place in fiction (as well as the interconnected nature of writing and reading, imitating and emulating, and learning from others – it's a never-ending journey). Look around you. What do you see, hear, smell, taste, touch? What does something actually feel like, for instance? How best to describe it? But with fiction it is not how you yourself would necessarily describe it, but how your characters would. This is the big difference, while these things are also closely linked. You, the writer, are trying to see things in the way your characters do. There are numerous creative writing classes premised on describing what you see around you, or the place you grew up, or somewhere that means a great deal to you. And in a way you continue doing this as your writing moves from a classroom situation, or fledgling approach, to something more sustained and professional. You keep looking around you, seeing familiar things, things that might move you, things that create deep feelings, and then you might begin to try to see those familiar things in different ways; how someone else might view them.

Defamiliarising the familiar is a key tenet of imaginative writing, and a way to invest your writing with a distinctive edge. Innovative, literary writing – writing that is aware of its syntactical as well as its thematic and storytelling ambition – can be reliant on telling the same old things in sparkling new ways. It's the avoidance of easy cliché, and the striving to see and say things differently, afresh, in ways that haven't been articulated before. Chandler's similes and metaphors were new, and certainly new to the genre, even if the 'views' he was describing, or the weather for that matter wasn't. Same goes for Ted Lewis and his rain. It's always rained, but who'd ever put it in such an obvious way right at the beginning of a novel? Leonard meanwhile was using his characters to speak in ways that made us see them, while also enabling us to understand how writing for the screen works, and how important humour is to an entertaining and engaging read (to be explored further in Chapter 8). Plus, you also feel that Leonard was reminding writers not to take themselves too seriously.

This particular theme – one of debunking 'literary' pretension – was obviously captured in the passage by Jim Thompson. These were his thoughts about writing, as much as *Get Shorty* is laden with Leonard's approach to craft. Arguably, one of the most respected literary giants of the modern era, Margaret Atwood, also has a dig at 'literary' pretension while articulating, with humour, her appreciation of Chandler – the standout genre writer of his age. Her endorsement means a great deal, especially in the sense of bridging that 'genre/literary' divide.

Sense of place

Setting is sense of place, of being in the scene. If that sense of place is determined in part by the author's voice, then language, the very fabric of the writing, is intrinsically linked to setting. The action within the story arises in part out of place. More importantly, the events shouldn't seem wholly 'out of place' in that world; or at least, after perhaps some initial surprise or shock, they should be seen to be organic, natural, entirely possible in retrospect. Place, like character, has a personality, a 'voice', albeit one that is subservient to the 'voice' of the 'observer', the character, and also the voice of the whole. Place doesn't just need to earn its 'place' within a fiction, it also needs to be part of the story, the mystery, adding not just to atmosphere but also suspense. There are numerous ways that weather, for instance, can play a part. It wasn't just rain, when Lewis was contriving atmosphere: he gives us the mood of both place and character. While in the beginning of Rankin's *Let it Bleed*, we don't just have a car chase in treacherous conditions, but Rebus' sudden sense of mortality. I've focused on weather because of the opportunities it allows writers: in capturing a place, adding to the story and enhancing characterisation.

The sense of place can be controlled by descriptive passages, and dialogue (which can itself be descriptive, suggestive of place and character) and setting can also be used to build meaning, mood and momentum. Effectively, setting should be utilised to add to the suspense and narrative drive of your story. Commonly, crime series are dependent on place and identity, on recognition and familiarity, while also, in striking cases, defamiliarising the familiar. Crime writers and their series characters become synonymous with certain cities, territories, terrain. There are so many to choose from. The Spanish writer Manuel Vázquez Montalbán brilliantly captured Barcelona emerging from the horror of the Franco era with his Pepe Carvalho investigations. Such was his influence on the Italian writer Andrea Camilleri, Camilleri called his own series character Inspector Salvo Montalbano in his honour. Camilleri via Montalbano became synonymous with Sicily, albeit largely in fictionally named towns, on both page and screen.

Crafting crime fiction

Maj Sjöwall and Per Wahlöö brought 1960s and early 1970s Stockholm alive, including the darkest corners, with their ten Martin Beck novels. Henning Mankell then took on their mantle with his Inspector Kurt Wallander series, set in the small Swedish town of Ystad. These two series are not just responsible for what became the Scandi Noir crime fiction wave, they also shifted the ground on which crime fiction, or detective fiction, operated, to a cold, dark reality. Realism and the crime novel were never more 'realised'. Actual cities, towns and streets were portrayed, along with highly believable and often disturbing cases and procedures. The term 'police procedural' became increasingly known and popular across Europe and the world (though American writer Lawrence Treat's 1945 novel *V as in Victim* is commonly regarded as the first police procedural). Writers were increasingly challenged to create highly engaging characters and captivating 'plots', as well as to follow correct or recognisable procedures. Description also depended on resource and research, or fieldwork. Setting took us into the mortuary, the forensic lab, not just the police car and HQ. It took us to court, to prison, to every imaginable crime scene, often painstakingly portrayed.

It also took us, when done well and convincingly, to the aspects of drudgery and tedium associated with policing. Again, Sjöwall and Wahlöö did not hold back on the more mundane aspects of the job. There are numerous descriptions of nothing happening for days, weeks even. For instance, this line comes from the first novel in the series, *Roseanna*: 'It had been an uneventful and dreary day, full of sneezing and spitting and dull routine.'[16] *Roseanna* is written in a very lucid, succinct and straightforward way, with little embellishment. Modest from the word go, Martin Beck is described, without any flair, as such:

Setting and description

> Martin Beck wasn't chief of the Homicide Squad and had
> no such ambitions. Sometimes he doubted if he would ever
> make superintendent although the only things that could actu-
> ally stand in his way were death or some very serious error
> in his duties. He was a First Detective Inspector with the
> National Police and had been with the Homicide Bureau for
> eight years.[17]

The paragraph continues: 'There were people who thought
that he was the country's most capable examining officer.'
Martin Beck would never consider such a thing of himself,
however. Yet Beck's and the authors' landmark strength lay
in the slow uncovering of a corrupted and perverted welfare
state. Sweden then was supposedly anything but. Indeed, it was
largely regarded as the model for a caring and well-educated
society. Beck, courtesy of committed Marxists Sjöwall and
Wahlöö, also notably reminded us of the common nature of
murder and murderers. 'Words like repulsive, horrible, and
bestial belong in the newspapers, not in your thinking. A murderer is a regular human being, only more unfortunate and
maladjusted.'[18]

While the procedural aspects of the ten-novel Martin Beck
series can be slow, mundane, largely to the book, with Beck
himself suffering from endless bad stomachs and a frosty home
life – all matter-of-factly described – humanity surges through
the novels, spotlighting what's really intrinsic to the genre. Life
and death, and one another.

Forensics

Val McDermid, a former journalist and crime reporter, as so
many crime writers are, has long recognised the importance

of proper research, specifically in the area of forensics. Her *Forensics: The Anatomy of Crime* is a must for any crime writer tackling criminal investigations and procedure. In the introduction she outlines the idea that 'the application of science to the solving of crime is the reason I am gainfully employed', and that crime fiction 'only began with an evidence-based legal system'.[19]

Forensics can be both description and setting, adding to the environment, atmosphere and sense of place of a novel – indeed, the very character of a novel, as distinct from the protagonist(s). One way of looking at this is as solid ground, or space that lends identity, authenticity, if not accuracy, to a fiction. We're setting our fictional stories, our characters loose in real situations, places and environments.

Yet the writer has to get this right: all these places and procedures, this science, not to mention all manner of legal matters (which obviously change from territory to territory); or at least, make them believable. Readers tend to go along with a scenario if it feels and sounds right, so there is no need to worry about producing something that's wholly accurate. Sticking entirely to the facts – not so much in relation to place, but procedure – would invariably be very dull, which is why there are lines in the Martin Beck series that cleverly mention the tedium and days stretching out with no leads or progress, without us actually seeing them, or without us having to read pages and pages about nothing happening. Days, weeks, even months can go by in just a sentence; the use of time management is descriptively and structurally very smart. Though this was before DNA, vast databases and digital technology sped up many procedures, Sjöwall and Wahlöö, like McDermid, recognised the fact that science and technology aren't everything. 'I can't let the technology seduce me – the heart of the book has to be about characters', McDermid has said.[20]

There is another side to this as well. Understanding and researching such science, particularly in the case of forensics, or computer science in relation to databases and cyber-crime, can also be very hard and diverting work. There will always be someone who knows more and knows better, which is why we strive for authenticity, especially if you work to the maxim that less is more. We're writing fiction, not an essay for a science journal or a legal website. Too much research, too many facts, as McDermid clearly acknowledges, get in the way of characters, and seeing as characters control plot, then no amount of science will make for an engaging read. Fancy knowledge is a sideshow. There'll always be someone controlling, directing, discovering, stumbling, and it's their searching, their chasing, their interpretation that matters. Besides, an abundance of so many 'clever' facts, or police procedural regulations, sticks out like a sore thumb. Knowledge is not clever in itself – it's what you do with it.

You can also spend a huge amount of time researching something for it never to make it into the story, or the final edit. I know writers who become completely obsessed with trying to get something 'right'. I've found that the most efficient way of researching for me is to allow the plot to dictate the information I need. I'm directed by what I need to know, and when I need to know it, and research accordingly as the writing progresses.

Period settings

Historical fiction, that is contemporary fiction set in the past – and let's not forget that time can be as pertinent and demanding as place – requires a whole raft of skills and resource. From a syntactical point of view, most historically-set crime fiction is written with the contemporary reader in mind: shortish sentences and paragraphs, limited or clearly demarcated POVs, with a narrative line, or timelines following linear routes. The Victorian trope of wavering POV, and often a faux narrator, are less commonly adopted. However, writers such as Stuart Turton (*The Seven Deaths of Evelyn Hardcastle*)[21] and Eleanor Catton (*The Luminaries*)[22] are innovatively playing with such tropes and creating highly contemporary crime novels set in the past.

Writers of more traditional historical crime fictions will also nevertheless need to consider aspects of modernity, psychology and consciousness in relation to character. In a literary sense we think the way we do because of how others have thought before. Placing characters in a setting that pre-dates modern psychology and, for example, Freudian analytical thinking, would logically involve trying to get into their headspace – arguably a place that regarded the self in quite a different way. Every aspect of our being is in some way the sum of what has gone before. If you remove decades and centuries of thought and reasoning, of understanding, of being, we find different ways of thinking, different desires and survival strategies. By reading novels and other kinds of texts written in the historical period we are writing about we can encounter conceptions of the self and how society functioned – and even see how those authors set their own work in times past. However, adopting historical space is a licence, a contemporary compromise, as writers will always be looking over their shoulder with hindsight and invariably be instilling current, informed thinking. Culture is ever-dynamic, while literary culture and crime fiction in particular couldn't be more pertinent, more current – in part because of the general swiftness of its production and dissemination.

Yet, historical crime fiction is vastly popular; perhaps because it adds to the sense of escapism, of being drawn into 'another' imaginative world, which might operate on very different terms. Numerous writers pull it off in myriad ways. One of the most interesting and popular current approaches is Abir Mukherjee's Wyndham and Banerjee series of novels, set in Raj-era India. The first in the series, *A Rising Man*, is set in 1919, and begins:

> At least he was well dressed. Black tie, tux, the works. If you're going to get yourself killed, you may as well look your best.
>
> I coughed as the stench clawed at my throat. In a few hours the smell would be unbearable; strong enough to turn the stomach of a Calcutta fishmonger. I pulled out a packet of Capstans, tapped out a cigarette, lit it and inhaled, letting the sweet smoke purge my lungs. Death smells worse in the tropics. Most things do.[23]

We're on the streets of Calcutta, in the POV of Captain Wyndham of 'His Majesty's Imperial Police Force'. Wyndham is soon joined by Surendranath Banerjee, a young sergeant 'with an accent straight off a Surrey golf course', and who's otherwise known as Sergeant Surrender-not Banerjee. Banerjee is the product of a recent government policy to 'increase the number of natives in every branch of the administration'. In the mouth of the brutally mutilated body of the *'burra sahib'*, Wyndham comes across a balled-up note. It says: 'No more warnings. English blood will run in the street. Quit India!'[24] What follows is a twisty plot, playing with post-coloniality. Wyndham, an ex-Scotland Yard detective and First World War veteran looking for a fresh start, increasingly relies on Banerjee's local knowledge, warmth and intelligence. It's a highly entertaining and atmospheric piece of detective fiction that goes some way to rewriting and readdressing historical prejudices and ignorance.

The title comes from a line from Rudyard Kipling's poem 'City of Dreadful Night'. Mukherjee admits to a very complicated relationship with Kipling, not least because of Kipling's overt racism and support of the colonial system of which he was firmly part. Yet, Mukherjee also admits to drawing on Kipling for 'a glimpse into that time and place'.[25] So here's the thing: could *A Rising Man* have been written in 1919? Obviously not, and it's not just the thematic considerations, character depictions and postcolonial approach to colonialism that make this a very contemporary novel, with a historical setting. It's the language, the syntax, even the graphic depictions of violence that move the form, the genre forward a century. From the first page:

> The body lay twisted, face up and half submerged in an open sewer. Throat cut, limbs at unnatural angles, and a large brown bloodstain on a starched white dress shirt. Some fingers were missing from one mangled hand and an eye had been pecked out of its socket – this final indignity the work of the hulking black crows who even now kept angry vigil from the rooftops above. All in all, not a very dignified end for a *burra sahib*.[26]

Popular Indian crime fiction didn't come into existence until the 1930s, and was largely due to the writer Sharadindu Bandyopadhyay introducing us to the Bengali detective Byomkesh Bakshi. Bengali crime fiction went on to dominate and endlessly reinterpret the detective novel for the rest of the twentieth century across the Indian subcontinent. In the Anglophone world of 1919, however, we find crime novel of the

year going to American Isabel Ostrander's *Ashes to Ashes*. This is
how that novel begins:

> 'Well, that's the situation.' Wendle Foulkes' keen old eyes nar-
> rowed as they gazed into the turbulent ones of his client across
> the wide desk. 'This last batch of securities, absolutely all that
> you have left of you inheritance from your father. Leave them
> alone where they are and you are sure of three thousand a year
> for yourself and for Leila after you.'
>
> Norman Storm struck the desk impatiently, and his lean aris-
> tocratic face darkened.[27]

Three years earlier, John Buchan had brought us *The Thirty
Nine Steps*, with this opening:

> I returned from the City about three o'clock on that May after-
> noon pretty disgusted with life. I had been three months in the
> Old Country, and was fed up with it. If anyone had told me a
> year ago that I would have been feeling like that I should have
> laughed at him; but there was the fact. The weather made me
> liverish, the talk of the ordinary Englishman made me sick, I
> couldn't get enough exercise, and the amusements of London
> seemed as flat as soda-water that had been standing in the sun.
> 'Richard Hannay,' I kept telling myself, 'you have got into the
> wrong ditch, my friend, and you had better climb out.'[28]

Great to see the weather appearing so chillingly; but who
uses the word 'liverish' nowadays? Or the phrase 'you have got
yourself into the wrong ditch', even if they're writing histori-
cally set fiction?

Three years after the publication of Isabel Ostrander's now
largely forgotten *Ashes to Ashes*, Agatha Christie introduced us to
Tommy and Tuppence in *The Secret Adversary*. Christie herself
gives us a little foretaste in an epigraph. '*To all those who lead
monotonous lives in the hope that they may experience at second-hand the*

delights and dangers of adventure.'[29] The beginning of Chapter 1, subtitled 'The Young Adventurers, Ltd', introduces us to the protagonists, as such:

> 'Tommy, old thing!'
> 'Tuppence, old bean!'
>
>   The two young people greeted each other affectionately, and momentarily blocked the Dover Street tube exit in doing so. The adjective 'old' was misleading. Their united ages would certainly not have totalled forty-five.[30]

Note the authorial, or omniscient narrator, aside from the language. As has been variously acknowledged, Christie drew inspiration for amateur detective duo Tommy Beresford and Prudence 'Tuppence' Cowley from Ostrander's series characters, ex-cop Tim McCarty and fireman Dennis Riordan. Again, we could be discussing this in the previous chapter ('Imitation and limitation'). However, setting is as prone to imitation and emulation, if not parody, as the weather and all manner of descriptive tricks and tropes. The key point here, however, is the nature of the past, and historicism, and where inspiration and influence lie.

The sentence right at the beginning of Abir Mukherjee's *A Rising Man* that stands out to me is: 'Black tie, tux, the works.'[31] The phrase 'tux', short for tuxedo of course, became popular in 1920s North America. It was not a common British colonial term at all. 'Dinner jacket' or 'black tie' would have been used. Yet, here we have a now common term we all understand, being used in, frankly, the wrong place at the wrong time. Do we mind? Not at all, because *A Rising Man* is an excellent contemporary crime novel, with a historical setting, operating on a number of levels. It feels authentic and accessible to the contemporary reader. What it's not is a parody, or even a fiction trying to be a period piece. The novel is especially knowing in its relation to time and place, and could only have been written now.

Mukherjee has spoken about his personal and familial links to Calcutta, the era, and his recent visits there, and how these provided the real inspiration (as noted above). Kipling and his abhorrent attitudes to race provided something to write around and against, while attempting to write a more truthful interpretation of time and place, of history. The novel, as is often claimed, can be a way to search for a greater truth. Essentially, with Mukherjee's series we have connection and conflict: a deeply felt and personal sense of place, time and injustice. That he has made such good 'entertainment' out of it is testament to his skill as a writer of 'contemporary' crime fiction. And it is just this conflicted sense of connection and identity, feeling unsure about a circumstance or situation and questioning it, that can provide the spark that your fiction needs. In the same way that we draw on others for creative inspiration for our characters, our relationships and feelings to them, and perhaps our understanding or misunderstanding of certain relationships, be they functional and dysfunctional, loving or troubling, so a similar approach can and often enables a greater concept of setting and place.

Setting as character

As has been mentioned, settings have characteristics, personalities that coincide with, or run alongside the 'homegrown' characters. Many writers and critics talk about settings as being characters in their own right; as powerful, for instance, as the protagonist(s). However, like character and plot, and the umbilical cord that links them, so we can add a third element to the equation – place (and by place I'm also referring to era/time).

Place/setting is all part of the imaginative world that is being created by the writer. This world has to be convincing, and operate according to its own rules and dimensions. Any procedural aspects, forensics or legalities, for example, need to be stamped by the locale. For instance, weather needs to be appropriate, possible, even if it's unseasonal or freakish. But most importantly the character of the place needs to chime (even if in purposeful discord) with the characters, the protagonists. This is why I like to think of setting as an extension of the character and the dominating viewpoints, rather than something more separate or distinct. Obviously, the POVs do the 'seeing', and it's the characters' moods and agendas that largely do the 'feeling'. Description brings it all together. The 'higher power', or real control and driver, is of course the author. And the more the author 'sees' and 'feels' a place, invariably the better it will be rendered.

The 'purpose' of the place, why a fiction is set somewhere, and why a place might enable a greater pull on the 'plot', can be further enhanced by an author's strength of feeling for a place, and or era, which as in Mukherjee's case, can arise from personal, historical connections. Of course, for a place you don't know well already, on-the-ground research and online research can achieve a lot. However, we all know there's nothing like being somewhere, or having been somewhere, to bring a place alive in our own minds. Indeed, where we were born, where we grew up, how we grew up, what we witnessed, who was around us, can instil great emotions. And it's those emotions, particularly if they are conflictual, troubled, questioning, which can be the spur for fiction, for fiction that means some-thing, at least to you. Plot, character and setting, all wrapped up in personal history.

Lived knowledge

We have discussed writing what you know, and not being afraid of writing about what you don't know; we are creating fiction, after all. We want to create new and exciting criminal worlds, which operate on their own terms. However, setting, I've always believed – and by extension description, because that's how you 'describe' and capture a place – needs feeling, con-nection, knowledge, and knowledge beyond simply acquired knowledge. By this I mean lived knowledge. This can be of great inspiration to your fiction.

My second novel, *Bank Holiday Monday*,[32] had a backstory (there'll be more on such structural devices in the next chapter) involving a character who'd suffered a traumatic experience in Australia. That part of Australia was described in some detail – the sense of it and so forth. I'd never been there, but wanted to draw an analogy with a vast, open stretch of dry land back in England. It was misplaced. I know I never got to grips with those scenes – just as I knew, when co-writing *First Frost*, that I couldn't really 'see' Denton. Indeed, I even went to the length of drawing a small map of the town, to help my geography (which was included in the published work). For my novel *My Criminal World*, which I wrote straight after *First Frost*, I knew I had to return to familiar territory, albeit armed with some more practical detective fiction resource and writing experi-ence. So I began at my desk, literally: 'As ever, I'm probably staring out of the window, at flowers, at foliage anyway …'[33]

Crafting crime fiction

I'm doing this as I write now, on a beautiful, early spring morning. Clear sky, soft sun, slight breeze.

For *My Criminal World* I stepped out of my front door; I considered my job at the university up the road: the concrete campus with its walkways and shadows; my colleagues there, with their then focus on 'high literature', and seemingly insurmountable canons. For some, genre was almost a dirty word. I looked more carefully at the route I took walking my children to and from school. I thought about our neighbours and local friends; the shops and pubs, parks and services, at exactly what life would be like in this environment if I were a successful genre writer, a bestselling crime writer operating outside the academy, but with close links to it. The character David Slavitt came to mind. An endlessly hospitable host and keen cook, I also gave him a lovely academic wife: star of her department at the university up the road.

Academics are more than happy to turn a blind eye to popularism, if it means a good meal, or so I had the subsidiary characters in my novel behave. I also gave David chubby fingers, and an increasing sense of paranoia; he doesn't think he can write another bestseller and nor does his forceful agent, while he's beginning to suspect his wife of having an affair. How could he blame her? Then the young man – a student no less – is found dead, and the police begin to ask David more and more questions. This half of the novel was set in a world I knew pretty well: one right on my doorstep.

The other element to the novel is the 'crime novel' David is writing. This is a short police procedural set in a coastal town: effectively the town I was born in, Great Yarmouth, and a place that has long haunted me because of its physical and historical beauty, and more recent deprivation, along with a number of troubling family connections. I'd already visited this terrain in my first novel, which was not a crime novel, and would visit it again in a later crime series (discussed in Chapters 6 and 7). The police procedural aspects feature a crooked detective, Britt Hayes, who's in a relationship with a mysterious former hitman, Howie Jones.

The novel within that novel, titled *Kristine*, begins with the discovery of a naked female corpse on a desolate stretch of scrubby sand dunes, sandwiched between a run-down cara-van park and the cold, grey North Sea.[34] This was in direct acknowledgement of and in homage to Sjöwall and Wahlöö's *Roseanna*. Also, at the time of writing *My Criminal World*, which is effectively a psychological thriller wrapped around a police procedural, there was much urgent and necessary debate about the depiction of violence towards women in crime fic-tion and drama. This resulted in the setting up of the Staunch Book Prize, which celebrates the best crime novel where no female character experiences violence. The award continues to be controversial, with many arguing that it's not realistic and too confining. Notably, as Val McDermid has stated: 'When women write about violence against women, it will almost inevitably be more terrifying because women grow up know-ing that to be female is to be at risk of attack. We write about violence from the inside, from the perspective of the victim. Men on the other hand do not grow up with the notion of themselves as potential victims, so when they write about it, it's from the outside.'[35]

What I did know about when writing *Kristine* and *My Criminal World* was Great Yarmouth: the town, the characters, the weather. I'd grown up with the atmosphere of the place deeply lodged in my mind, in a not wholly pleasant way. There were wonderful and intriguing aspects to the town, just as there were some horrendous goings-on: the local press can be a great resource for factual criminal activity. Of course, strictly speaking, this wasn't for me to observe and depict, but my characters. Yet, and back to an earlier point, I found while writing them that these characters were a 'natural' part of the place, even if they'd drifted there or found themselves there inadvertently. The 'crimes' they perpetrated and investigated, and the greater 'crime' of the place, the town (the most deprived in the region), or effectively crime orchestrated and enabled by the state, were, I felt, true. This feeling came from my long association with and knowledge of Great Yarmouth, but of course in *My Criminal World* my feelings were channelled through the crime writer David Slavitt's first-person perspective, who then had to channel it through Britt Hayes and Howie Jones' third-person subjective POVs.

The layers of feeling and association, of identity and connection to a place (and even an era), can be the basis for a great many settings that mean something to a writer. In turn, these deeply felt connections can be utilised in such a way that they will then mean something to the reader. This should also be the case even if the reader has no connection to or very little knowledge of that place. The reader is being transported to a world that might be familiar, or very unfamiliar. The job of the writer is to make it seem fresh to those who know it well, and engaging and relevant to those who don't know it. Pack it with 'felt' meaning and such a setting really begins to sing.

We all know what weather is. What rain is. It's just how that rain can rain, or look in the hills. The rain in Great Yarmouth often comes in off the sea horizontally. Cloud meets water. Fog and fret are never far away. Strangely, a number of *My Criminal*

Setting and description

World's online reviews complain about the weather. 'Why does it have to rain so much?' 'Why's it so cold and damp?' Or even this about the language: 'Why does everyone swear all the time?' To these questions and complaints, I can only say: have you ever been there?

5

STRUCTURE AND DEVELOPMENT

No plan, no plot is Lee Child's well-known practical mantra, which also speaks to Jack Reacher's philosophy and way of being.[1] Or, as detailed in Heather Martin's authorised biography, *The Reacher Guy*, Lee Child would say blithely, 'I never plot.'[2] Stephen King, we also know, greatly distrusts the idea of 'plotting', because, as he says in *On Writing*, he believes 'plotting and the spontaneity of real creation aren't compatible'.[3] Patricia Highsmith, as we also know, didn't just believe that a plot should 'never be a rigid thing', but that a plot should not even be 'completed', or wholly considered when the writing begins. 'I have to think of my own entertainment, and I like surprises', she wrote. 'Rigid plots, even if perfect, may result in a cast of automatons.'[4]

What's striking from not just these writers, but many more, is this fear of rigidity. That the more that's 'known' before a novel is completed, the less surprise there'll be. That the artistic, creative spontaneity, which appears to be consciously, or subconsciously bound up with 'literary' worth – even among great genre writers, many of whom are deeply sceptical and even abhor the concept of 'literariness' – might be damaged

Structure and development

and diluted by any such early consideration. Ian Rankin has an interesting approach to plotting and planning. As he told UEA students when he was a visiting professor at the university in 2016: 'The first draft tells me the story. The second draft tells the reader.' In other words he writes the first draft for himself, trying to work out what the story is, then he embellishes and articulates the material with the reader in mind. Rankin also revealed that his first draft is often only 40,000 words or so; well under half what the finished/final manuscript might be. As such, he said, you could consider the first draft as a 'blueprint'.

The right shape

However, with the above thoughts and quotations in mind, we need to consider what we might mean by 'plot' and 'structure', and how this then might be 'developed'. Louise Doughty, author of the often labelled 'literary thriller' *Apple Tree Yard*,[5] and a champion of both writing and storytelling, often writes in a non-linear way, and only when she has amassed a novel's worth of material, and feels she has all the necessary words, scenes and chapters completed, will she begin to order the narrative, which often involves multiple timelines and POVs. Indeed, with *Apple Tree Yard*, as she told creative writing students at UEA, she printed out all the material she had, and then spread it out on the floor of a large room, before physically moving scenes and chapters around and finding the right 'shape'. This shape involved consideration of both the most logical and most surprising, but also fulfilling and entertaining, storylines for the novel.

Lee Child, meanwhile, only ever wrote in a linear way, with most of his novels involving one timeline, and with the ultimate aim of getting Reacher from A to B, or really A to Z, while uncovering all manner of crimes and conspiracies and exacting his own form of justice. According to Heather Martin's biography, *The Reacher Guy*, Child 'thought of structure as a retrospective delusion in the mind of the reader, an illusion of intentionality'.[6] She quotes Child: 'I start with the first line, then I think OK what's the next line, then I keep going and one hundred thousand words later usually the story has worked itself out.'[7] Yet, story and plot are not necessarily the same thing, while structure and development are also often separate, distinct, though closely linked aspects of a crime novel. If we look at that sentence by Child again it reveals more of his process. 'I keep going and one hundred thousand words later usually the story has worked itself out.' So he knew that his Reacher novels were going to be around 100,000 words. This is a highly significant consideration in relation to structure.

Word count

It's not for nothing that there's a common analogy between running a marathon and writing a novel. It's about structure and narrative timelines as much as pacing. It's about going the distance. (We might also like to think of a middle-distance run as a novella or novelette, and a sprint as a short story.) How many words will my novel be? I always ask myself this question and know quite closely before I start writing whether it will be 60,000 words or 75,000 or 80,000 words. I often ask other writers and students this, and am always surprised and somewhat alarmed when they either don't know, or say it will be however many 'chapters' or 'pages'. Chapter size only means anything if we know roughly how long that chapter will be, word-count wise. Pagination is almost entirely irrelevant if we don't know the font and font size, or indeed how much white space has been included.

If we consider ebooks, the closest we generally get in relation to the length of a novel, or where we're at, is percentage. As a reader, what does 24 per cent read of a novel really mean? Then we get the calibration of how many reading hours are left. Again this is a strange, almost abstract calculation, because it is not so much the amount of time you might have left of a novel to go, but when you will be reading it, when you'll have the time to read it, and how you are concentrating during those periods. Such AI calculations in relation to reading speed cannot account for wavering concentration, or engagement, let alone aspects of narrative drive, suspense and authorial pacing and rhythm. At least not yet.

As Lee Child implies, somewhat surprisingly, in *The Reacher Guy*: the aim is to instigate a nicely linear tale, but you mustn't arrive at the ending too soon.[8] His sense of pacing, and the need for rhythm and balance – to enhance enjoyment, as well as engagement – appears to trump an all-out, onward, breathless rush to the finish. We all know when an author puts their foot down too hard, and the ongoing rush, or narrative drive, actually gets in the way of enjoyment. I've found Robert B. Parker's Spenser novels to be just a bit too quick. It's like eating a gorgeous meal too quickly. It can make you feel sick, even if you don't get to the end, which questions the very premise of a thriller being thrilling from the beginning to the end in a relatively short space of time. Pacing, as we'll explore further in Chapter 6, is a complex balancing act, linked to plot and characterisation, suspense and mystery, as well as structure and syntax. If a Lee Child Reacher novel is averagely 100,000 words long, at what points on that journey do key plot twists arise, and where or when might such a novel turn a corner? How are these things even considered by novelists such as Child, who do little or no planning in advance?

I find that, as a writer, the ebook 'read so far' percentage is actually significant and helpful to contemplate. If we think of a novel as an architectural structure, then maths and physics are crucial. Balance and control – syntactical and thematic – largely determine the success of the whole. This is also connected to the concept of genre, the crime genre especially, and reader expectations of length and form. That a crime novel – and we can even further break this down to sub-genre – should be a certain length is obviously a problematic and overly prescriptive idea. However, habits and expectations arise . If we look at the length of the twentieth-century European crime novel, they began somewhat small. The detective fiction of Georges Simenon and Agatha Christie came in on average at between 40,000 and 60,000 words per novel. The Americans, interestingly, often kept things even smaller; perhaps in part because their fiction developed from the pulps where word count and pay were intrinsically linked. Early work by James M. Cain – for instance *The Postman Always Rings Twice* and *Double Indemnity* – was remarkably short. Both those 'novels' weigh in at under 35,000 words, which is often cited as being the lower limit for a novella. More generally, novellas are commonly regarded as being between 20,000 and 50,000 words, while a novelette (a rarely used term) sits at around 10,000 to 20,000 words, and a short story anything under 15,000 words.

Of course, these numbers and labels are a construct of the publishing industry as much as writers, critics and academics. However, authorial intention in relation to the length of the

Structure and development

novel can be vital. Crime novels grew in length as the twentieth century progressed, with 400- to 500-page tomes becoming commonplace. But it wasn't necessarily always value for money. Some plots and characters became bogged down with baggage and backstory. Part of this was a publishing industry concept that people liked the idea of paying the same for more – the 'more' being more pages. These pages or extra words were often not integral to story, plot and characterisation/development. Brevity and succinctness had gone out of the window in place of just more stuff.

Obviously, some texts require great length to accommodate the diversions, the layers and multiple timelines and POVs. But a crime novel that moves with pace and purpose, menace and motivation? Especially one that is coherent, and convincing from start to finish? While Lee Child might have liked the idea of not reaching the end too quickly, while also not plotting or planning as he wrote, he did, nevertheless, invariably follow a linear route, and one that took up, on average, 100,000 words. His Reacher novels also, significantly, follow a short timeline: just a few hours, days or weeks at the most. There is *61 Hours*, of course, which gives you the fundamental structure in the title.[9]

Timeline

My own obsession with word count stems from my training and first job as a journalist. At one point I wrote a books column for the *Daily Mirror*, and because of various design and layout issues, the word count was averagely 382. I could soon hit this without ever having to look at the word-count bar at the bottom of the screen; knowing just how to articulate and shape my argument, the points I wanted to get across, and the conclusion within that space. My approach to writing fiction has become much the same. I set out to write a novel already knowing the distance, the shape (particularly in relation to timeline and key events), and to an extent, the conclusion or ending. As such, I know mostly where I am percentage-wise, before I've got anywhere near the end.

Crucially, to this sense of word count I also know the timeline: over how long the novel will take place, how many hours, days or weeks, and whether there's more than one timeline or narrative thread, and how such a structure may cohere. Lee Child likes the linear tale, not least because that's how he plots, plans and structures: on the go. Situating a linear tale within a short time frame is also a canny consideration, and one that more than suits the modern and contemporary crime novel. Investigations are now so much quicker because of technical advances, than, say, when Maj Sjöwall and Per Wahlöö were writing. Readers are perhaps more impatient. We're used to bingeing on fast-paced TV crime series. The digital world we now inhabit seems to spin quicker and quicker. On the one hand there might be 'readerly' time to encompass, or at least instil in relation to pacing and rhythm, so as not to rush an ending. On the other, we have to consider the intrinsic time within a novel: what's happening on the page, the rising tension, and what might be happening off the page, and in between the scenes and drama. This 'dead' time, or white space, is perhaps the most problematic for the genre. How can a story move with pace and purpose if there are chunks of unrecorded, unarticulated time taking place within the narrative timeline, albeit off page?

New paragraphs, line breaks, chapter breaks, part breaks are all and often used to denote the passing of time, along with shifts to other timelines and POVs, without crushing us with unnecessary details and observations, or dead time. But what of the story, what of the characters? Are they just resting in these periods, are they on holiday from the 'plot'? The more crime-orientated my fiction has become, the tighter the timelines. However, this can also be a problem, as too much focus can be spent on the moment, the scene, without moving things forward. It comes back to balance and a sense of the whole – those 60,000, 70,000, 80,000 words. What does the writer know from the outset regarding not just word count but key aspects of structure, on top of all the other plot, character and POV considerations and decisions? Highsmith put it somewhat abstractly in *Plotting and Writing Suspense Fiction*:

> Careless as I may sound about plotting and writing, I do believe in seeing ahead one chapter I'm writing, and this is more than a day's work in the writing usually. There are some beginning writers who can go romping on and fill two hundred pages in no time, but much of the time, an editor does the work for them, pointing out inconsistencies and actions out of character. It is both lazy and insensitive for a writer to write like this. A writer should always be sensitive to the effect he is creating on paper, to the verisimilitude of what he is writing. He should sense when something is wrong and, as quickly as a mechanic hears a wrong noise in an engine, and he should correct it before it becomes worse.[10]

Highsmith goes on to talk about the importance of sequence and how to order key events or situations and knowing what should come next, at least for the two or three steps ahead. She believed that a writer's mind had 'a way of arranging a chain of events in a naturally dramatic, and therefore correct form'. Citing Aeschylus and Shakespeare, she explained that this dramatic way of arranging events was 'manifest' in the sense that it was 'instinctive'. However, she also maintained that it was a product of 'practice' and 'discipline' too.[11]

Developing threads

Development, or the developing of ideas and threads, is a process closely bound to 'plotting'. Adding to or 'thickening' the plot with elements of surprise, menace and suspense further enhances drive, and increases reader engagement and the ultimate sense of fulfilment. In Chapters 1 and 2 we looked at Aristotle's ideas around drama and structure, in relation to plot and character. Basically, the beginning, middle and end, or as I labelled the parts in my novel *My Criminal World*: 'The Wrong Beginning'; 'The Fatal Middle Bit'; 'Another Kind of End'. There was a metafictional reason for this, and that was the suggestion that the writer, David Slavitt, and by proxy me, the author, wasn't entirely sure how best to do this. This is something of an eternal question for the writer. We know also that Aristotle, in his *Poetics*, outlined the six elements of Athenian tragedy (and I always think they are worth repeating; indeed the lifelong journey of learning to write is nothing short of one repetition after another; it's how we 'learn', how we learn anything, particularly language): plot, character, reasoning, diction, song and spectacle.[12] We also know that this has been variously interpreted and reinterpreted and adopted by all manner of storytellers and screenwriters, and is most commonly rephrased as: situation, complication, crisis, climax, resolution.

Screenwriters further talk about 'beats' and what needs to happen by a certain point, or page on the script. These are structural underpinnings, as much as they are bound up with plot and plot development. John Yorke, in his seminal *Into the*

Structure and development

Woods: A Five-Act Journey Into Story, has a chapter on the three-act structure followed by a chapter on the five-act structure, with specific screenplays/movies broken down accordingly. Midpoint comes either in the middle of act two (if a three-act structure) or the middle of act three if a five-act structure. The midpoint is also the moment for a 'breakthrough' or a reveal of 'key knowledge'. The importance of change is highlighted in every step of the way, from 'no knowledge' and 'awakening' to 'reawakening' and 'total mastery'.[13] In other words, acts are about not-knowing and knowing, and how such information impacts on character. While Yorke, like many other screenwriters and theorists, appears to advocate quite formal structures (and the so-called 'beats' do need to occur on certain pages, or distance into the story), there's still a strong demand for characters to change and develop, especially in relation to motivation and desire.

However, if we take Lee Child's line (quoted in *The Reacher Guy*, but also variously delivered in person on a number of occasions at literary festivals) we get something of an opposite view:

> I say bullshit to the character arc – I'm not trying to get an MFA here. I'm trying to do for people what I love for myself.[14]

What that *is* is 'the same but different'. Haruki Murakami was asked by the *Guardian* what he liked about Lee Child's Reacher novels, and he replied: 'Everything's the same!'[15] So if we have John Yorke on the one hand advocating the necessity of change, and Lee Child on the other implying everything needs to remain unchanged or stay the same (certainly in relation to characterisation), and Patricia Highsmith in the middle with her ideas that developing an idea is 'not always logical', and that arranging events was largely 'instinctive', and even that 'good books write themselves',[16] what are we to make of planning (intrinsic plotting and characterisation aside), and significantly, structure?

Structuring

Highsmith did also admit that 'practice' and 'discipline' were crucial to the arranging of events. She was actually keener on structure and balance than the way she describes her approach might suggest. She liked to 'be aware of chapter length', not that there were any 'laws about chapter length'. However, to Highsmith, a chapter was like a 'little "act"' in a play, and had to have a 'dramatic or emotional bang to it'.[17] If we think of such a chapter, or 'little act', as being made up of a number of scenes, we are beginning to sense structure, particularly if we then consider the chapters to be grouped into larger acts, or possibly parts. Of course, the level of surprise we need as writers from our own work (in order to create a plot that is surprising) might determine a much more casual or 'instinctive' approach, while other writers might be trying to keep things, character-wise, as much the same as possible. Whichever we choose, we are still in a form that is determined by structure: usually a beginning and an end, with a number of words in between.

In *How to Write a Mystery* Linwood Barclay puts it like this:

> When I write a book, I feel as though I am building a house. I'm the carpenter. I am banging this thing together, one stud at a time. If literary writers are the gardeners, crime writers are the contractors. A genre in which a well-constructed plot is critical demands practitioners who know enough to measure twice, cut once.[18]

Structure and development

That Barclay decides to draw a line between literary and crime writers is perhaps distracting. Barclay is making a key point – using the analogy of building a house to building a plot, and by my interpretation of what he means by plot here to be in part structure. It's interesting to think semantically for a moment and of the various meanings of plot: notably a 'plot of land', or a 'building plot'. From a blank space come all manner of structures and uses, meanings and sustainment; ways of living and engaging and being entertained, if not ways for dreams to be fulfilled. Chandler was particularly adept at observation, description and turning something physical into something full of metaphorical dread and menace. I wonder whether Chandler thought in fact of indoor and outdoor spaces, imagining his characters in and out of rooms, gardens, hothouses and mean streets. Structure is intrinsic and visible, holding the book together from the outside in and the inside out. It holds in place the scenes and chapters, giving shape to the whole, and amounting to how the fiction is constructed, fitted out and capped off.

Significantly, Chandler was among many writers who embarked upon a process of salvage, reclamation and renovation. Indeed, before we explore that point, let's just consider his approach to plot and structure. In his introduction to *Trouble is my Business*, a collection of his short stories, he wrote: 'The ideal mystery was one you would read if the end was missing.'[19] To him 'scene' (as we've seen) outranked 'plot', and he would have been more than happy if the last scene or two were simply not there. In that introduction he also talks about crime fiction, or the genre as he knew it, relying on formula, and his and others' desires to break out of that formula. Formula is inherently tied to structure, and even more linked to development, along with reader expectation. He stated: 'To exceed the limits of a formula without destroying it is the dream of every magazine writer who is not a hopeless hack.'[20] The 'magazine' reference here belonged to Chandler's commercial connection to the pulps such as *Black Mask* – the original breeding ground for noir and hardboiled fiction.

While Chandler was a great advocate of not 'plotting' or outlining, and letting the character and situation seemingly take him at will, he did have two tricks up his sleeve: one rather random, the other much more structurally orientated. As he stated in the essay, in regard to a flagging plot: 'When in doubt, have a man burst through the door with a gun.'[21] Perhaps more considered and useful is what he said in a letter to Dorothy Gardner, secretary of the Mystery Writers Association, in 1956.

> Any book which is any good has to turn a corner. You get to the point where everything implicit in the original situation has been developed or explored, and then a new element has to be introduced which is not implied from the beginning but which is seen to be part of the situation when it shows up.[22]

Significantly, Chandler's first novel began life as two short stories, 'The Killer in the Rain' and 'The Curtain'.[23] He effectively took the best bits from both and spliced them together, culminating in both a plot and character amalgamation. There are numerous academic studies on *The Big Sleep* and the two short stories identifying where the joins are more successful, more obvious and less successful. As a notoriously slow writer (and late literary developer), Chandler hated wasting anything. That he then went on to contemplate his process, identifying the idea of 'turning a corner' to enhance a plot, appears to stem from an almost accidental, or parsimonious approach to creativity, process and not wasting words. Put simply, two short stories stuck together end on end would clearly illustrate such a corner or shift. Obviously his approach was more thought-out and integrated. Yet the broad idea struck, and resonated.

The American short-story writer Grace Paley was a great advocate of coupling storylines and plot ideas, even suggesting such a process could be crucial to overall meaning. She expanded in *The Paris Review*:

> A story is made very often of two stories, until you have one story sort of half-contradicting another or corroborating another … separately each story would be less interesting, and two stories together really make a third story.[24]

Paley went on to explain that it was then in part up to the reader to imaginatively complete the 'story' and cement, if you like, those two stories into one. At a talk at Bennington College, as recorded by the writer Anna Hood in the journal *The American Scholar*, Paley was a little more succinct, and also suggestive, when she said:

> Every story is two stories. The one on the surface and the one bubbling beneath. The climax is when they collide.[25]

The reference to 'climax' I take to mean a somewhat surprising, unexpected, even magical conclusion, borne out of forces being guided more by structural imperative – the need for joining two things together, not least for the sake of the length of the whole – than creative 'literary' design. In a way, it's back to that Attridge notion of something being done intentionally ('by an effort of the will'), and something that happens without warning to a passive, though alert, consciousness through the process. Mysterious? Yes, though perhaps not necessarily in the crime fiction sense. Another great American short-story writer, teacher and thinker, Eudora Welty, has this to say in her key essays 'On Writing': 'Every good story has mystery – not the puzzle kind but the mystery of allurement.'[26] She goes on to offer something quite prescriptive:

> Beauty comes from form, from development of idea, from after-effect. It often comes from carefulness, lack of confusion, elimination of waste – and yes, those are rules.[27]

And what rules indeed, especially in relation to 'form' and 'elimination of waste'. Reclamation is as much a legitimate form of trying to eliminate waste as is cutting unnecessary passages, asides, descriptions, explanations and exposition. Form and structure go hand in hand. It's how and when you sense the whole that requires care, consideration and clarity, even if you arrive at that sense of the whole by a lengthy, circuitous route. The sharpness that all writers of crime fiction (with purpose) strive for might begin in a very elusive way, but I'd argue that the sooner you settle on the edges of that sharpness, that blade, or the right form, the more time and angst you'll save in the long run.

The wrong shape

Before writing *My Criminal World* I spent some time on a story about a woman who kills her husband, largely in a rage and on the spur of the moment, just before they're meant to be hosting a dinner party. The fictive present follows her horror at what she's done and her attempts to keep the facts, and the body, from her dinner-party guests. The narrative then ran on for many thousands of words as I tried to incorporate the backstory leading up to the present, and then as I tried to make sense of the present and what was to happen to her. This became overly digressive, and a bit confused. Complications such as her children and friends should have provided fuel, though only seemed to create drift and diversion. Exactly what did she want and what did she want to get away with? Had I thought about this enough prior to beginning writing?

A draft went on for many thousands of words – indeed I got up to around 45,000 words before my enthusiasm and energy for the project really started to flag. I liked the working title: *What You Should Not Miss*. However, I couldn't escape the sense that the story was so premised on the opening – this body in the bathroom, while the house was full of guests, and children, and a perpetrator wracked with guilt, fear and panic, but also a steely sense of relief – that anything after it would be a something of an anti-climax. The project began slipping away from my daily word-count deadlines and then my attention.

Until, that was, I was asked to write a short story for a magazine. *What You Should Not Miss* came to mind. Previously, all my published short stories were written to order/commission, and a number of them were culled from speculative beginnings of novels. I'd never got as far with a project as *What You Should Not Miss* and not continued to the end of a full draft. (I had set myself a 80,000 word-count target for the novel. I was 35,000 words short as it was.) However, not wholly prepared to let *What You Should Not Miss* go, and being presented with an opportunity in the form of this commission, I decided to cut and shape the material I had into a short story. A very short story as it turned out. Here it is:

Crafting crime fiction

The Wrong Goose

I

She wipes her mouth, her forehead, with the palm of her hand. Wipes her hand on the front of her blouse – not thinking.

Looking down, Chloe sees her hands are clean, amazingly, but clammy, and a smear of perspiration has appeared across the front of the delicate, cream-coloured material. The blouse was a present, from Paul, last Christmas, exactly a year ago. She's hardly worn it. It was obviously expensive, carrying a fancy label – though to her it has always felt cheap.

In a hurry, it was the first thing she grabbed from the wardrobe. Of all the things to put on. She'll never wear it again. In fact she'd like to rip it off right now, have a very long shower, and then put on warm, untainted clothes, grab the kids, and drive away, fast up the A11. Though that can't happen.

Lifting the fabric away from her stomach, her skin, trying to waft it, to dry it, Chloe catches her face in the huge mirror above the large sink. Oh, she's getting used to the fine lines round the eyes, the hint of sagging, the pallor, even if Paul never did. You are young and then you are old. No middle age for her.

But there's another look on her 42-year-old face, a look she's not seen before. And this look, this face, suggests not panic or terror, but triumph. There is a flicker of freedom staring back at her. Some seasonal cheer. With a shudder she also notices some speckles of blood in the bottom corner of the mirror.

Not turning around, never, she lets go of her blouse, lets the thin material cling once more to the soft flesh of her softening stomach, and quickly and very carefully steps out of the en-suite, closing the door firmly after her.

Before she's reached the kitchen, she finds herself coming to a stop in the hall, outside the kids' games room. Her flush of success suddenly evaporates. It is as if, for that brief time, she were possessed. Of course she was.

The noise of electronic warfare is seeping from under the door – new presents, new wars being enacted. Young human sounds too. As if Christmas wasn't expensive enough.

Structure and development

2

'Hi, it's me. Where the hell are you, you bastard?'

It had gone straight to answerphone again. Fran stabs the red end-call button. Throws the phone across the bed. She is livid, with herself mainly. She shouldn't have called him, again. So much for her resolve. How long did it last, 20 minutes? Half an hour?

Pull yourself together, girl. But this other voice begins to reverberate in her head: *easier said than done, easier said than done.*

She knows she should go back downstairs, join Don, the others, for pudding and more brandy. But her heart is not in it. Her heart is elsewhere.

3

'Sorry guys,' Chloe says, stepping into the kitchen, which opens out into air and dark glass. She looks down at her silly blouse, from a different life, sees that the sweat has all but dried. She considers her hands again; sees once more that they are clean, but ridiculously pale. Almost blue. The word bloodless comes to her.

Looking up she takes in the large table at the far end of the room, and the four people clustered around it.

'Is everything OK, Chloe?' Izzy, her sister, mock shouts from the echoey distance.

'Yeah, fine. But Paul's decided to go for a walk. I'm sorry, he's ruining everything.'

'Don't be silly,' says Izzy. 'Dad was always smashing plates, going off in huff on Christmas Day.'

Chloe tries to smile back, but can sense she's grimacing. She feels naked, transparent, and hurries forwards.

'It's you and the children we're really here for,' says Izzy, who had never much liked Paul. 'Why did you ever move to this charming little city?' She laughs.

'It was Paul's idea, his work,' Chloe says, not laughing.

'Do you think he ever regrets it?' Ash, Izzy's husband, suddenly says.

'He's hardly ever here,' whispers Chloe, pleased she got the tense right. She takes the seat next to Izzy, which, once she's sitting, realises wasn't where she was sitting before. It was Paul's place. She just stops herself from getting straight back up. 'Too busy, seeing –'

'Oh my God,' shouts Izzy, looking, staring towards the door.

A small boy has appeared. His face drained, blood on his hands, his front.

4

The phone is in her hand again – over the last few months it's become part of her. She's checked the news. Checked there've been no major incidents. Checked there's no obvious excuse for his silence.

Fran stands, having made a decision. She knows where he lives. She's explored it thoroughly on Google Maps, more than once. Big house, on the outskirts of the city. Only two hours away, if she drives fast.

She'll sneak out. Now Don's on the spirits it'll be fucking ages before he notices she's gone anyway.

Determined, she heads for the door. If Paul won't leave his family willingly, she'll drag him out, alive and kicking. What's Christmas for if you can't be together, with the person you really love?[28]

All those thousands of words came down to 873. The titled changed too, while a somewhat sentimental ending was slipped in, because it was for a December/Christmas publication. Two women involved with the same man. One wants him dead, and indeed executes her wish, albeit in a moment of rage (off page here in the short story), while the other woman wants him very much alive. As such, it could be seen as a classic love triangle, gone murderously wrong. But is there anything else to say than in those 873 words? How far can you elaborate on such a scenario, especially as the story starts immediately after the violence, the drama? Indeed, it was just this immediate situation – a compromised dinner party – that I wanted to explore. Also, importantly, the structure became much clearer in the heavily cut and reduced form. The original, the novel-in-progress, had conceivably become bogged down with mis-direction and a lack of clarity, conviction and intent. In the longer form, the structure had been far too loose. It was only by such radical cutting that a proper shape appeared; a shape with sharp edges, involving two POVs and, effectively, two storylines. It was quite possibly always a short story. It just took me a while to realise.

Settling on those edges, the correct form for a fiction can be an almost hopelessly daunting task, especially for a beginning writer, and even more so for a writer who 'sees where the words take you'.[29]

That short quote is taken from a recent novel by Julie Myerson, titled, intriguingly, *Nonfiction*. The unnamed narra-tor is a writer, who at one point explains to a creative writing student: 'I never know anything. I rarely understand a word of what I'm writing. Seriously, I always write from a place of complete darkness.'[30] Darkness seeps into every aspect of *Nonfiction*. It is noir without overtly knowing it, and certainly without being labelled and marketed as such. The story and impending apocalypse accelerate. There's little mystery, except perhaps the existential mystery of existence, and why some people develop addictions. There's little mystery to the overriding sense of building fear and horror, except perhaps in relation to timing, and to when the worst possible thing to happen will actually happen. This is because we know all along that it will happen, despite desperately hoping it won't.

Crafting crime fiction

Planning and outlines

While intentional noir and by extension crime fiction is what this book is all about, even exquisite, non-genre short story writers such as Paley and Welty considered form and development as crucial structural devices. As this chapter suggests, there are ways of contemplating form, structure and development, while also considering plot, character and POV, within the crime fiction genre. That is presupposing, however, that the writer is aware of being in the genre, which most definitely isn't always the case; Louise Doughty and her novel *Apple Tree Yard* being an excellent example.

When I write, I begin with word count and try to fit everything into that. My story outlines, in bullet points, take up no more than two or three A4 pages. They are determined by over how long the main storyline takes place: a day, a week, and so on. Then, I'll add what I think might be key markers, or events that need to happen on certain days. Prologues, and even more rarely epilogues, are not considered until the first draft is down. I read somewhere that a prologue should be suggestive of where the plot is at about the two-thirds marker. (You can even directly lift a brief section from that point – this works very effectively for Megan Abbott in *Dare Me*.)[31]

If your prologue implies too much of the ending, you'll ruin the surprise and the suspense. Anything too abstract will add unnecessary ambiguity. Many fledgling writers simply begin with a prologue, before considering much else. Such prologues can be a good way of setting a tone and getting into the story. However, in my experience, an early prologue will almost always be superseded or rendered redundant by the time a full draft is completed. By all means write one if it is what gets you going, but don't overly adhere to it, and don't rely on it to do all the immediate heavy lifting. If you deem it necessary to get the reader immediately into a point of crisis or extreme tension, you could take a leaf out of Megan Abbott's book and select material from later in the story once you know the direction of the whole, if not after you've completed it.

Some crime stories make good use of multiple timelines, or more than one narrative thread. With *What You Should Not Miss*, I incorporated two narrative threads, though running along the same timeline. Some books revisit a particular time or scene from various points of view – in other words a sort of Groundhog Day approach (such as *Tony & Susan* by Austin Wright,[32] or even, to an extent, *Gone Girl* by Gillian Flynn[33]). So there are some options to choose from if you want to work with two or more narrative threads: each narrative shift can either carry the story forward in relation to time, effectively passing the baton on, or cover the same ground or time, though from a different perspective. Louise Doughty's *Apple Tree Yard* employs both approaches to build a complex yet highly engaging narrative. Indeed, the book also uses both past and present settings, as the whole of the novel is effectively wrapped around the conclusion of a court case.

Often, however, narrative threads might occupy quite different timelines – perhaps years, or decades apart. In detective fiction, cold cases can very effectively be articulated in this way. Val McDermid's *The Skeleton Road* is a good example. Cold-case detective Karen Pirie tries to identify the remains of a body found in a building renovation. The story takes us back twenty-five years to the Balkans War and the cover-up of potential war crimes.[34]

Crafting crime fiction

Multiple timelines can be a very effective way to bring key, often highly revealing events in the past to life by bringing the reader into a different 'fictive present': taking the reader straight to the moment, the heart of the action through a different POV. Paula Hawkins' *Girl on the Train* follows Rachel, Anna and Megan's stories in a nonlinear, though clearly marked way: each chapter being announced by the name of the narrator and the date.[35] We go backwards and forwards until all stories effectively collide. Such an approach can be more engaging and dramatic than memory, which logically can never quite render dialogue accurately, and if used properly will be inflected with all that's happened and been considered since. Our memories are tainted, of course, which can also be used as an effective device of misdirection, or intended misinterpretation. Though, logically, who can remember exactly what someone said years ago, except perhaps for the odd line?

There are numerous technical ways to incorporate backstory and key moments, so let's look at when it's best to do so, and when not.

A flashback is effectively the fictive present in a different time/timeline, and is quite different in essence to memory. Yet, a text that employs too many sudden flashbacks might jar, and also raise questions about whether you have the right structure: would it actually make sense to have this narrative incorporated into its own differentiated timeline? There is also the idea that backstory is filler, and not closely enough aligned to story development. How much is necessary? Should the term even be considered? Forward momentum, I believe, is the most important structural and story development consideration, however many timelines and narrative threads are involved. I try not to think of 'backstory' as such, but 'forward-story'. What best

Structure and development

will propel the narrative? Can a dip into the past accelerate the story in the present, or the main narrative thread? And how should that shift be articulated? As discussed in Chapter 2, all characters should be rounded, and carry with them aspects of their past – just as we all do. But what fits into the narrative, and in a succinct, purposeful and coherent way, should be a matter of careful choice, and, as suggested here, dependent on structure and development.

Multiple timelines and narrative threads

Another novel I've been working on for a number of years was originally premised on a dual timeline. The 'present' timeline followed a middle-aged hairdresser, Gregory, whose life is suddenly torn apart by the unexpected appearance of his stepbrother, Daniel, who had emigrated from the UK to Australia decades ago. Also firmly in the frame is Sophie, Gregory's sister, who's recovering from breast cancer, and more tangentially, Adam, Gregory and Sophie's younger brother. Daniel was always a threatening, menacing and unstable character. Now back in the UK, in Gregory's small, provincial city, he begins to threaten and blackmail. Daniel has also has a strange hold over Sophie. The blackmail relates to an event that happened when they were all teenagers, on a holiday in rural France. This was in 1978, when Gregory's mother and Daniel's father had recently got together. This was their first holiday as a new 'family'. None of the teenagers had been abroad before, and Daniel quickly leads them astray. They steal from isolated farmhouses, local stores and begin joyriding. One farmhouse, inhabited by a very old and sick woman, is especially well-stocked with powerful prescription drugs.

Behind Gregory's back, Daniel has also embarked upon a sexual relationship with the unconfident 15-year-old Sophie. However, Sophie is often left out of Daniel and Gregory's escapades. Meanwhile, the younger Adam spends his time with an Instamatic camera, taking photos. Then the old woman gets shot dead with a hunting rifle Daniel and Gregory found in her house. Unbeknown to them at the time, Adam's there to capture it, having snuck up with the perennially left-out Sophie.

The first draft of the novel involved alternating timelines/narrative threads: the present predominantly told from Gregory's POV, with the past being told from Sophie's POV. The idea was to build tension from both, leading up to the murder in the past and the full ramifications of an attempted blackmail plot in the present. Each chapter, of around 5,000 words, switched between the POVs and storylines. The key to such an equal dual structure is to load both storylines with largely equal doses of narrative drive, surprise, suspense and mystery. Crime plots with triple or even more storylines require the same engagement from all threads, especially if those threads are weighted, word-count-wise. Engaging a reader in all the POVs/voices and threads is the challenge. Invariably readers tend to attach themselves and engage intimately with one POV/character over another. On top of this, each thread has to pull its weight independently and collectively. The overall balance between such narratives can be hard to achieve. The more fragmented and/or episodic a narrative is, the harder it is to create strong and coherent narrative drive and suspense, plus mystery.

This novel was originally called *Now Freak* (a period homage to Chic's disco track 'Le Freak'), and then *Run Free* (from the Candi Staton song 'Young Hearts Run Free'). However, getting that balance right proved difficult. The question, 'Whose story is it?' became louder in my head. Also, the setting, including the period, was so tied in with the characters and plot, I began questioning the present timeline altogether. The real story was in the past. The present was an add-on, which was struggling to make itself wholly necessary, as well as gripping, suspenseful and entertaining.

After a lot of consideration, and significantly, rereading Ian McEwan's noir novella *The Cement Garden*,[36] I decided to ditch the present timeline, and to follow a largely linear narrative, capturing just the two weeks of the holiday from Sophie's 15-year-old perspective. Impressionable and wayward teenagers seemed the strongest and most authentic aspect of the work: not least because I'd been there. I bookended this with two very brief and revealing passages from Adam's POV; or more accurately the POV from the cheap lens of his Kodak Instamatic. While Gregory no longer has a POV, he is still a key character, along with Daniel, as unwilling and willing perpetrators, respectively.

However, Sophie is the main victim, and the survivor, in numerous ways. The text now runs to just 32,000 words, and as such it is a novella: a fantastic form for a fast-moving, intense, linear crime narrative. The final version centred around a short space of time, an exotic, but stifling setting, and a protagonist with everything to live for, and everything to lose. I also retitled the work *Hot August Night*,[37] after the Neil Diamond live album: Neil Diamond being Sophie's mother's favourite singer. I like to think those songs provide something of soundtrack to the narrative.

Again, and in retrospect, to arrive at a successful structure took me too long, and too many drafts. Was this due to a lack of planning, or trying to be too complicated? However, it was another good lesson in reclamation, trial and error, persistence, and not being afraid to radically cut. However, I believe now that much time could have been saved with stronger planning and a better sense of the sort of crime fiction and effect I was striving for. In structural and developmental terms, why not be simple? Why overcomplicate matters? It is worth remembering that some projects and ideas won't sustain their suspense and menace for enough word count to become novels, but could work much better as novellas perhaps, or even short stories.

6

PACE AND FLUENCY

James Patterson

'Pace, pace, pace' is what James Patterson says is the most important factor in writing a crime thriller.[1] He built his whole empire, his 'factory', on the premise. All his various co-writers are charged with this instruction. He then meticulously edits the manuscripts as they come flooding in, cutting all unnecessary words of description and dialogue. His various writers are of such experience that they tend to know a good deal about how to pace and self-edit. Yet, making that narrative as taut and succinct as possible invariably needs other hands, other eyes. It's what editing is all about (editing will be discussed in depth in Chapter 9). However, our duty as writers of crime fiction, I believe, is to nail that sense of pace and momentum; of thrilling, terrifying, suspenseful forward drive. British crime writer Mark Billingham, as we've heard, talks about trying to get his texts as 'tight as a drum' before he's happy. It's a good analogy.

Patterson thinks, as a writer and more commonly as an editor, from scene to scene. He suggests there's no particular formula to his work except that 'when you pick up a Patterson book you'll not be able to stop reading'. Indeed, Penguin Random House, Patterson's UK publisher, came up with the strapline: 'The pages turn themselves.' All Patterson's work is defined by ultra-short paragraphs that continually push the story along. He implies that he lets his own emotions and instincts tell him whether something works. Yet as a former advertising executive – he was chief executive of J. Walter Thompson, North America – you can't help but feel that his 'instincts' are greatly informed by experience and understanding of the type of story he wants to write, and how that story will be received. He might say, 'I always do it scene by scene, section by section', but he continually asks himself the questions: 'Am I hooked? Are the surprises continuing?'[2] This is from the opening of *22 Seconds*, the 22nd Women's Murder Club novel, co-written with Maxine Paetro:

> Cindy Thomas was working at the dining table she'd bought at a tag sale down the block. It was cherrywood, round, with a hinged leaf and the letters *SN* etched near the hinge. She traced the initials with her finger, imagining that the person who'd left that mark was also a journalist suffering from writer's block – and Cindy was a blocked as a writer could be.[3]

We get straight into the scene, with some sharp description that amplifies the characterisation. Three short sentences in and we know Cindy has a problem. Things really begin to accelerate in the next paragraph, showing us exactly what sort of novel we're dealing with.

> Her full-time job was as a senior crime reporter at the *San Francisco Chronicle*. She'd been covering the violent murders of a killer unknown. And then, at the end of his crime spree, caught by the police, this unrepentant serial monster had asked her to

write the story of his life. And that's what she was doing – trying to do – now. It would be easy for her agent to sell this idea for a true-crime thriller about Evan Burke. He was a savage and highly successful at getting away with his skills. According to him, he was the most prolific killer of the century, and Cindy didn't doubt him.

Unrepentant, savage and 'highly successful at getting away with his skills' – what could possibly go wrong? Cindy Thomas is the series' 'up-and-coming' journalist. The Women's Murder Club cast also includes Lindsay Boxer, a homicide detective in the San Francisco Police Department, Claire Washburn, Chief Medical Examiner for San Francisco and Yuki Castellano, a top city lawyer. They all variously rely on and play off each other, professionally and domestically. It's a great series set-up, while the novels follow a clear pattern of short prologue (sometimes, as here, with more than one clearly labelled part) detailing a situation a few days in/ahead, then we begin the novel in effectively the fictive present with Chapter 1; in this case nine days earlier. Chapter 1 begins:

A lifelong veteran of US intelligence agencies, Lindsay Boxer's husband, Joe Molinari, now worked from home as a high-level consultant in risk assessment, port security, and advanced cyber threats.[4]

The word count for the paragraphs from Chapter 1 onwards is significantly less than that for the prologue (parts 1 and 2), featuring between one to three short sentences. The chapters come in at no more than two and half pages. *22 Seconds* incorporates 112 chapters. Patterson's journey from writer to editor found him concentrating on the story first, and how that moved, and the words themselves second. During the interview he said of his first novel *The Thomas Berryman Number*: 'I felt *Berryman* had a

lot of good sentences. A lot of times you get people writing wonderful sentences and paragraphs and they fall in love with their
prose style, but the stories really aren't that terrific. Berryman
was better written than the story.'[5]

On a micro-level for Patterson it's about being in the scene.
'If I don't feel I'm in the scene for this kind of writing, I don't
think it works.' The phrase 'this kind of writing' asks lots of
questions. This kind of writing, meaning Patterson's novels, or
novels of that type? Crime novels more generally? As you will
have gathered by this point, my mantras are: pace and purpose;
menace and motivation. If we think that, for now, 'purpose' can
be covered by plot, character (and to a strong degree structure
and development), what do I mean by 'pace'? Is it separate from
'menace and motivation', or, as will be discussed in Chapter 7,
mystery and suspense? In part, pace is where motivation meets
descriptive economy. So stick to the point.

Being succinct

As illustrated by Patterson, and just about every other significant
crime writer, descriptive economy and being succinct and economical with all aspects of the writing are crucial. This means
cutting not just unnecessary chapters, scenes, paragraphs and
sentences but all unnecessary words. Anything unnecessary to
plot, to character development, to enabling the reader to be 'in
the scene', can be regarded as extraneous and should also probably go. Interiority and over-elaborating on a POV character's
thinking or state of mind might well sink an otherwise decent
story. Every close read-through (there will be more on this in
Chapter 9) should be able to identify flab, and that's before a
good professional editor might get their hands on it.

Pace and fluency

Yet pace is not predicated solely on economy. Cutting and cutting doesn't necessarily make for coherence, let alone fluency, and without that, pace is almost meaningless. Stephen King, clearly obsessed with ditching unnecessary words (having learnt a great deal about economy from, among others, William Strunk and E. B. White),[6] despite his novels stretching to many hundreds of pages, is also very aware of the need for coherence, fluency and 'graceful narration'. From *On Writing*:

> I would argue that the paragraph, not the sentence, is the basic unit of writing – the place where coherence begins and words stand a chance of becoming more than mere words. If the moment of quickening is to come, it comes at the level of the paragraph.[7]

King also talks about good writing being dependent on 'style' and 'graceful narration' along with 'plot development', the creation of 'believable characters' and 'truth-telling'. Graceful narration and plot development – all obviously bound up with strong characterisation – are what used to be regarded, and especially in non-genre critical and practical approaches – as narrative drive. Pacing can actually be as much to do with syntax as content, or plot development, with all the add-on aspects of mystery and suspense. Further, there is the sense that information management – giving the readers just enough, and not only reveals but description, too, so they can question and interpret themselves, even expand the fictional horizon in their minds – can greatly add to engagement, and thus pace and drive. Fine information management helps a reader to be a willing and active participant. If we've been allowed to be part of the equation, if we've been pulled in, then we as readers can hasten the journey.

Crafting crime fiction

'Pacy' is a term critics (and publicists) love to attribute to a given text. A 'page-turner' (let alone a book where the pages turn themselves) is obviously full of pace. We also know what 'fluency' means in relation to writing; simply and primarily words, phrases, sentences that don't jar and stumble.

While fluency is determined by syntax, it is also bound up with continuity and plot/character coherence. To expand, fluency means paragraphs and scenes, chapters and parts that cohere. Writing that is not only sharp and succinct but flows with effortless ease. Writing that even surprises with its quiet descriptions and adept use of adjectives, punctuation, metaphor and simile. Dialogue that is in character (however diverse and idiosyncratic those characters might be), yet also happily believable within the context of the novel, the novel's setting, or world, if you like. Artfully relayed dialogue, and smart use of vernacular and dialect, is especially vital to overall fluency.

So while pacing and fluency can be quite different, and indeed while fluency can exist in a literary or writing sense, almost on its own (think of a dream sequence or a long passage of exquisite description, think of a poem, at least a certain type of poem!), pacing is more thematic and content driven. Yet, pacing is also, as we know, concerned with syntax and brilliantly sharp and economical prose. Lee Child talks about the need to 'instil relentless forward motion'.[8] Words alone, or as few words as possible, can't do that on their own. It's what those words, within the context of the narrative, mean. Surprisingly few critical and practical guides to writing identify 'pace' as a standalone subject. Linked with fluency it becomes even rarer and conceivably more complex and abstract – perhaps, because it's so difficult to identify,

Pace and fluency

determine and then implement practically. However, we do have a sense of what 'pace' means in relation to a crime novel.

Invisible fluency

Perhaps obviously, fluency, especially within the crime fiction context, is much more about writing that doesn't draw attention to itself than writing that does. This is not to say that Patterson's championing of story over prose is the only consideration that matters here, because the story has to be told well. To do that the writing has to work. In many ways it has to work harder to be unobtrusive, to be compelling, engaging, and yes, practically pacy as well. The marking criteria for the Crime MA that I run currently includes this:

> We expect you to demonstrate an exclusive and sophisticated knowledge of the literary languages of crime fiction and to be able to master whichever of these languages you choose to use. We expect you to exhibit a sophisticated use of English grammar and punctuation. We will expect the breadth and depth of your reading, and practical understanding, to be evident in your range and control of the languages with which you write.

The paragraph is effectively a breakdown of the elements of 'fluency'. The concept of pace is not spelled out here; however it lies between the lines: the choice of 'language'; the 'sophisticated' use of grammar and punctuation; 'range' and 'control' alongside serious reading 'resource' and 'practical' understanding.

Crafting crime fiction

Catton and Cain

Try this for a beginning:

> The twelve men congregated in the smoking room of the Crown
> Hotel gave the impression of a party accidentally met. From the
> variety of their comportment and dress – frock coats, tailcoats,
> Norfolk jackets with buttons of horn, yellow moleskin, cambric,
> and twill – they might have been twelve strangers on a railway
> car, each bound for a separate quarter of a city that possessed
> fog and tides enough to divide them; indeed, the studied isola-
> tion of each man as he pored over his paper, or leaned forward
> to tap his ashes into the grate, or placed the splay of his hand
> upon the baize to take his shot at billiards, conspired to form the
> very type of bodily silence that occurs, late in the evening, on a
> public railway – deadened here not by the slur and clunk of the
> coaches, but by the fat clatter of the rain.[9]

We are in New Zealand, in 1866, and this is the beginning
of Eleanor Catton's vast, sweeping, extraordinary, dazzling
Booker Prize-winning novel *The Luminaries* (2013). The protagonist, Walter Moody, has arrived in New Zealand to make his
fortune on the goldfields. He stumbles upon a gathering of
twelve local men, who are meeting in secret to discuss a series
of unsolved crimes. Moody is pulled into the mysteries through
a network of fates and fortunes, which stretch beyond physical
realms to the astrological and metaphysical (and metaphorical)
depths of the universe. The hardback edition is 832 pages long.
It's split into twelve parts arranged, though not at all equally,
word-count-wise, around the astrological chart. The beginning
paragraph above is in fact mostly just one sentence. But this
sentence displays everything you need to know about fluency.
Look at the control, the range, the use of language, grammar,
punctuation, literary resource and practical understanding.

Pace and fluency

Look how the setting is brought alive, the sense of mystery and external menace. We even get some rain!

In this extract we have fluency and an idea already of pace and drive beyond the syntax. Why are they gathered here in this smoking room? Why is there this sense of silence, of isolation despite the numerically suggestive size of the gathering? Consider the word 'conspired', and how Catton then rounds all this off with a hint of humour in such a descriptively powerful phrase: 'the fat clatter of rain'.

While *The Luminaries* could be considered a work of crime fiction, it's more commonly regarded as a prizewinning literary novel. The sheer size of it, along with its wildly expansive period and astrological canvas, and the fact that the timeline shifts back and forth between 1866 and 1865, could classify it as anything other than a fast-paced, linear, tight timelined crime narrative. Yet, Catton is heavily influenced by crime fiction, and indeed drew greatly upon James M. Cain's *Double Indemnity* for plot inspiration. *The Luminaries* contains a femme fatale, or wronged woman, and a number of double-crossing and hapless male suitors and adversaries. Greed, jealousy, betrayal, murder – it's all there. Plus, a back and forth, or at least a bookended timeline.

Here's the beginning of *Double Indemnity*, published some 77 years earlier in 1936:

> I drove out to Glendale to put three new truck drivers on a brewery company bond, and then I remembered this renewal over in Hollywoodland. I decided to run over there. That was how I came to this House of Death, that you've been reading about in the papers. It didn't look like a House of Death when I saw it. It was just a Spanish house, like all the rest of them in California, with white walls, red tile roof, and a patio out to one side. It was

built cock-eyed. The garage was under the house, the first floor
was over that, and the rest of it was spilled up the hill any way
they could get it in. You climbed some stone steps to the front
door, so I parked the car and went up there. A servant poked her
head out. 'Is Mr Nirdlinger in?'[10]

There's no rain, but there's plenty of menace ('this House of
Death') and the prose is especially succinct and direct. We have
short sentences, which are light on sub-clauses. There are no
semi-colons or en dashes. We are brought into the story by
a first-person narrator looking back from the perspective of
someone who knows how the story will play out.

Both first paragraphs are almost exactly the same length: *The
Luminaries*' runs to 147 words, *Double Indemnity*'s to 149 words.
However, the latter features ten sentences, to *The Luminaries*'
two. What does this tell us about pace, fluency, genre and
intent? What does it tell us about James M. Cain's first career
as a reporter, becoming Professor of Journalism at St John's
College, Annapolis? Or, for that matter, Eleanor Catton's
career beginnings studying for an MA in Fiction Writing at the
International Institute of Modern Letters (Victoria University
of Wellington, New Zealand), followed by an MFA at the legendary Iowa Writers' Workshop, which at that time did not
'teach' genre or crime fiction?

Obviously, we know exactly where we are with *Double
Indemnity*, including the type of novel, or actually novella to
come – there are just 137 pages of my Orion paperback edi-
tion, and around 35,000 words. We also might know that *Double
Indemnity* followed James M. Cain's first novel, *The Postman
Always Rings Twice*, which had immediately established him as
a crime writer; a writer of shocking, disturbing noir. Indeed,
The Postman was tried, unsuccessfully, for obscenity in Boston,

Pace and fluency

while being hailed as a masterpiece by writers across the genre, and across the globe. Albert Camus said it inspired him to write *L'Étranger* (*The Stranger*); while Cain himself acknowledged the influence of Émile Zola's 1868 novel *Thérèse Raquin* on *The Postman*.

With *The Luminaries*, we are in very different territory. While those first sentences speak volumes about fluency, the pacing is of an entirely different nature. In many ways it prepares us for a very long novel with shifting POVs and timelines, where the narrative drive builds and then breathes, builds and breathes, but never at a breathless rate. This is where we need to consider syntax in relation to the whole, as well as the type of fiction or crime fiction we are aiming to produce. Just how fast do we want it to flow? How do we want to pitch the pace? How heavy the foot on the accelerator, if you like? We need to think about when to apply the brakes, as well.

Tempo

Patricia Highsmith thought of it as 'tempo'. 'It is part of the plotting, and of the effect one intends to make, this decision about tempo.' She explains further in *Plotting*:

> Partly it can be called 'style,' and as such is natural and unstudied, and has to do with the temperament of the writer. A very fast or slow tempo should not be attempted, if one feels strained and unnatural writing in it. Some book are nervous from the start, some slow all the way through, underplaying, analyzing and elaborating on the events. Some start slowly, pick up speed, and rush to the end. Can you imagine a suspense story by Proust? I can. The prose would be leisurely and involved, the action not necessarily so, and the motivations analyzed thoroughly.[11]

Crafting crime fiction

Highsmith was adamant that such a consideration of 'tempo', or pace as I prefer to call it, should be largely natural and unforced. 'A writer should arrange the events in his story in the most amusing and entertaining sequence, and the right tempo of the prose, slow, fast or medium, will probably come of itself.'[12] The majority of writers, though, from committed crime writers to more experimental 'literary' authors (who might just happen to write crime narratives without initially knowing the thematic 'genre' they're aiming for), do consider tempo or pace and organise their sentences, paragraphs, chapters, and so on accordingly. This is where content meets craft, or more practical considerations. And then later, the whole publishing juggernaut might kick in to add its voice to the type of novel lying between the covers.

Sometimes, as with Louise Doughty's *Apple Tree Yard*, the publishers, and author for that matter, might not initially know what they are dealing with. *Apple Tree Yard* was initially published as a non-genre, contemporary literary novel. Eleanor Catton's *The Luminaries*, a novel deeply embedded with murder and mystery, has never strictly been promoted as a crime novel. Yet *The Luminaries*, like *Apple Tree Yard*, began to be seen as such by readers, really ahead of critics. This was even while Catton herself began to talk about her influences and interests in the genre, and Cain in particular. This then adds another dimension to the genre/literary debate, and indeed to any debate about authorial intent or knowingness and informed reception. Who speaks for the work? The author, the reader, the critic, the publishing machine? From Eliot to Stein, Barthes to Foucault, there have been more than enough writers, critics and theorists discussing such matters, not least in relation to the 'death of the author' and Barthes' idea that the work sits outside a writer's orbit. Foremost, I'm interested in authorial intent from the

Pace and fluency

get-go, and the writer's world. This is what we writers can do something about.

Authorial intent

Sara Paretsky's V. I. Warshawski series has only ever been private-eye/detective novels. The cover of her 2012 novel *Breakdown* features the strapline: 'It starts with a dare and ends in murder.' The first chapter is titled 'Graveyard Shift', and the first paragraph reads:

> Rain had turned the streets a shiny black. It coated windshields with a film that cut visibility to inches, and tuned potholes into lakes that trapped unwary drivers. All month long, Chicago had been hit by storms that put as much as three inches of water on the ground in an hour, but left the air as thick and heavy as a wet parka. Tonight's storm was one of the worst of the summer.[13]

Forget what Elmore Leonard had to say about the weather, of course, and look at how Paretsky makes the weather so heavy and menacing. In total we have 312 words and four sentences, all loaded with atmosphere. Even without a clear sense of whose POV we are in, we know the fictional territory. Rain turning the 'streets a shiny black' broadcasts a slippery menace. We can already sense the dangerous, terrifying tangles to come. Yet, it's the next paragraph, now clearly from V. I. Warshawski's POV, that gets the plot moving:

> I'd come up empty in all the likely spots: bus stops, coffee shops, even the sleazier nightclubs that might not have carded a bunch of tweens. I was about to give up when I saw lights flashing in the cemetery to my right. I pulled over and rolled down my window. Above the rumble of rain on my rooftop I could hear high-pitched chatter and bursts of nervous laughter.

Crafting crime fiction

Where Catton used 'clatter', though pre-loading this with the adjective 'fat', Paretsky gives us 'rumble' to describe rain. We're down a word, an adjective, yet we're then quickly moving forward to 'high-pitched chatter' and 'nervous laughter' in the same sentence. We're moving forward with descriptive, or technically syntactical speed and plot development. Paretsky knows the type of novel she's writing – she's written quite a few, all highly successful – and the confidence and conviction of her writing speaks volumes in not so many words. Paretsky and her V. I. Warshawski series were also landmark in addressing the detective or P.I. genre gender issue, transforming the role and image of women in crime fiction. She was also instrumental in founding the Sisters in Crime organisation, which supports and promotes women within the genre.

Heavily influenced by Paretsky is the Scottish crime writer Denise Mina, who's written a number of series with female 'detective' leads. Her most visceral, angry and shocking novel is the blistering, award-winning *The End of the Wasp Season*, featuring a heavily pregnant DS Alex Morrow amid a tangle of murder, suicide and two vulnerable, impressionable and disturbed teenage boys. A brilliant forensic investigation, led by Morrow, who has a talent for 'spotting lies and liars',[14] overlays a profoundly moving story about the frailty of family, and 'how easily, despite all the parts being in place, everything could suddenly turn to shit'.[15] Though it's Morrow's investigation the POV shifts between a number of characters, including the initial victim and the perpetrators. The pace has plenty of rhythm, moving from slower moments of tormented reflection to furious, violent action and bitter outbursts. It is a stunning example of register, and scale, and how and when to shift gear. Here is Morrow reflecting on who the real perpetrator is, Lars

Pace and fluency

Anderson, and accusing him of 'killing' the actual perpetrator, Lars' son Thomas:

> It was the hardest interrogation she'd ever done. Low before she started, tired before she started, she saw the despair in Thomas Anderson and knew what he was thinking though he said very little. Lars had killed him over the ice cream. Lars had wiped out his significance and his identity over the ice cream. Lars had wiped out the meaning of his mother. There was another. He had wiped out the significance of him having another son, loving another son, and she knew from her own experience that what haunted him more than anything was the suspicion that his father loved the other son and was kind to him and proud of him. Danny had that same look in his eye, a lack, a suspicion that there were children in the world who were beloved when he wasn't. That's what she couldn't look at in him. That's what she had avoided all these years.[16]

Morrow brings her thinking round to Danny, her wayward, criminal brother, her own family. She moves from a professional investigation to a deeply personal issue in one paragraph. This is exactly what can make detective fiction so strong, intimate and engaging: the exploration of feeling, connection, being and belonging. Through studied, syntactical repetition Mina ups the pace and intensity, the narrative drive, until we reach an almost unbearable point. Mina does the same when describing violent action and the aftermath of violence. *The End of the Wasp Season* begins, however, just before the central murder, making the reader witness to an utterly terrifying scene of intrusion, fear and a fight for survival. Here's the very beginning from the POV of the soon-to-be victim:

> The silence startled Sarah from a hundred-fathom sleep. She opened her eyes to the red blink of the digital alarm clock: 16.32.

The yips of small dogs came from one of the gardens down-hill, insistent, ricocheting off the ceiling and around the curved room.

Quiet. The radio was off. Sarah routinely left the radio on in the kitchen when she was here, tuned to Radio 4. The conversational coo took the edge off the emptiness. Heard from another room it gave the impression that the house was full of charming, chatty people from Hampshire. Burglars might find that strange in Glasgow but it was plausible in the exclusive village of Thorntonhall. Sarah left strategic lights on too: hall, stairs, anywhere that couldn't be seen into. She had a talent for making things seem.[17]

The last sentence is particularly considered, given how the narrative develops and the police, except Morrow, quickly assume all the wrong things about Sarah and what had led to her murder. In other words, in relation to herself, Sarah made things seem otherwise than they really were. The first scene also ends before the real violence begins. Indeed, most of the violence is told retrospectively. Mina imposes a distance rather than a prurience, and because of that distance the violence is in many ways colder and more brutal. Morrow describes the crime scene, the body, as she sees it:

Morrow's weight shifted half an inch and, confronted with the full sight, she lost her breath. She had expected disgust, had defences against that, but against sheer, suffocating pity she had nothing.[18]

To Morrow, the victim's 'vulnerability was unbearable'.[19] *The End of the Wasp Season*, which has emotional echoes of fellow Scottish writer Iain Banks' groundbreaking and incendiary *The Wasp Factory* (1984), is a relatively long book, running at just over 400 paperback pages.[20] And while structurally complex with multiple POVs, including flashbacks, pace at both

Pace and fluency

a micro- and macro-level is remarkably controlled, especially given the emotional charge running through the work. This collusion of syntactical skill and content make for a troubled, uneasy, but utterly engaging fluency, along with pace that builds steadily, and is often blistering. Let's call this narrative drive, then, an overarching term that engages us and pulls us along (if not quite turning the pages for us). It involves character motivation, conflict, plot twists, pacing, even dialogue: all the usual suspects. This is distinct from the occasionally used term 'narrative pace', which broadly refers to the speed with which key events within the story unfold. This is in fact a rather basic concept, reliant on the amount of text used to cover a certain period of time: the shorter the text, but the longer timespan covered somehow meaning an acceleration of pace; while detailed description can be used to slow the sense of time passing. Hopefully, the above extracts from Mina and Paretsky, along with Patterson and co., are illustrative of a more complex, studied and effective approach: pacing and fluency as distinct from both 'narrative pace' and the much broader 'narrative drive', which, in fact, can be quite purposefully leisurely.

Narrative drive

The closest E. M. Forster got to defining 'narrative drive' was in relation to 'Pattern and Rhythm', in his *Aspects of the Novel*. Such considerations, inherently abstract, should come, he wrote, 'after story and plot, and revolve around repetition and variation which work together to combine the whole, with the resulting chords leading to a larger and more meaningful existence' (or story).[21] He also explored aspects of 'narrative drive' in the chapter/essay on 'The Plot'. Here, of course and notably for us, Forster elaborated on the importance of surprise and mystery to plot, and the organisation of events dependent on and subsequently determined by causality.[22]

Mystery and suspense, both of which include elements of surprise, are the focus of the next chapter in this book. But we need to get there first. With 'pace and purpose' being one of my two mantras, there came a time in my own writing when I felt I needed to, frankly, up the pace. My desire to embark upon a crime series had yet properly to materialise. I was perhaps still a little too uncertain of the type of fiction I wanted to write, what I was aiming for, what I was capable of. Authenticity in fiction comes from knowingness and integrity. It comes from doing what you can do best, being true to yourself and your specific talents, or so I believe. While readers might well be the best judges of that, authorial design is very much part of the equation. And design, or intent, comes from experience and practice, resource, desire and ambition.

By design

I wanted to write a series, but I didn't want to write a police procedural, or any form of detective fiction. My novel *My Criminal World* had given me an entrance, a window, into a setting and various situations regarding characters and a criminal milieu. But the metafictional element, the writer writing his next crime fiction, was too knowing, too conceptual, especially coming from a creative writing professional. It was time I ditched the thinking around the purpose, I decided. It was time I took on board what I'd learnt from *What You Should Not Miss* and *Run*

Pace and fluency

Free/Hot August Night, as well as all that I'd learnt from my previous, crime-influenced novels. Along with, of course, everything I'd read before and in between.

Chandler was still sitting there as the crime series writer I was most influenced by. Yet there were also the landmark ten Martin Beck novels by Maj Sjöwall and Per Wahlöö: what form, what function! Plus, I couldn't ever forget Elmore Leonard's humour and the way he captured the criminal mentality, the way he wrote from an engaging criminal-protagonist perspective, even if he didn't write crime series. Maybe, though, of most significance at the time was watching, albeit belatedly, *The Sopranos*: all six seasons and 86 episodes over one winter.[23] Here was a series, like Mina's *The End of the Wasp Season*, that was about family first, crime second. Or rather it was how crime, personal and professional, intimate and organised, impacted, by design and circumstance, on family and the individual members of that family, and extended 'family'. There was humour, and humility, along with a serious amount of menace and violence. Motivation was determined by greed and survival. Also, in relation to Tony Soprano, there was an existential sense of being and belonging: just who was he and why was he suffering panic attacks?

My mother was a writer and one of the main reasons why I wanted to be one, too. She brought me up. Matriarchs have shaped my life, and in that I include my paternal grandmother, who influenced my first (non-crime) novel *Gorleston*.[24] For good and bad! While *My Criminal World* featured a strong, maverick, female cop, Britt Hayes, straight detective fiction was not what I was after for my next book. Heavily influenced by *The Sopranos*, I realised I wanted to get closer to the crimes, the perpetrators. But not necessarily violent criminals.

Crafting crime fiction

A maverick matriarch was what I hit upon, a female crime boss, who might also come up against an adversary like Britt Hayes, or indeed Britt Hayes herself. So my Goodwin Crime Family trilogy was born. Richard 'Rich' Goodwin was an old-style, organised crime boss, based in Great Yarmouth. Fraud, coercion and drug and people trafficking were his specialities. The deprived, corrupt (at least fictionally) seaside town of Great Yarmouth provided plenty of scope and visually stunning backdrops. 'Rich' Goodwin was on a mission to build, with US mafia backing, a super-casino. He had plenty of rivals, one of whom has murdered him just before the first novel begins. This leaves his wife, Tatiana ('Tatty') Goodwin, to emerge from a Temazepam haze and take over the helm. She could have chosen to disappear into a simpler life, but something tells her that she was always smarter and tougher than her despicable husband. Besides, she has three grown-up children to help her, along with Rich's right-hand man, the ever-loyal Frank. Frank's into men and gardening, and sees Tatty and her children as the family he never had.

To signal a clear and determined shift to purposeful, dedicated crime fiction, albeit from the criminals' perspective, a decision was made with my agent and publisher to use a pseudonym. We settled on Harry Brett – Brett being my mother's maiden name. The first novel in the series, *Time to Win*, was written quickly, with strong intent, and with the POV shifting between Tatty, her children (Zach, Sam and Ben) and Frank – to keep it in the family, so to speak.[25] Using a pseudonym had the strange effect of liberating 'me', or liberating my old writerly habits, from me. It was a revelation, and hugely enjoyable. Here's the first paragraph:

Pace and fluency

> There was a time when the sound of rain was comforting, calming. Now it pissed her off. It was autumn already, she remembered. September 1. It was not her favourite month. She let the patter swirl around her head for another few minutes, realising she was listening out for something else. Breathing, snoring. But it wasn't there. She lifted her head, opening her eyes. Propped herself on her elbows. Rich wasn't there.[26]

OK, the bloody rain seeped in. Of course it did (which inspired a few further negative comments on Amazon). There is an inherent danger in trying to capture a place and a set of people in a noir crime thriller. It can be bleak. It's not for everyone. However, that's not to say it was not right and appropriate and authentic for the 'fictional' world that had been created. However, my principal concern in the writing of *Time to Win*, and the subsequent novels in the trilogy (detailed in the next chapters), was pace, and trying not to sound like my former, questioning and somewhat metafictional writing self, the me of my previous novels. This novel had to be different, yet also authentic. Pace and fluency are invariably determined by plot, as well as the prose style and syntax. I was attempting to use all the various components and then put them all back together, practically, on the page, in a different, simpler, and hopefully more honest and straightforward way. A new identity helped me, and made me feel that perhaps this was the writing identity I should always have had.

Drive

The great contemporary American noir writer James Sallis was perhaps being more than knowing when he titled his arguably greatest work *Drive*. A very short novel, though a touch longer than a novella, *Drive* is a lean, dark mystery, or neo-noir, that takes the concept of pace and runs with it for its full, brief length. It's about a stunt driver by day who moonlights as a getaway driver at night. This is the beginning:

> Much later, as he sat with his back against an inside wall of a Motel 6 just north of Phoenix, watching the pool of blood lap toward him, Driver would wonder whether he had made a terrible mistake. Later still, of course, there'd be no doubt. But for now Driver is, as they say, in the moment. And the moment includes this blood lapping toward him, the pressure of dawn's late light at the windows and door, traffic sounds from the interstate nearby, the sound of someone weeping in the next room.[27]

The message here is one of momentum and being in the moment, or as Patterson would have it, 'being in the scene', which is another key consideration of pace and fluency, or, more broadly, narrative drive. This extract, this novel, so aptly titled, could just well be where pace and fluency meet narrative drive. The mystery takes the back seat, until it climbs over and makes its presence felt. You should never have to wait for too long.

MYSTERY AND SUSPENSE

Surprise

Mystery and suspense? Well, where's the surprise? It's part of mystery and suspense. It can't easily be unpicked by the reader, if the writer applies it with care, subtlety and calculation. However, it can easily be inserted, exploited and contrived. As we know, Chandler famously said: 'when in doubt have a man burst through the door with a gun'.[1] Even though Chandler was addressing the idea that he never outlined and liked to let the character and situation take him at will, clearly he found surprise a good way of getting him out of a plot hole, or seeming dead end. It's what you do when you're stuck. It's also what a crime writer might do if they feel they need to inject not just surprise, but pace and often action as well. Highsmith was also a great proponent of the seemingly casual and arbitrary surprise: 'I have to think of my own entertainment, and I like surprises'[2] – as if somehow they just popped into her head. For some writers, surprises do have a habit of popping into our heads when writing. The skill, or the knack, however, is in deciding whether to fall for them. The writer must decide whether they enhance the mystery, and probably suspense as well, or whether they are a distraction, which might cause a series of knock-on problems, including necessitating some rewriting of earlier sections.

Surprise, ironically, is often expected in a crime novel. However, it's a device to be used with caution. Mystery in its broadest definition is inherently bound up with sudden appearances, occurrences, connections, coincidences, strange reveals: surprise, in other words. Such surprise might add new questions for the reader (and writer) to answer, or complicate and enrich the greater question already in play. The surprise may well be difficult, conflictual, sometimes adding threat or menace to the current situation. It's here that surprise more obviously tips into suspense. It can be a raising of the stakes: often, it's a way of increasing jeopardy. *The Talented Mr Ripley* is full of surprises, not least when Marge arrives in Venice, at Ripley's palazzo, out of the blue. We don't fear that Ripley's double life is about to be busted, as much as what Ripley might suddenly do to Marge. You could say this was a surprise, then, with a twist.

In essence both mystery and suspense often incorporate surprise and are so intertwined – who is that person knocking on the door, or who is that person bursting into the room with the gun, and why? Suspense could come from the fear of the occupant(s) of the room, or the new threat that they might pose to the person bursting into the room. Will they be shot, maimed, killed, or kidnapped and dragged away? Or might they stage a fightback? Might they turn the tables on an innocent 'investigator'? A character suddenly in peril, in fear for their life: this is suspense. Jeopardy like never before. When will it ever end? The mystery, if you like, is how that situation arose and how it might be resolved. This obviously goes beyond surprise, with the sense of suspense carrying through the heightened scene.

Mystery and suspense

Mystery unravelled

Lee Child talks about asking questions and delaying the answers as being the fundamentals of suspense, and instilling that 'relentless forward motion'.[3] As we know, he sees it on a micro- and macro-level – a series of smaller questions under the umbrella, or umbrellas, of larger questions. But this of course is also mystery. Things are not what they seem; as purported by Jim Thompson, it's mystery distilled. It's mystery before we might even know it's mystery. When we realise such, then surprise and suspense kick in – if they haven't kicked in already. E. M. Forster put it like this in *Aspects*:

> The facts in a highly organised novel ... are often of the nature of cross-correspondences, and the ideal spectator cannot expect to view them properly until he is sitting up on a hill at the end. This element of surprise or mystery – the detective element as it is sometimes rather emptily called – is of great importance in a plot. It occurs through a suspension of the time sequence; a mystery is a pocket in time, and it occurs crudely, as in 'Why did the queen die?', and more subtly in half-explained gestures and words, the true meaning of which only dawns pages ahead. Mystery is essential to a plot, and a cannot be appreciated without intelligence. To the curious it is just another 'And then –' To appreciate a mystery, part of the mind must be left behind, brooding, while the other part goes marching on.[4]

Forster was adamant that memory and intelligence – recollection and understanding – were key to engaging with and effectively enabling a novel to exist and work. In other words he understood the importance of the reader to the equation. Interestingly Forster also recognised the impor-tance of the writer, the 'plot-maker', to 'leave no loose ends'.

Crafting crime fiction

'Every action or word in a plot ought to count; it ought to be economical and spare; even when complicated it should be organic and free from dead matter.'[5] David Lodge in his chapter on Mystery in *The Art of Fiction* talks about the effect of suspense being 'what will happen', and how this can be converted to 'enigma' or 'mystery' – 'how did she do it?'[6] These two questions, he states, are the 'mainsprings of narrative interest and as old as storytelling itself'. That we find them in this book, in Chapter 7, as opposed to say Chapter 1 or 2, is an attempt to distinguish them from simply being something wholly integral to the crime novel – which of course they are to varying degrees – but also to being something more specific and loaded, and far more pliable and practical. Yes, they could be seen as part of 'development', as much as 'pace', or narrative drive. They happily sit within plot and character, obviously. Yet they can also be further, and intrinsic, considerations of the crime novel, and especially a crime novel that moves with 'menace and motivation', 'pace and purpose'. Let's consider the concept of mystery as a way of enhancing a crime fiction, and of stamping genre intent on the writing.

In the US, the term mystery is still pertinent to crime fiction, or the crime thriller. Mystery Writers of America has been going since 1945 and is responsible for the hugely influential Edgar Awards, among many other initiatives. In his introduction to the recent *How To Write A Mystery: A Handbook From The Mystery Writers of America*, Lee Child talks about the four pillars or corners of the genre as being mystery, thriller, crime fiction and suspense. Writer and editor Neil Nyren simplifies this in his chapter, 'The Rules – And When To Break Them':

Mystery and suspense

Mysteries are about a puzzle. A crime is committed, usually murder, and the protagonist has to weave their way through the clues and suspects to finally arrive at a solution. It's a more cerebral endeavor, and the key question is 'Who did it?'

Thrillers are about adrenaline. Something bad happens, with the certain promise that more – and probably even worse – bad things will happen unless the protagonist can prevent them. The stakes can be intimate (one person's life) or huge (the fate of the world), the protagonist can be an ordinary person or a superhero. Whatever the case it's the suspense that drives the book, the chase, the scramble, and the key question is 'What happens next?'[7]

Both Forster and Lodge propose that mystery is integral to narrative, fiction and the novel in general. Nyren, like many, many others, spells out the specifics of a 'crime' mystery, which effectively dates all the way back to Collins and Poe, and came to the fore in the Golden Age. Crime fiction as puzzle. Mystery as riddle. Nyren's analysis of the thriller gives the basis of 'crime thriller' as suspense: the chase, the jeopardy. As he rightly then explains, it is now very common for crime fiction to contain both elements – a riddle and a chase – with all sub-genres flowing from these two paradigms.

'Mysteries' can be full of suspense, while 'thrillers' can be full of mystery. Again, however, it's the type of mystery and suspense that we need to try to identify, if we are then to use that understanding in our own practice. It's where we want to put the emphasis in our works-in-planning and progress. This is a fundamental genre, or sub-genre decision, preferably arrived at before too much planning and writing. These are the concepts, the decisions we need to make up front, in order to ward off any risk of an over-reliance on unplanned surprise, or surprise for surprise's sake. Further, I'd suggest checking, or keeping in check, extreme or unjustified (and unplanned) sudden action and violence. Action and violence alone, as we've heard from Chandler among others, don't make for strong crime fiction. Violence has to be earned, justified. Ultimately, it has to be coherent to the world of the novel, if not the scene itself; and this is where you might introduce an element of surprise, leading to suspense.

Menace

Mystery and suspense are hardly exclusive to crime fiction: we can all name countless examples of equally mysterious and suspenseful works of non-crime fiction. Think of horror, sci-fi, even romance. Think of non-genre or so-called literary fiction. Any fiction that moves with pace and purpose is invariably imbued with mystery and suspense. It's the menace and motivation – especially the menace, and the more murderous the better – that begins to determine the genre. Certainly, 'fusion crime fiction', where the crime genre is combined with various other genre and sub-genre elements, is becoming particularly popular. One example is supernatural crime fiction by the likes of Sarah Pinborough (*Behind Her Eyes*) or Charlaine Harris (Southern Vampire Mysteries/ True Blood), and of course sci-fi crime fiction has long been a trope: from Philip K. Dick's *Do Androids Dream of Electric Sheep?* to China Miéville's *The City & The City*. But what element tips the genre balance? At what point do we decide something is more sci-fi-, or fantasy-leaning? Where does the term 'crime' fit in, particularly if we are dealing with other worlds or alternative universes? Obviously, we can include an investigation into a crime, just as we can up the suspense and fear: a life in peril, for instance. But the writer must decide how, and why, and to what degree.

The other factor pertinent to both mystery and suspense is the question that I believe trumps them all. It follows on from (and adds to) to the key questions, 'Who did it?' and 'What next?' It is the question that adds real meaning to any mystery, and it is simply this: 'Why?' Why did someone do such a thing, what are the consequences and what might they, or others do next? On a literal level 'why' is integrally linked to 'who did it', just as it is to 'what next'. It's up to the writer – ahead of the reader – to outline possible scenarios and states-of-being, even if misdirection is also being brought into play, and indeed in that case, especially so. It's up to the writer to create that character, or characters, to carry those questions and ultimately to answer them. They need to provide answers, even if those answers are in fact further questions. The reader might think they are a step ahead, or have alternative ideas and conspiracy theories about what lies beyond the surface level of what they are reading, more than the scenario suggests. The writer must remain in control of what the reader is reading between the lines, fully aware that they are enabling (or encouraging) the reader to think such things. The writer created this suspenseful mystery and this world, and they need to know how it looks on the surface, and be a step ahead of what the reader might conclude, while allowing the reader the space to reach those conclusions. In many ways, the more the reader feels enabled and possibly even in command, the better the job the writer has done – at least of creating a certain type of crime fiction. As was the case, certainly, for classic detective or Golden Age crime fiction.

Crafting crime fiction

First steps

In a basic, classic mystery, a crime will have been committed, most commonly a murder, and a plot could centre on the investigation of who might have committed it. Red herrings or a few MacGuffins (a red herring without any legs) would be thrown in the way. The mystery, on the tin, would eventually be solved, with smart readers working out who the perpetrator(s) really is(are) some time before the end. This would be in the vein of Agatha Christie et al. At the far opposite end of the same spectrum, we might have a novella like Martin Amis' *Night Train* – a blatant homage to gritty, mid-century modern detective fiction and ultimately a serious metaphorical and metaphysical study of existentialism. The stuff in the middle, that is neither a replication or a dynamic, parameter-breaking homage, or an entirely, genre-infused new way forward, is what most of us produce and where genre-comfort of a certain sort might lie. However, just because we could be dealing more with knowns, rather than unknowns, or reader expectation and identification, it doesn't mean our 'mysteries' shouldn't strive for difference, originality and spark. Besides, how do we actually incorporate the known elements of the genre, anyway?

In his groundbreaking, though now dated, essay 'The Typology of Detective Fiction', the structuralist critic Tzvetan Todorov asserted that classic detective or 'mystery' fiction followed two superimposed timelines: one chronological, the other reverse chronological.[8] One follows the attempts to solve the crime, while the other follows the events leading up to that crime; this could be portrayed through memory, interview, interrogation or flashbacks, even imagined scenarios by the super-intuitive investigator. Laid out in parallel (not that they

necessarily are) we have the investigation or reconstruction portraying the events leading up to the crime, and thus the mystery
is eventually solved. One way of approaching the planning
and plotting of such a mystery is to chart the events and situations that lead to the crime. Overlay this with how those events
might be discovered, and then with these two central storylines
mapped out, decide how best to tell the story and from whose
perspective. Just who is telling the story plays a very significant
part in amplifying mystery, and also suspense. Both are created
through narrative withholding, which is greatly exploitable by
playing with the limits of POV.

For instance, switching a POV from one character to another
can offer a completely different version of the same story. Who
might be misinterpreting what has happened? Who is revealing
what, and to whom? Here it might be appropriate to use an
unreliable narrator (and this is just as useful a tool for writing
non-crime fiction, as it is entirely bound up with POV). In any
case, such discrepancies might be factual (to do with whether
they are telling the truth about the 'facts') or more emotionally
charged (to do with how they interpret the facts). Either option
can add to questions of reliability. While these concepts are
ostensibly narrative in nature, they can be readily exploited for
dramatic purposes, creating layers of information and misinformation, and playing with how and when this information is
revealed. In part, this goes back to the idea of questions – the
very premise of mystery and suspense. Ask a question and delay
the answer, until the reader isn't just on the edge of their seat,
but is practically tearing their hair out wanting answers.

For an example, dip into any crime novel and you'll be surprised to see how much dialogue and exposition is riddled with
'mysterious' questions; or rather, questions that enhance the

'mystery'. Pulled from my shelf and almost opened at random, this is from roughly halfway into Leye Adenle's *When Trouble Sleeps*, his follow-up to the award-winning *Easy Motion Tourist*, and which also features Amaka, the self-appointed saviour of Lagos' sex workers:

> Ambrose walked ahead of Amaka down the dark, unlit corridor in his mansion. Yellowman walked behind them. Ambrose stopped in the middle of the corridor where moonlight poured in through a window overlooking the front yard. He turned to Amaka. 'Did you bring it?' he said.[9]

Now look at the next few sentences for a studied lesson in delaying the answer, and how to amplify the mystery, and suspense:

> Amaka looked at Yellowman. Light from the window cut across his body from the shoulders down. In the shadow, his neck and face were a pale grey. He held his hands behind his back where he stood a couple of metres away but still within earshot. She looked at Ambrose. 'Can we be alone?' she said.
>
> Ambrose gestured to Yellowman and the tall figure withdrew into the shadow. Amaka waited to hear the door shut, then she turned to Ambrose.

This next section then adds to the complexity of information and misinformation at stake. Further, it exhibits Adenle's control of the material, and the manipulation of 'mystery'. One question is answered while others/bigger questions are then posed.

> 'I have a confession to make. I don't have the memory card but he doesn't know that. You just have to tell him exactly what I described to you and he'll be convinced you've seen the videos. He'll have no choice but to withdraw his candidacy. Can deal with him as a civilian, but if he becomes governor, he'll be too powerful and he'll have immunity.'

Mystery and suspense

'Immunity does not mean he cannot be investigated. Gani
Fawehinmi vs Inspector General of Police. 2002.'

'You're a lawyer?'

'No. I'm a politician. But I know the law when it affects me.
How did you lose the memory card?'

So while we think a question, the question of where the
memory card has gone, has been answered, Adenle then ramps
it up again, with a further question: 'My handbag was stolen at
Oshodi. It was in it.'[10]

Who stole Amaka's handbag? Was this part of a larger
conspiracy? Question upon question, mystery upon mystery.
However, not conforming to the ultimate Todorovian structure and not tying everything up too neatly might just allow
your novel to breathe with life. Frankly, life is messy. Things
are always unresolved. Despite the need to be aware of balance, coherence and consistency, practical and thematic
neatness overall isn't necessarily wholly fulfilling, and certainly not nowadays with modern crime fiction. In fact, often
what's left out, what's intentionally missing, can impart the
most lasting impression: mysteries that go unanswered. Yet,
beware – leave too many questions unanswered, leave the
ending too open, and you won't be doing your job. Reader
dissatisfaction could be profound. Ambiguity could look like
authorial laziness, or lack of control, while meaning will be
diminished.

Balance

Like so many things in relation to writing fiction, and crime
fiction especially, it comes down to balance, and authorial
control. We teach a module, A Theoretical and Practical

Approach to Crime Writing. Students are guided through embedded extracts and various opportunities to submit work and ideas. The Mystery and Suspense seminar, prepared by my colleague Tom Benn, has the message: 'The success of every mystery might be in finding the right balance between what to put in (and where), and what to omit.' In part, this riffs off a Lodge line in *The Art of Fiction*: 'Enough information must be fed to the reader to make it convincing when it comes, but not so much that the reader will easily anticipate it.'[11]

If we think of information feeds to fuel mystery, then in some ways we are also considering 'surprises': information, perhaps, that we hadn't seen coming, rather than necessarily more obvious and blatant actions; guys popping up with guns. Another way of thinking about the information that fuels mystery is as something that is unpredictable with foresight but inevitable with hindsight. The key to implementing these new threads, ideas, actions, questions (invariably) or effectively 'mysteries' – and again do think of umbrellas, and loops of questions and answers; small umbrellas with big umbrellas above them – is to regard these smaller mysteries as being in service to the story. As Tom Benn puts it:

> A mystery should always be in service of a story. A story in service of a mystery is a story in service of nothing – and most readers can tell. This is why mystery (the device rather than the genre) should be seen as another essential tool at the writer's disposal, rather than the engine for an entire novel.

The converse to information feeds and that drip, drip of 'mystery' fuel is the withholding of information. That important information is withheld either from the protagonist (possibly, though in a less charged way, from a subsidiary character), or the reader, or both. The knack here is to allow the reader the room to either think something is missing, or realise something was missing, but not be wholly surprised later on when it's revealed. Too much authorial toying with the reader can create a lack of connection, and not least annoyance. If you can see the authorial workings, if you can even sense them, then the author is being too present, and not subtle enough. In a way, this is not unrelated to prose style and an overly 'writerly' syntax. The author is saying, hey, look at me, isn't my mystery clever. Put the 'seeing' and 'not-seeing' (or knowing and not-knowing) into the perspective of the protagonist/narrator, and then you will have both connection on the part of the reader, and effective mystery. On the Crime MA we use a simple exercise to get students thinking about this narrative withholding. It is this:

> Begin a story in the first person, describing an inhabited house from the perspective of a thief. Don't mention that the narrator is a thief; don't show the narrator in the act of stealing. (But your narrator might have already stolen something or be about to steal.)

A more 'literary' approach and exercise to 'mystery' as suggested by Andrew Cowan in his *The Art of Writing Fiction*, asks a student/fledgling writer to use an earlier draft of their automatic writing, and attempt to turn this into the start of a short story. To do that, Cowan suggests, you should 'aim to depict the mysterious'.

> Whatever your character is doing, your description should suggest that something ominous is about to occur. Your character should sense that something is amiss, and your reader should share the uncertainty (without becoming confused).[12]

Crafting crime fiction

Further guidance is provided by the comment: 'You may change the point of view to first person, but remember to place the emphasis on precise sensory detail.' Cowan suggests elsewhere that a 'writer's chief interest or purpose will be to dwell in the realm of the uncertain, exploiting the possibilities of mystery, ambiguity, complexity'. For him, it's precisely this kind of uncertainty that will draw the reader into the fictional world and hold them there. But Cowan also raises questions: 'how to depict the mysterious without becoming confusing? How to suggest ambiguity without seeming muddled, or complexity without seeming contradictory?'[13]

I've included these comments because I think they illustrate where aspects of 'mysteriousness' (or if you like, ambiguity and complexity) can take over, or in effect take the place of purposeful and considered mystery, certainly in relation to crime fiction. One of the purposes of this chapter is to consider mystery as a practical device to enhance plot (in all its senses) and genre identity, as opposed to mystery as something 'mysterious', ambiguous and perhaps unnecessarily complex. Or something that stems from a writer's 'literary', likely uncharted, exploration of 'being' or a state of being, and desire to express this through writing. There, you might find a writer withholding aspects of information or causality (in relation to events) because they simply don't know, or don't know yet. Enhancing this element of intrigue or mystery in a non-genre, or markedly 'literary' fiction is arguably practically and thematically far easier than carefully placed information, withheld and revealed to increase suspense and pace. This respect for the craft of suspense is one reason I'm wary of surprise – particularly surprise for surprise's sake.

Mystery and suspense

The unexpected

Whatever I think in general terms about surprise and mystery, it's true that ideas for plot surprises, quite unexpected, quite unplanned for (indeed, surprising), might well pop into your head while writing. This can happen even if you are the most diligent and forward thinking of plotters and planners: a writing control freak (as someone once called me). It can also be hugely important and ultimately relevant and rewarding.

So here's the thing: despite all that has been discussed above, don't immediately discount those surprises or sudden twists (reveals, withholds, unexpected appearances) that can suddenly come to mind. They might well have come to mind because you are concentrating hard, thinking every which way about your work-in-progress and something in your subconscious, which is wholly on point, comes to the fore. Such 'connections', regardless of process and anything predetermined, can make writing the highly enjoyable and endlessly discoverable journey that it should be. But nevertheless, I would stress caution, pause for a moment, and consider all that's gone before and was planned to come after. Does this new idea fit? Is it really right? Does it add to the mystery, the suspense – could it come to be seen as integral, organic, fundamental – without adding unnecessary complexity and deviation, and a huge amount of rewriting? As long as it adds to the key elements of what you're writing, you might be onto something.

You might also come up with a red herring, or purposeful misdirection, or even a totemic MacGuffin – they too can pop into a writer's head, during a hard writing session. They might well flow naturally out of the current direction of the narrative. However, red herrings (unlike MacGuffins, which have always seemed a bit cheap and forced to me, perhaps because they were borrowed from the silver screen) will need resolving to a point: just how far, and for how long will they remain active, even if in the background? They can't seem to be overly casual, abrupt or unlikely. Such deviation needs to be as warranted as real plot movement, or, as Chandler would imply, turning a corner. One way of thinking about red herrings is to regard them as 'alternative possibilities', and to stay logical to the thought processes of the characters in context. An investigating character, say, or a character under threat, or a perpetrator. While misdirection and added complexity from these sources can of course add to the sense of suspense (as well as mystery) – more threat, more jeopardy, more at risk, more questions to be answered – there are other, more practical steps that can be considered.

Breaks and cliffhangers

Simply, chapter and line breaks can have a huge effect. These are how cliffhangers can be highlighted. End a scene on a dramatic point, probably involving some action, which is not resolved or has not evolved as far as it could go, then cut the scene. Pick up a different narrative thread or timeline, or simply use the white space to jump forward or back in time, or to a different POV and moment. Here's an illustrative line break, then chapter ending from Adenle's *When Trouble Sleeps*:

> He tucked his pistol under his shirt and retrieved the Uzi and spare clips. He put a clip into each pocket of his jacket, then checked both ends of the road. He got out of his car, held the weapon under his jacket, and crossed the road.

Mystery and suspense

He kept his eyes on the gate as he crouched down to pick up an empty shell from the ground, and sniff it. He put it into his pocket and searched around him. His eyes fell on a spot in front of the gate. He walked over, crouched again, and touched it. It was wet. He rubbed his fingers together and sniffed them. He pulled out his Uzi and aimed it at the gate, backed up towards his car, got inside without taking his eyes off the gate, and started the engine.

This is from Yellowman's POV. We then have a line break, before picking up with Yellowman again:

The lookout behind the gate lowered his pistol. He kept close to the ground as he crept towards the house.

The chapter, Chapter 49, which is only two pages long, then ends. We pick up with Chapter 50 and Amaka's POV:

Amaka's eyes darted towards the door.
'Who's that?' she said.
The handle turned and it began to open. She sat up in the water, reached for a towel and covered herself. 'Who's that?'

Then what about this for both suspense, but also misdirection and making us realise we're elsewhere entirely?

Eyitayo entered the bathroom. She was in a blue kimono and she had a bottle of wine and two glasses in her hands. 'It's just me,' she said, using her bum to shut the door behind her. Amaka returned the towel to the rack and sank back into the bathtub.[14]

There are 110 chapters in *When Trouble Sleeps*, most averaging only two pages in length. Many chapters also incorporate line breaks. There are numerous POV shifts, while it's firmly Amaka's story, or rather the story she's involved with, which increasingly becomes one of survival (along with resolution).

Crafting crime fiction

While practical, structural effects – such as line breaks and chapter endings – can be integral to shifting POV and time-lines, they can also maintain mystery and sustain threat. On a macro-level they help shape the whole, adding to the pace and rhythm. Where you end a scene can offer dramatic possibilities, another way of adding meaning and purpose. The white space of a novel can be as important as the words themselves. OK, this is not poetry, but it's all part of punctuation, grammar, syntax, the prose itself, and moving the narrative forward, hopefully with pace.

If we now consider the perceived threat to Amaka in the above extract, we are also dealing with immediate threat, risk, jeopardy, or in other words, suspense. We fear for Amaka. We think Yellowman is about to burst in with an Uzi. While mystery is premised on the how, and the why (as Lodge put it, 'how did she do it?'), suspense is of course premised on whatever next, or, 'what will happen?'[15] Having said that, just wanting to know what will happen might not necessarily be very suspenseful. It could be a certain sort of itch. At some point we really want to know where this story is going, what might have happened to so and so, but we're enjoying being in the moment or the scene enough not to rush. Conceivably, in such a scenario, the writer is doing a good enough job of capturing a mood, a moment, a setting, a scene for the reader not to need to rush. Ideally, the prose will also maintain purpose, and enough narrative drive for the reader not to be bored.

Rush of adrenaline

Though what of that rush, that sense of adrenaline readers love to feel? What makes us sit up, sit on the edge of a seat,

Mystery and suspense

lean forward, and read faster and faster, while our hearts begin to thump? Suspense, far more than mystery, inspires physical feelings in the reader. Interestingly, practically applying or incorporating suspense on the page can also require describing physical aspects of action and violence, or certainly impending violence. While suspense can be tied up with an urgent need to know what will happen next, what might be revealed next, what might be answered – as opposed to questioned – next, it is perhaps at its most obvious and intense when we fear for a character, a protagonist, or a narrator we have become intimately engaged with and connected to. Will they be harmed, caught, kidnapped, murdered? In the third person, this can be done simply by alerting the reader to a threat ahead; the protagonist, say, might be walking slowly, carefully, observantly down a dark street, but still not know who might be lurking behind a corner. Yet the reader does. What we might not know, though, is if they will escape harm. Or what they might do to the assailant.

Popular Anglophone suspense fiction – that is fiction, often melodrama, which was designed to induce feelings of horror or trepidation in the reader – came to prominence in the mid- to late nineteenth century and was a category all of its own, under the banner 'sensation literature'. It stemmed in part from neo-gothic, horror (ghost) and romance stories, and led to adventure fiction and of course the thriller, along with the 'mystery' novel, which developed into detective fiction. One of sensation fiction's key premises was to use contemporary settings and scenarios with deeply allegorical or abstract elements. 'Mystery', and especially unease, came from the known mixed with the deep 'unknown'. Subject matter could include adultery, theft, kidnapping, insanity, bigamy, murder. Anthony Trollope is credited with saying that such fiction should be 'realistic and sensational … and both in the highest degree'.[16] Perhaps the best-known example and a key precursor to crime fiction is Wilkie Collins' *The Woman in White*. Other notable sensation texts include *Lady Audley's Secret* by Mary Braddon, *Foul Play* by Charles Read, and *The Mystery of Edwin Drood* by Charles Dickens. Sarah Waters has acknowledged the influence such texts had on her novel *Fingersmith*, while Eleanor Catton has also credited the sensation genre having in part influenced *The Luminaries*.

So if we go back to one of crime fiction's earliest premises, even before the thriller and the detective novel emerged, diverged and then variously merged again, we are left with the idea of realism and sensationalism combined to the 'highest degree'. In relation to genre, in relation to creating the maximum effect, 'sensationalism' should not be seen in a disparaging way. Let's think of it as a further device to engage, and perhaps more pertinently to excite, thrill, terrify. It's not just 'what next', but 'whatever next'. As mentioned earlier, raising the stakes is a sure way to up the emotional temperature if not the suspense at a given moment. In practical terms, this could involve an unexpected reveal, or a rug being pulled out from under a central character. Or it could involve a more specific and seemingly possible physical threat. Make it life and death, not a petty theft. Your reader's connection to that character is key: jeopardy is at its greatest when we care about or are fully invested in the person who is in trouble. Certainly, we are programmed to feel empathy for those who are weaker or less fortunate than us, or those who are in trouble, particularly not of their own doing. So, it's important to encourage that connection with the central character(s), but remember: the reader should never feel manipulated. Crime writers need to beware of being mawkish or oversentimental.

Raising the stakes

Obviously in truly suspenseful fiction, jeopardy should ramp up as the novel progresses. Depending on the strength of the effect you are going for, it could well reach unbearable proportions. Yet, it mustn't spin relentlessly out of control. Louise Welsh, author of crime genre-defying novels such as *The Cutting Room*, *Tamburlaine Must Die*, *The Girl on the Stairs* and *The Second Cut*, has a great line on suspenseful action. 'Remember, action, like sex scenes, is a series of events – keep it hot and interesting.'[17] The thing is, action is largely surface. It is what lies beneath that will provide the resonance: character, motivation, context, voice, subtext, narrative tension/conflict, connection ... Action is also not simply suspense. On a basic level it is things, happening. It can be a way of amplifying suspense, and the moment, or the situation. And any such suspenseful (what next) situation should involve elements of the broader mystery (how, why), at least on a deeper level. Ruth Rendell, with a solid track record of intelligent police procedurals behind her with her Inspector Wexford series, and numerous standalones, also wrote more psychological suspense-orientated fictions under the name Barbara Vine. She was particular on the importance of suspense, while being somewhat abstract in its application, as she told the *Guardian*:

> Suspense is my thing. I think I am able to make people want to keep turning pages. They want to know what happens. So I can do that. Mind you, I think this ought to apply to any fiction, because however brilliant it is in other respects, you don't want to go on reading it unless it does that to you.[18]

Crafting crime fiction

Rendell put down her approach to suspense as 'a sort of withholding', which could be taken to be the asking of questions and the withholding of answers. Yet, questions invariably contain elements of 'hows' and 'whys', and as such are the bedrock of mystery. Mystery inspires questions and, conceivably in crime fiction, answers and then some sort of resolution. This is the case even if the questions are not explicit, and as perhaps Rendell might have been suggesting, rely more on a 'withholding', so that it's only a matter of time before the reader realises what might be being withheld, and the questions that could possibly stem from that.

Smart crime fiction, as we know, is not just about establishing facts (whodunnit), or putting a puzzle together; and for the reader possibly even ahead of the author, or final reveal. It's about establishing character in tandem with plot (the character as plot in action), so the questions (or implications/or the dawning of questions) are not just suspenseful, but meaningful, pertinent, purposeful. They need to be well judged and well placed. Conflict is as important to suspense as cliffhangers, red herrings, pacing, atmosphere, raising the stakes; all the other means and devices discussed so far. Invariably, ultimately, suspense and mystery are as intrinsically linked as plot and character. All this requires planning, consideration, careful implementation (even if, of course, your surprises are to appear shocking, random, out of the blue). What they must not appear to look like, however, are authorial, spur-of-the moment additions!

Building such an approach to surprise, to mystery, to motivation, around a series can require even more planning and consideration, especially on the macro-level, and especially if that series is grounded in realism (as opposed, for example, to elements of the supernatural or fantasy). Certainly, I found that

Mystery and suspense

when I was writing the second and third novels in the Goodwin Crime Family series, all the key questions in relation to mystery and suspense required even more attention.

Series suspense

Mystery and suspense in a series is also determined by micro- and macro-levels of questions, surprises and threats, along with reveals and answers. The series form means that the macro is greatly expanded, and possibly ever-expanding if you don't know how many novels the series will end up having. You can carry key questions – such as love and desire, paternity, or the identity of a shadowy crime figure, or the police mole – from book to book. But there should also be a sense of getting closer to some of the answers. OK, a question or two might then lead to a long-form red herring, with the reader being thrown back to square one. Or such threads of mysteries could be answered in part here and there, and be a long-form way of turning a corner, taking us into new territory, say on book three, or book eight. However, the surprises, and the way mystery and particularly suspense is handled, all need to remain as new and as fresh as possible from book to book.

Reliance on tricks the reader has already seen to raise the temperature and increase suspense will quickly fall flat. How many times can a protagonist be kidnapped, for instance? Series characters don't necessarily change or develop a great deal from book to book. In the case of Jack Reacher, or Inspector Maigret, they change barely at all. But their situations need to. And these need to be fresh and seem original. If the series characters are on more of a developmental trajectory – such as Ian Rankin's John Rebus, or Liza Marklund's Annika

Crafting crime fiction

Bengtzon – ageing inspector and struggling crime reporter and mother, respectively – the bigger questions, those that keep us invested in the characters, will be on a more enveloping trajectory. A trajectory that will need, ultimately, to encompass the whole story of however many novels, or the mega-narrative, as it's beginning to be known. Again, the specifics of suspense and mystery will play their parts in both micro- and macro-ways.

Planning The Goodwins involved mapping the first three novels before a word was written – albeit in brief, bullet-point ways. Key structural decisions were made before the writing began: each novel would take place over a short period of time, just four or five days. Each novel would take place during a different season. Each novel would be told from the perspectives of members of the Goodwin family, along with some sections from Frank, the family's right-hand man. While it was always going to be the story of Tatty rebuilding a criminal empire in the deprived environs of Great Yarmouth, while also rebuilding a sense of herself and personal purpose, each of the three novels contains a key thematic and perspective difference. This difference centres on Tatty's three grown-up children: Zach, Sam and Ben. The first novel, *Time to Win*, finds Tatty's youngest, Zach, desperate to prove himself independent of Tatty and Frank. His fledgling coke-dealing business and plans to turn a rundown caravan park into a weekend rave scene go spectacularly wrong, along with his secret relationship with the daughter of his mother's cleaner. Book two, *Red Hot Front*, has a subsidiary plot following pregnant Sam as she relocates to Great Yarmouth with her super-smooth, international financier boyfriend.[19] Except the boyfriend is not all that he seems, and Tatty has to deal with him, risking her relationship with her daughter forever.

Mystery and suspense

Book three, *Good Dark Night*, has a subplot involving Ben's return to the fold, and with serious ambitions for the Goodwin family business.[20] A former currency trader, and somewhat shy City boy, Ben has not reckoned on the ferocity of the rival local criminal gangs, and finds himself, much to Tatty's horror, kidnapped. Further danger arrives with Tatty's former brother-in-law, who always had a very different take on family.

Raising the stakes by using a mother's relationship with her children was the aim. With the workings of the crime empire overlapping the domestic situations, having a focus on a different grown-up child in each book allowed for clear, distinguishing and intrinsic mystery. Who are each of these characters, and just what do they really know about their parents, their upbringing? How do recent reveals change their relationships with their mother, and each other? What did they want in the past, and what do they really want now? It meant that suspense could also be handled differently, with each of the grown-up children capable and vulnerable in quite separate ways. Ultimately, Tatty can learn more about herself, as a mother, a 'business' person, a criminal, from each of them, and from each of their crises. Where are her real loyalties? What does she need to do to rectify the past?

Each book has various inciting incidents, rising tensions and climaxes. Each book is steeped in place and character, with the two concepts being so ingrained they are unbreakable. Plot and character work as one, ultimately across a three-book structure (with each book also roughly involving a three-act framework).

The surprise, if that's quite the right word, or the real mystery's resolution, at the end, is that any answers are far closer to home than perhaps the characters, and hopefully readers, ever thought. The sense of suspense along the way was always closely considered. I hoped to inspire in the reader a sense of urgency, fear, excitement, sensation. In the end, it is always best judged by the reader. Sensibilities vary. Readerly resource and expectations vary. Still, we all know when we've read a good book.

Has the writer done a good job? This is probably the hardest thing for a writer truly to know about their own work, especially before it's gone out into the wild.

8

ENTERTAINMENT AND ENGAGEMENT

Practical and thematic considerations are graspable. We can discuss and use the key devices of writing crime fiction, from plot and point of view to mystery and suspense. Theme and content are also within the writer's control, if sometimes more easily identified and claimed with hindsight. Do we ever know what our fiction is really about thematically until the book is finished, until others might spot things, patterns? Conceivably, our work will speak to different people in different ways. I'm always struck by students who set out to write a fiction, even a crime fiction, about such and such a theme, before they've even considered or planned who the key characters will be, even where and when it might be set. Often, they are more concerned with polemic and issues (social/political/ecological, and so on) than necessarily fiction which is operating for fiction's sake; that is for the sake of a good read. Or rather, fiction that allows the characters to do the thinking, the situations to create the drama, and the issues, as such, to arise organically. (Even though invariably these will be determined by the author's preoccupations and subconscious. Just don't force it!)

Crafting crime fiction

Sticking with the basics – menace and motivation, pace and purpose – encapsulated through the devices and concepts explored in the previous seven chapters is not necessarily easy, though more of that in the next and final chapter, 'Craft and editing'. However, all are variously in the control of the author. Yes, talent and instinct will play huge parts, along with determination. But how can we devise and plan for reader enjoyment? How can we consider, while devising and writing, 'entertainment' and 'engagement'? Is it even up to the writer to determine how captivating, thrilling or amusing their work is? It is up to the writer to use all their knowledge and talent to create the sort of fiction they want to create. As much as a writer might desire to write 'entertaining' and 'engaging' fiction, it's a very imprecise science. How exactly do you set about entertaining an audience, engaging a reader, when a good chunk of the equation falls to the reader and reader response? Call this the 'unknown', if you like. Do you ever really know what effect your work will have on others, what the reception might be?

The process for a more established writer is arguably easier and less random. You might have an agent, sub-agents, editors and publishers and various teams of marketing people to advise based on their professional experience, before the work is published. You could be well into a series and know largely what works. But it's the writer and the writer's approach that comes first, and so that's what we'll explore here. We also need to acknowledge ourselves as readers, and the truth about what we enjoy reading.

Entertainment

For now, let us consider 'entertainment' – this factor of our writing that we both can and seemingly cannot specifically control. Entertainment is something we all have some experience of and ideas about as consumers of fiction. Why do we read? Why do we seek out certain types of books? There are books we read to be entertained, and those we read for other reasons. The crime fiction genre, actually like the novel itself (back in its most obvious manifestations in the eighteenth and nineteenth centuries), was premised on entertainment, and being 'novel', or new. Slowly, like the novel, crime fiction became more complicated and nuanced – and arguably more necessary than ever. From social realism to social justice, the personal to the political, myriad sub-genres and fusions, and all manner of syntactical succinctness, flair and innovation, the form developed new ways of doing and saying important things about life and death, about being, identity and belonging; giving rise to new voices, with new urgency.

Significantly, the concept of entertainment within the genre has never been forgotten. Along with my defining features of crime fiction (menace and motivation, pace and purpose), I could also add 'entertainment and engagement'. It's a popular genre for a reason, and all the better for it. Crime fiction should be highly captivating, even if sometimes violent. It should be enjoyable, and it should take you to new places, new, highly dramatic situations. These will often be uncomfortable situations; though some writers choose to balance them with more comfortable, exotic experiences. In other cases, comfort could come from a certain sort of resolution, even if that resolution is in part open-ended. We know the joy that Golden Age detective

fiction, or solving the puzzle plot, gave to a whole era of readers, and is still giving to readers today. Put simply, crime fiction
should be something you turn to, so you can turn away from
your everyday. However, that does not mean it shouldn't help
explain the everyday – it might well be a heightened version
of it. There are ways of doing this that are more captivating,
mysterious, thrilling and enjoyable for the reader than others.
The everyday in extremis, if you like. Making entertainment
out of disturbance, violence, suffering, or devious criminal acts
has always been the challenge.

Natsuo Kirino's *Out* and (the already cited) Paula Hawkins'
The Girl on the Train, two of the most shocking and internationally popular crime fictions of the last twenty-five years, are
certainly sombre, oppressive examples. *Out* begins:

> She got to the parking lot earlier than usual. The thick, damp
> July darkness engulfed her as she stepped out of the car. Perhaps
> it was the heat and humidity, but the night seemed especially
> black and heavy. Feeling a bit short of breath, Masako Katori
> looked up at the starless night sky. Her skin, which had been cool
> and dry in the air-conditioned car, began to feel sticky. Mixed in
> with the exhaust fumes from the Shin-Oume Expressway, she
> could smell the faint odour of deep-fried food, the odour of the
> boxed-lunch factory where she was going to work.[1]

And this is after an epigraph by Flannery O'Connor: 'The
way to despair is to refuse to have any kind of experience …'

The Girl on the Train begins with a short paragraph given a
whole page of its own, with no chapter number or heading:

> She's buried beneath a silver birch tree, down towards the old
> train tracks, her grave marked with a cairn. Not more than a
> little pile of stones, really. I didn't want to draw attention to her
> resting place, but I couldn't leave her without remembrance.

She'll sleep peacefully there, no one to disturb her, no sounds but birdsong and the rumble of passing trains.[2]

In *Out* we have an almost sensory overload. In *The Girl on the Train* we are already alerted to a female's unofficial final resting place. Both novels become more meaningful and pertinent, and really get going in their second paragraphs, as the questions pile up. From *Out*:

'I want to go home.' The moment the smell hit her, the words came into her head. She didn't know exactly what home it was she wanted to go to, certainly not the one she'd just left. But why didn't she want to go back there? And where did she want to go? She felt lost.

From *The Girl on the Train*, another short paragraph given a whole page of its own:

One for sorrow, two for joy, three for a girl. Three for a girl. I'm stuck on three, I just can't get any further. My head is thick with sounds, my mouth thick with blood. Three for a girl. I can hear the magpies, they're laughing, mocking me, a raucous cackling. A tiding. Bad tidings. I can see them now, black against the sun. Not the birds, something else. Someone's coming. Someone is speaking to me. Now look. Now look what you made me do.

Menace seeps into both beginnings, along with strong suggestions of crimes. Both novels feature female protagonists pushed to the murderous edge. Both were deemed cutting-edge, landmark books on publication. Both were adapted into highly successful films and spawned numerous spin-offs. Both were also regarded variously as popular crime fiction around the world, especially *The Girl on the Train*. *Out*, Kirino's first novel to be published in English, has always been seen as more 'indie', and 'challenging', probably because of the level of violence, sex and various cultural gaps between Japan and the Anglophone world. Read it, if you haven't. As *Time Out*, stated, it's 'sensational'. Or as *USA Today* said: 'No gritty urban American tale of violence can match the horror of *Out*.' *The Girl on the Train*, meanwhile, became one of the beacon texts of the emerging sub-genre known as Domestic Noir, with a more traditional and singular sense of feminist and 'vigilante' justice. As for enjoyment, or entertainment – the very endings of both give clues to this. Please excuse the possible spoilers, though I'm not sure either example gives too much away plot-wise. From *Out*:

> She punched the elevator button. She would go and buy an airplane ticket. The freedom she was seeking was her own, not Satake's, or Yayoi's, or Yoshie's, and she was sure it must be out there somewhere. If one more door had closed behind her, she had no choice but to find a new one to open. The elevator moaned like the wind as it came to meet her.[3]

From *The Girl on the Train*:

> I get into bed and turn the lights out. I won't be able to sleep, but I have to try. Eventually, I suppose, the nightmares will stop and I'll stop replaying it over and over and over in my head, but right now I know that there's a long night ahead. And I have to get up early tomorrow morning, to catch the train.[4]

In many ways, both stick to the tone of their beginnings. These endings are also syntactically coherent with their beginnings. Though both endings are clearly optimistic, suggesting freedom, a tomorrow – a sort of resolution, if not quite happy days. Even true noir – from the likes of James M. Cain, Dorothy B. Hughes and Jim Thompson and neo-noir from, say, Hawkins and Kirino – can be entertaining. But I'd suggest that the entertainment comes from a chilling thrill of being taken to such extreme situations, which invariably end in violent outcomes.

Entertainment and engagement

Graphic (even if appropriate) depictions of violence are certainly not for everyone. However, the reader, at least survives.

Pushing it

Portrayals of truly sadistic serial killers provide particularly strange 'entertainment', to my mind. Despite coming from the sparkling, seemingly pristine frozen north, Jo Nesbø has taken the sub-genre into ever-darker places. The shocking, disturbing extract below (and this is a content warning) comes from a short way into *The Leopard*, where a terrified young woman has a ball-like contraption stuffed into her mouth. She's told not to pull the wire that it's attached to, or to try to dislodge it. She's struggling to breathe. After many agonising hours and minutes, she pulls the wire:

> The needles shot out of the circular ridges. They were seven centimetres long. Four burst through her cheeks on each side, three into the sinuses, two up the nasal passages and two out through the chin. Two needles pierced the windpipe, and one the right eye, one the left. Several needles penetrated the rear part of the palate and reached the brain. But that was not the direct cause of her death. Because the metal ball impeded movement, she was unable to spit out the blood pouring from the wounds in her mouth. Instead it ran down her windpipe and into her lungs, not allowing oxygen to be absorbed into her bloodstream, which in turn led to a cardiac arrest and what the pathologist would call in his report cerebral hypoxia, that is, lack of oxygen to her brain. In other words Borgny Stem-Myhre drowned.[5]

Nesbø was largely responsible for the term 'torture porn' coming into existence. Inevitably, though it took a few years, there was a considerable backlash against this kind of fiction – and especially against the strong bias towards depicting violence against women (as discussed in Chapter 3). Arguably his version of Scandi noir, or the serial-killer thriller, attempted a certain sort of realism, as opposed to Thomas Harris and Val McDermid's hyper-realism – the creating of worlds we know are highly imaginative fictions (even fantasies in the case of Harris' Hannibal Lecter). The more imaginative and heightened the characters, such as Harris' Hannibal and McDermid's Angelica, the more we know we're in an alternative, or largely fictitious world. Even such extreme and extremely violent characters as these have their 'charms' and attractions – Lecter especially so. In the case of Nesbø's serial killers, charm doesn't often come into it. Here we are in a more real world, where killers are profoundly unpleasant. In all these cases, the writers' aim is to bring fear and terror to the everyday, and often the weak and vulnerable. Pleasure, or 'entertainment' from such fictions, is, as suggested, a matter of taste, as well as being a matter of escapism. Maybe, for some, the closer to reality, the more terrifying and 'entertaining': triggering the adrenalin rush of fear, but from a place of safety (both narrative, in the hands of a trusted author, and physical). Horror films work in similar ways.

The hero serial killer

Perhaps as a result of the backlash against such extreme, sadistic and 'realist' violence in some seral-killer crime fiction, there's been a resurgence of the 'hero serial killer': the entertaining and engaging serial killer, or vigilante serial killer, both on page and on screen. Jeff Lindsay's very successful Dexter series began with the novel *Darkly Dreaming Dexter*, and features vigilante psychopathic killer Dexter Morgan, who operates under 'Harry's

Entertainment and engagement

Code'.[6] He only kills those who deserve to be killed and who have escaped legal justice. 'A serial killer with a heart' is one cover line. Luke Jennings' creation Villanelle, a Russian-born hitwoman, first appeared on the page in *Codename Villanelle*.[7] As in the case of Dexter, it took an excellent small-screen adaptation and some fine acting to gain the series global presence and success.

Even so, credit needs to go to Jennings for coming up with the idea. Villanelle is also, of course, accompanied by an equally engaging nemesis in the form of MI5 agent Eve Polastri. None of these characters or any of the situations are particularly 'real', and the entertainment comes from the extravagance, the audacity and the outrageousness of the characters, which propel the plot. It's crime fantasy, or crime fiction as highly imaginative literary 'entertainment'. No one really gets hurt. The violence is almost cartoon-like, with little attempt at gritty realism. We are in alternative worlds determined by other rules. Lindsay and Jennings are only two such writers to stretch their imaginations, the imaginary worlds of their novels, and the parameters of the genre, for the sake of entertainment, as opposed to literary expression. They are not trying to change the world, but entertain the world. And they are doing it very well.

Empathy

In the case of *Out* and *The Girl on the Train*, where seemingly 'real' worlds and identifiable characters and situations are being realised, entertainment (and engagement) come from connection, understanding and empathy. We can see all too clearly – certainly by the end – how such relationships might develop and destruct. We put ourselves in others' shoes, and shiver. We might also 'enjoy' the feeling – if the text is effective and doing its job – of exacting bloody justice. The vicarious pleasure of inhabiting the minds and mindsets of certain characters, especially as they go about doing dreadful, but conceivably understandable things, has long been recognised. Happier endings than beginnings also provide some comfort. (Even though that would then not make it true noir.)

The pleasure or entertainment factor coruscating through a proper noir is arguably harder to fathom, but could be to do with witnessing someone else's, often deserving, implosion. Many people's literary taste simply takes them to the dark stuff. Plenty of readers 'enjoy' getting into the head of sadistic serial killers. Done well, a story can bring understanding and empathy to the disturbed, the challenged – people who some might determine as 'evil'. However, for me to be 'entertained' I need my serial killers – like Dexter or Villanelle – to be larger than life, heightened, fantastical. I need to be taken to imaginary, but entirely coherent and convincing, situations and worlds. Fiction is imaginative writing after all, crime fiction especially so.

Misdirection

While the entertainment factors of *Out* and *The Girl on the Train* are various, to do with not just resolution but revenge and retribution, the founding text of the Domestic Noir sub-genre, Gillian Flynn's *Gone Girl*, has a very different take on what constitutes crime fiction 'entertainment'. It's sardonic, playfully cynical, metafictional and funny throughout. It's also political in its gender and social constructs and critiques. It plays on so many levels it's no wonder it's been variously interpreted, loved and loathed. Landmark books tend to attract the widest spectrum of responses. That *Gone Girl* contains the twist of all twists further adds to its technical feats and know-how, and obviously to its powers of reader 'engagement'. As regards entertainment, as *The Times'* critic put it: 'You think you're reading a good, conventional thriller, and then it grows into a fascinating portrait of one averagely mismatched relationship.'[8] At the time of publication I reviewed the novel for *the Daily Mirror*, saying: 'This is Flynn's third novel and she's more than found her voice, creating taut, thrilling, deeply intense narratives about characters very much on the edge.'[9] In *Gone Girl*, misdirection is Flynn's calling card, and that also goes way beyond plot. We think we are reading a dissection of a terminally dysfunctional relationship, but we are also reading a romp. You can practically hear Flynn laughing between the lines.

'I am penniless and on the run. How fucking noir', declares Amy Elliott Dunne three-quarters of the way through.[10] If you are one of the few people who still hasn't read the book, be alert here please to the spoiler: by this point, the reader has already learnt that the 'girl' they thought was gone because she was the victim of a crime is actually gone because she has carefully planned and executed one. Misdirection is a useful device for creating and enhancing surprise, mystery and suspense – the key factors in ensuring reader engagement. It can also be highly entertaining. Look how we, the readers, have been fooled. This is a strangely satisfying experience. You think you know something, that you are onto a trail, a clue, a reveal, about to catch the culprit, only to be shockingly informed otherwise. It's not easy to pull off, and certainly not on the scale that Flynn achieves. Not only are we misdirected, our connection to one of the principal characters is completely altered. Can we continue to believe in them, and actually enjoy the rest of the novel? We can, and do, but it also means re-evaluating all that's gone before, along with, perhaps, several of our own pre-conceived, possibly prejudiced ideas. This allows for rereading and revisiting, and also enjoying the work in different, adapted forms, such as on screen. That the story can survive such a twist is further testament to the engaging and entertaining plot, characterisation, prose and premise. Also important here is the book's deep connection to the current social debates, the contemporary world we live in.

The academic Clive Bloom has described popular fiction as that which 'most becomes its period and which is most caught in its own age'. He has added that it is not just a 'barometer of contemporary imagination', but of all that is 'ephemeral artistically'.[11] That popular fiction also needs to be 'ephemeral artistically' further adds to the sense of capturing the moment, and the inherent dynamism of the crime fiction genre. Jokes date, we all know that. By extension, humour can age. Themes and content shift with the times. However, the need to be entertained, the need for imaginative 'escapism', is inherent, and continues.

In *The Bloomsbury Introduction to Popular Fiction*, Bran Nichol tells us that one function of so-called 'popular' fiction is to provide a moment of escapism amid the monotony of ordinary existence, while literary fiction's key function is to 'enrich our lives, or teach us something we did not know'.[12] This is a well-worn argument. As notoriously cited by Chandler in his essay 'The Simple Art of Murder' (1950), we have Dorothy L. Sayers writing in her introduction to the very first *Omnibus of Crime* (1929) of the detective story: 'It does not, and by hypothesis never can, attain the loftiest level of literary achievement.'

Entertainment and engagement

According to Chandler in his essay, Sayers suggested (and elsewhere) that this is because the detective story 'is a 'literature of escape' and not 'a literature of expression'. Chandler goes on to chastise Sayer, saying he, like Aeschylus, or Shakespeare, or Sayers herself, doesn't know what the 'loftiest level of literary achievement is'. He suggests that more powerful themes will provoke more powerful performances, and that a literature of expression and a literature of escape was just 'critics' jargon'.[13]

Vitality

For Chandler, a sense of energy, connection and life, was key. 'Everything written with vitality expresses that vitality ...'[14] This is a sentiment that echoes all the way down through the twentieth century and on to James Patterson (among many other best-selling writers). 'Be in the scene', as we know Patterson implores. For any work of fiction properly to engage the reader, it needs to come alive.

Somewhat conversely, for Chandler, and actually for Sayers too, 'escape' was crucial. As his (arguably justifiable) diatribe towards Sayers draws to a conclusion, Chandler states: 'I hold no particular brief for the detective story as the ideal escape. I merely say that *all* reading for pleasure is escape ...'[15] Reading for pleasure is fundamental to popular fiction, including crime fiction. Why else read it? Why else write it? Though can you say that reading for pleasure and reading to be entertained are much the same thing? This is where entertainment and engagement are profoundly linked and quietly distinct.

Perhaps the most obvious example of an author trying to make a distinction between their 'lighter', more entertaining work, and their more 'serious' literary endeavours, is Graham Greene. Greene wrote 25 novels (if you include the very short *The Fallen Idol*), of which six he deemed 'entertainments'. He was using the term largely to describe what he regarded as 'thrillers' from his other work, in part to attract film interest. These were: *Stamboul Train, A Gun for Sale, The Confidential Agent, The Ministry of Fear, The Third Man* and *Our Man in Havana. Stamboul Train* was published in 1932 and *Our Man in Havana* in 1958. Then Greene gave up on the distinction, yet some of his novels outside the category, *The Quiet American* and *A Burnt Out Case*, published in 1956 and 1960, respectively, are as much 'thrillers' as *The Confidential Agent* is. *Brighton Rock*, published in 1936, two years after *A Gun for Sale*, is also the thematic extension of that earlier work, yet Greene never classified it as an 'entertainment'.

By contrast, *The Third Man* was initially written as a film treatment and script, with a strong eye on its 'entertainment' value. And of all his novels, the funniest, arguably most riotously entertaining, and with heaps of comic crime thriller undertones and overtones, is *Travels with my Aunt*, published in 1969. The novel follows boring, staid, retired, suburban bank manager Henry Pulling, as he's 'pulled' into a life of international travel, adventure and criminal enterprises by his eccentric 'aunt' Augusta. The novel has aged quite badly in places. Still, you can see the enjoyment and energy with which it was written. The dialogue sparkles, the situations surprise, the descriptions sing. This comes from part one, as they head towards Istanbul, following various encounters with the pot-smuggling adventures of Augusta's one-time young lover 'Wordsworth', and a pot-smoking, privileged young American hippy called Tooley; a moment of calm then:

Entertainment and engagement

For some reason an old restaurant-car with a kind of faded elegance was attached to the express after the Turkish frontier, when it was already too late to be of much use. My aunt rose that day early, and the two of us sat down to excellent coffee, toast and jam: Aunt Augusta insisted on our drinking in addition a light red wine though I am not accustomed to wine so early in the morning. Outside the window an ocean of long undulating grass stretched to a pale green horizon. There was the talkative cheerfulness of journey's end in the air, and the car filled with passengers whom we had never seen before: a Vietnamese in blue dungarees spoke to a rumpled girl in shorts, and two young Americans, the man with hair as long as the girl's, joined them, holding hands. They refused a second cup of coffee after carefully counting their money.[16]

Greene described *Travels with my Aunt* as 'the only book I've written for the fun of it'.[17] As mentioned in the introduction here, I've long contemplated the correlation between writing 'for the fun of it', or rather simply enjoying the writing process, and the 'fun' factor, or enjoyableness of a novel. Is it possible to write an 'entertaining' novel if you are not entertained or enjoying the experience of actually writing it? We might enjoy moments, aspects of the writing process (including all the planning, plotting and research). However, invariably there'll be times when the energy lags, when the ideas stall, when you think you might be going down the wrong avenue. There'll be times when just writing a sentence becomes a chore; times when you'll be, frankly, sick of your own voice (even if you are trying your hardest to inhabit other voices). Persist, however, if you can, with bringing some fun, some joy and some entertainment to the process, and you may find it'll rub off on the work in question.

Crafting crime fiction

Entertainment value

But will it rub off, and in any case, how do we judge the entertainment value we are striving for? What is meant by entertainment and the effects we are trying to achieve, wherever on the literary-genre spectrum? Specifically, where do we want to pitch our fiction in relation to 'lightness', 'humour' and 'comic' twists and turns, along with plot twists and turns? And where or when do we want to head down darker paths? Entertainment in relation to crime fiction isn't of course a simple matter of 'lightness' versus 'darkness'. Dark crime fiction can of course be deeply entertaining, diverting, shocking and addictive. 'Light' crime fiction – now referred to as 'cosy', or indeed 'soft', as one of my current editors puts it – can also be extremely entertaining. Satire tends to darken the tone, but again it could well be highly entertaining. This will be determined by pitch – what are your authorial intentions? Where will you be sitting on that literary-genre spectrum? Entertainment doesn't happen by accident.

However, as we've seen already, of all the genres crime fiction is perhaps the one most loaded with contradictions. How can crime, murder, violence, psychological disturbance, be 'entertaining'? Engaging, yes, but 'entertaining'? Moving on from classic detective or Golden Age mysteries, with their arguably cardboard representations of character, and their overly complicated puzzle plots, their reliance on deduction rather than anything resembling empathy, we're back to the Sayers/Chandler conundrum. Cosy and confined verses the mean streets. Or are we?

Again, we find ourselves slipping into definitions, trying to create brackets, parameters, distinguishing characteristics and features. Yet, as we know by now, so much crime fiction defies easy categorisation – and that's just one of its many strengths. Even if we were to try to single out comic crime fiction we might quickly shift from farce to slapstick to satire. The phrase 'black comedy' would soon raise its head. But does something have to be comic, or light, to be entertaining? No, of course not. In fact, comic crime fiction is one of the hardest sub-genres to gain good market traction. If you want to be commercially successful, most industry figures will tell you to avoid trying to be funny. But there are notorious exceptions.

Being funny

Janet Evanovich cornered a market with her long-serving, gung-ho, larger-than-life protagonist Stephanie Plum. Carl Hiaasen continues to capture Florida in all its extravagance and ecological fragility, with often hilarious characters and situations. Hiaasen makes an immediate comic statement with the double-word titles of his novels, such as *Strip Tease*, *Skinny Dip*, *Basket Case*, *Stormy Weather*. His beginnings are brilliant at getting the reader not just into the scene and the mood – day- and date-specific – but the complication as well. This is from *Razor Girl* (2016):

> On the first day of February, sunny but cold as a frog's balls, a man named Lane Coolman stepped off a flight at Miami International, rented a mainstream Buick and headed south to meet a man in Key West. He nearly made it.[18]

In this opening from *Nature Girl* (2006) we get a place, a character, a crime, a victim, a motive and a cover-up:

> On the second day of January, windswept and bright, a half-blood Seminole named Sammy Tigertail dumped a dead body

in the Lostmans River. The water temperature was fifty-nine degrees, too nippy for sharks or alligators.

But maybe not for crabs, thought Sammy Tigertail.

Watching the corpse sink, he pondered the foolishness of white men. This one had called himself Wilson when he arrived on the Big Cypress reservation, reeking of alcohol and demanding an airboat ride.[19]

And I can never resist revisiting the action-packed opening of *Skinny Dip* (2004), which tells us all we need to know about Joey Perrone's complicated situation:

> At the stroke of eleven on a cool April night, a woman named Joey Perrone went overboard from a luxury deck of the cruise liner San Duchess. Plunging toward the dark Atlantic, Joey was too dumbfounded to panic.
>
> I married an asshole, she thought, knifing headfirst into the waves.
>
> The impact tore off her silk skirt, blouse, panties, wristwatch and sandals, but Joey remained conscious and alert. Of course she did. She had been co-captain of her college swim team, a biographical nugget that her husband obviously had forgotten.[20]

Elmore Leonard was in many ways the pioneer of modern comic crime fiction, with his wildly colourful characterisation, whip-smart dialogue and eye for detail. This is the beginning of *Freaky Deaky*:

> Chris Mankowski's last day on the job, two in the afternoon, two hours to go, he got a call to dispose of a bomb.
>
> What happened next, a guy by the name of Booker, a twenty-five-year-old super-dude twice-convicted felon, was in his Jacuzzi when the phone rang. He yelled for his bodyguard Juicy Mouth to take it. 'Hey, Juicy?' His bodyguard, his driver and his houseman were around somewhere. 'Will somebody get the phone?' The phone kept ringing. The phone must have rung

Entertainment and engagement

fifteen times before Booker got out of the Jacuzzi, put on his green satin robe that matched the emerald pinned to his left earlobe and picked up the phone. Booker said, 'Who's this?'[21]

Another novel I can never resist revisiting because it makes me smile from beginning to the end, is *Be Cool*, Leonard's sequel to *Get Shorty*. Leonard rarely went in for sequels and obviously never a series, but as a reader I feel he enjoyed writing Chili Palmer and his world, perhaps more than many of his other characters. And maybe he hadn't quite finished with satirising Hollywood. There was too much fun to be had. The details in the first paragraph of *Be Cool* tell you everything about Chili's elevated, sober state as an ex-loan shark turned movie producer.

> They sat at one of the sidewalk tables at Swingers, on the side of the coffee shop along Beverly Boulevard: Chili Palmer with the Cobb salad and iced tea, Tommy Athens the grilled pesto chicken and a bottle of Evian.[22]

Get Shorty starts with a story about Chili having lunch in Miami beach, at Vesuvio's on South Collins, and having his leather jacket ripped off. How times and circumstances change. But has Chili really turned a corner, is he really heading down the straight and narrow, eating salad, drinking iced tea? When I was fortunate enough to interview Leonard he told me that he wanted to write like Hemingway: replicating that economy and precision. 'But the problem with Hemingway was he didn't have a sense of humour', he laughed. Humour, as with comedy, so often relies on timing as well as pithy lines. Don't overstretch a point. End a joke at the end of a sentence or paragraph. End with the so-called pay-off line. Even taking a technical approach cannot solve the problem that humour, any such comedy, is invariably something of an acquired taste, and is

quite possibly bound by cultural understandings. You get someone's lines or you don't. While Leonard fans might also enjoy
Hiaasen, Evanovich might well have quite distinct admirers.
Oyinkan Braithwaite's searing satire *My Sister, The Serial Killer*,
with its genre knowingness, yet keenness to push boundaries,
has probably met a far wider audience around the world. Five
short sections in, we find this piece of the action delivered in
the form of a joke (Braithwaite's italics):

> *Have you heard this one before? Two girls walk into a room. The room is in*
> *a flat. The flat is on the third floor. In the room is the dead body of an adult*
> *male. How do they get the body to the ground floor without being seen?*[23]

In between some remarkably frank, funny and revealing
exchanges from Korede trying to deal with her (now notorious)
sister Ayoola's latest 'miscalculation', we learn how:

> *First, they gather supplies …*
> *Second, they clean up the blood …*
> *Third, they turn him into a mummy …*
> *Fourth, they move the body …*
> *Fifth, they bleach.*[24]

Kate Atkinson is another favourite author of mine who incorporates fabulously catty, cynical observations and one-liners in
her Jackson Brody PI series. Much of the biting humour also
comes from misdirection and strangely but insightfully placed
POVs. Often such shifts in narrative perspectives can add a
gentle warmth, which further emphasises the cynicism and or
satire. This is from the beginning of *Case Histories*, the first in
the series:

> How lucky were they? A heat wave in the middle of the school
> holidays, exactly where it belonged. Every morning the sun
> was up long before they were, making a mockery of the flimsy

summer curtains that hung limply at their bedroom windows, a sun already hot and sticky with promise before Olivia even opened her eyes. Olivia, as reliable as a rooster, always the first to wake, so that no one in the house had bothered with an alarm clock since she was born three years ago.[25]

POV is fundamental to satire, humour, comic writing and of course engagement. The character is the means of delivery, and it all depends on the sharpness with which they are seeing a scene, and with which that scene is being relayed and described. It's not that the character might find something funny or entertaining, it's not that we want to see a character being amused or even laughing at a situation or another character's joke or mishap, but it's through character, and the author's control of that character and vision, that the reader might be amused, entertained and engaged. If we think of entertainment as a thematic concept and approach, something dependent on pitch, register, lightness of content or perhaps 'cosiness', 'softness' and engagement as something more technical and bound up with craft, syntax, structure and all the other various devices from description to pace to suspense, we might more readily be able to practise what we strive for.

However, entertainment can also be technical and practical. It might be as simple as figuring out how best to relay a joke, and deliver the punchline. Or perhaps setting a scene using a character, and then adding a revelation that completely changes what we know about that character and makes us re-evaluate the scene. Perhaps they are actually only three years old; perhaps they are not human after all. In practical and technical ways, we can generate engagement by setting up our writing to surprise, to amuse, or to shock. But this is selling the idea of engagement short. The theme of your novel will also be key to engaging the reader almost as much as characterisation and situation.

Thematic choices

Following my Goodwin Crime Family trilogy, I longed to leave the damp, deprived and depraved British seaside well behind. I'd spent enough time working with dark, gritty realism, being blasted by the rain and familial betrayal and dysfunction. Prior to that I'd also had plenty of exposure to satire, suggestion and metafiction. I felt it was time for levity, laughter and sunshine, without the cynicism. I wanted to inhabit a fictional world on lighter, more comfortable, or certainly more luxurious terms. This would be a place where resolution and justice were possible, even if those ideals were not always to be legally enacted and enforced. It would be a place of work and play, with a solid, reliable protagonist, who wanted what was best, not worst. Remarkably, I realised, when I came to plan my next series, the only 'good' or non-criminal protagonist I'd worked with in my crime fiction was DS Jack Frost, who was someone else's creation. But the fictional town of Denton certainly didn't appeal for a revisit. I longed for exotic locations and a properly pleasant, modern and forward-thinking lead character; that is to say, an appealing, contemporary character. This would be, hopefully, someone readers could engage, sympathise and empathise with. Someone they could like. Someone they'd want to hang out with.

Accidental detectives

An old idea from my days as a travel journalist resurfaced. What about someone who travelled for work, staying in different, highly attractive locations around the world? Crime fiction from the perspective of a layperson investigator, or amateur sleuth, has long been a trope – Agatha Christie's Miss Marple being perhaps the most famous example. Naomi Hirahara, author of, among many other works, the Mas Arai mysteries featuring a crime-solving Los Angeles gardener and Hiroshima survivor, is clear about the genesis of particular investigators, or, as she puts it, 'accidental detectives'. This is from her chapter in *How To Write A Mystery*:

> Unlike police procedural or private investigator stories, the amateur sleuth finds the writer, not the other way around. No other mystery genre reveals more about the author's inner work, or personal life. In some ways, amateur sleuths are the ultimate insiders, because they originate from inside us or from a very specific community. However, they also are definitely outsiders, as they are the main crime solvers outside the work of established law enforcers or professional detectives.[26]

Hirahara goes on to explain that the main challenge facing the creation of these mysteries is to justify the involvement of such a protagonist in the storyline, and how this can become particularly amplified for a series. Believability and credibility might become very stretched. Yet the world, every bit as much as the protagonist, being created by the author needs to convince, compel and certainly engage (as well as entertain). There are numerous angles that need to be considered before embarking upon this sub-genre. What can such a character bring to the story that the police or authorities can't? What knowledge, expertise or 'superpowers' might they have that puts them in the ideal position to solve the chosen crimes? What life do they have outside the sphere of the narrative?

Crafting crime fiction

Amateur sleuths are a different breed to private detectives and investigators, even those more reluctant and accidental than others. Examples include John D. MacDonald's Travis McGee or Steph Cha's Juniper Song. Amateur sleuths are at the scene of a crime, or witness to a crime more by coincidence than design. In other words, crimes come their way, rather than them necessarily seeking them out, at least initially. For me, one of the key attributes of a believable amateur sleuth is the ability or necessity for them to be in the right place at the right time (or perhaps the right place at the wrong time). Even embarking upon such a sub-genre is to acknowledge a fictional (even fantastical) leap of imagination. While conceivably adding aspects of constraint in relation to how such an 'investigation' might be conducted, it can also open ways of thinking outside any normal procedural process. Being realistic goes out of the window. Being convincing, entertaining and engaging comes flying in. Plus, it's a clear statement of fictionality, of imaginative world-building, of, conceivably, introducing a reader to new terrain, albeit under the vast 'crime fiction' umbrella.

Amateur sleuths, from the curtain-twitcher to the vicar, have long been the natural inhabitants of the cosy. They're more than grounded in escapism. Indeed, they were invented to take us into ludicrous scenarios, where the flesh and blood (let alone any hint of torture and sadistic violence) were not particularly real. (And yet we lapped it up; except perhaps Chandler, who of course hated anything he considered to be 'cosy'; but how 'real' really is Philip Marlowe?) The thing with amateur sleuths of old was that for many readers it didn't matter whether the 'detective' was far larger, or smaller, than life, as long as the puzzle was solved in a satisfying and surprising way. Moving on a few decades, if not a century, we are much more demanding and discerning when it comes to our crime-solving protagonists, of whatever profession or speciality. They need to be more rounded, as well as a believable presence in the situation. Thriller elements, of suspense and jeopardy particularly, now often find their way into detective narratives, both amateur and professional. The endless dynamism, boundary pushing and blurring at the sub-genre edges have all played their part in reinventing and reinvigorating the concept of the 'amateur sleuth'.

My own character is Ben Martin, a hotel inspector for Hideaway Hotels, a collection of the most luxurious, exclusive and discreet hotels in the world. The plan was for each novel to be centred on a particular hotel that Ben would be inspecting to make sure they met Hideaway's exacting standards. He'd fly in for a short trip, three days or so, attempt to do his inspecting duties, including wiping a white glove over the furniture to check for dust and grime, while sampling the exquisite restaurants and bars, and coincidentally crimes would happen. He'd usually spot something untoward before the first murder, and, attention grabbed, be on hand to investigate and navigate the public and private sides of a fancy hotel. Being a former financial journalist and dedicated gourmand gave him certain advantages, along with an inherent curiosity and a long-held desire to be a crime writer. (Yes, a metafictional element has crept back in.)

A retinue of work colleagues, old friends, a teenage daughter and a lovely ex-wife dotted around the world would add to the characterisation, scaffolding, development potential and backstory. The recurring love interest would be provided by his boss, the CEO of Hideaway Inc, Emily Muller. And being the boss, Emily would have every reason to pop up in her group's hotels, not least to check on Ben. Other flames would invariably erupt, further complicating the solving of the crimes being committed, and often putting Ben in more danger. The Hotel Amagat, just outside Deià, Mallorca, is the location for the first in the series,[27] which was quickly followed by The Maverick, in New York's hyper-fashionable East Village.[28] The third novel finds Ben Martin in the middle of winter, snowed in, in the most exclusive and secluded hotel of them all, the architecturally distinct Hotel G, situated in the middle of the Mont Blanc massif, right on the border of France, Switzerland and Italy.

While all three hotels are obviously fictitious, all except the G can be located pretty much to the street or private road. The first two novels also provide plenty of armchair travelling as Ben's investigations, and misfortunes, take him beyond the hotels' respective grounds. The third in the series, *The Hotel Inspector: Massif de Mont Blanc*, becomes something of a locked-room mystery, as a series of suspicious deaths occur within the hotel grounds and property.[29] Because of a blizzard, no one can arrive or depart, including the authorities. As is the case in all the Hotel Inspector novels, Ben finds he can only hide his true identity and purpose for being there for so long. Then working with and without the help of the hotels' staff (a number of whom are not entirely innocent, naturally), and remotely with his back-up retinue of work colleagues and old friends and associates, he urgently, if somewhat luxuriously, tries to determine who the perpetrators are.

As with all 'amateur sleuth' mysteries, the endings are not necessarily obvious, and justice is somewhat various. The proper authorities don't always step in to conclude matters officially, and Emily Muller and her management team can't understand why Ben is always finding himself in the middle of such terrible situations and drama. Hopefully, however, the reader can enjoy the licence and the worlds of these novels, and be entertained and engaged. They are the least serious bits of imaginative crime writing I've done. They are deliberately escapist. But they are also deeply serious, and, to me at least, authentic, attempts at providing 'entertainment', maybe some exoticism, and of course engagement, all within the broad parameters of a crime fiction narrative. They aren't especially pushing the boundaries of the 'amateur sleuth' or cosy sub-genres, except perhaps by acknowledging the contemporary world and how people struggle to belong, regardless of position, possessions or income. As such, the intention is for them to ask questions about identity, and the struggle to achieve as well as survive, albeit with plenty of humour and 'lightness'.

My Swiss German editor describes the work as 'soft crime fiction', though to achieve the effect is actually very hard. Being entertaining is difficult. Being engaging equally so. Invariably, I don't get it right straight off (in many ways I'll never it get it right, which is why I keep trying). Lots of sharp editing comments and advice come back to me. The process doesn't necessarily get any easier, even if you are enjoying the writing, even if you are trying your hardest to be 'light and fun' in dark, criminal ways. Especially so, if you are also trying to make the whole mechanics, the writing and thinking, the plotting and planning, behind the words on the page seamlessly disappear. Can redrafting and editing, and making it all look so easy and natural, ever be fun, simple or even easy? Read on to find out.

9

CRAFT AND EDITING

Hard graft

The short answer, or my answer anyway, to the question posed at the end of the last chapter – can redrafting and editing ever be fun? – is 'no'! Yet many writers think so, and particularly enjoy the experience. I've always found redrafting and editing somewhat difficult, even painful. I wish it wasn't the case, because invariably there comes a point when others need to see what you are doing, when perhaps only others can offer true and helpful perspectives. It certainly helps if these others are resourced and informed, insightful and pertinent, and even more so if they are involved in the publishing or writing business. However, that's not a requirement, at least not until you are dealing with agents and publishers, and professional publishing platforms. Any and all readers' comments are useful, especially if a large audience is one of your ambitions for the book. It certainly helps to hear from a wide variety of people – think of how focus groups are organised. Think how reader reviews on Amazon are encouraged and displayed. But we can't all benefit from a focus group, or necessarily professional insight, at least not in the beginning or early in our careers.

My trouble with redrafting and editing quite possibly stems from my work as a journalist, and the often formulaic and dogmatic way 'story' might be advocated by a particular outlet. For newspaper writing, style rules and set ways of doing things were paramount. It felt like I'd done the work, only for much more work still to be done, while having to cope with some pretty chastising comments. My mother, a fiction writer, used to say you had to be tough to be a writer.[1] But she was referring, as she'd explain, to content, to theme, to addressing difficult issues, often in relation to familial dysfunction. She was saying that you shouldn't be afraid of offending people who might know you, who might think you are portraying them or certain situations specific to them. 'Do what's right for the story', she'd say. 'Tell it how it really is.' Interestingly, she largely went out of her way not to offend people close to her, arguably to the detriment, effectiveness and power of her stories. She knew what it took, but was not necessarily able to put it on paper. And this is the thing: however well we know, or think we know what it takes, most of us can't ever quite manage to do it exactly how we'd like to. There may be flaws in the content, theme or characterisation, or on the practical side, in the prose style, grammar or punctuation. At least, that is how it invariably feels once others see your work and the criticism, however well-meaning, begins to flow in.

Being a writer is exposing. We are opening ourselves up to criticism, from whatever quarter. It can make you feel terribly vulnerable. In many ways, my mother was leaping ahead a stage. As a writer I believe you have to be thick-skinned to take the more prosaic criticism as well, and especially at the beginning. Can you punctuate dialogue correctly? Why are you using so many adverbs? Your paragraphs are too long, your sentences too convoluted. Where's the pace? Then we might well get to: 'This character's boring; is he necessary?' 'This scene needs more drama.' 'I don't understand where this is going.' And on to comments such as this:

> It feels as if there is a lack of plot to me and that has the effect of making the pace feel slow almost all the way through. I think the plot is going to have to be more complex with red herrings etc. or you're going to need some sub-plots to keep the reader interested. There's a lot of treading water: a lot of talk about the weather conditions, the security arrangements but there's little action.

The above quote, and the lines in quotation marks in the preceding paragraph are from my literary agent in relation to my latest novel, which happens to be my fifteenth.[2] I wish they weren't there and I wish hadn't had to deal with them. But I'm also extremely grateful that they are there, and that my agent is smart and insightful enough, as well as always being professionally honest, to relay them. She has long been my first reader. Sometimes my drafts are in better overall shape than others, yet her advice is crucial, and this is before my editor sees the manuscript. Her advice can also be, even after all this time, somewhat deflating. This is to be expected. You have, seemingly, worked so long and hard on a novel, and you've reached a point where you feel it's done, finished, which is why you emailed it off. You might well be a little sick of it – even thoroughly sick of it – and not want to see it again for some time. But the editing process, and certainly the publishing process, might only just be kicking in. You then need all that commitment, energy and determination with which you embarked upon the novel at the beginning to come flooding back.

Yes, as stated, there are writers who enjoy the editing process, who feel that it is only when redrafting and editing that their novel takes proper shape. Ian Rankin talked at UEA about his first drafts being not much more than skeletons of the finished novels – often only running to 40,000 words out of the usual end result of 90,000 words. He wants to get down the key points and plot movements before adding more detail and diversions. Meanwhile, James Ellroy's plot notes or chapter breakdowns famously can amount to hundreds of pages – not much shorter in length than the finished manuscript.

Other writers try very hard to avoid lengthy redrafting and editing work, and proudly hand in (at least what they think might be) near-'perfect' manuscripts. Those writers will remain anonymous. Many are very well known, and there has been a sense within the industry, and among critics, that the better known, better-selling author becomes more powerful within the editing and production process, to the point that editors feel reluctant, even impotent to suggest any changes, however small. Some bestselling writers, particularly of series, begin to believe that they know best, and after a while they might well have been at a particular publisher's for longer than their original editors and copyeditors. They might know best. But they also might not, which is one of the reasons why novels in long-running series don't necessarily continue to get better and better. At what stage might someone suggest revisions are necessary, and will they be listened to? Should they be listened to? Who ultimately knows best? The question that might then arise would be: best for who? A writer might go off on a tangent quite purposefully. However, at some point the writer will

Crafting crime fiction

need to defer that judgement, even if only to the reader, having bypassed (or ignored) all manner of editing advice.

The essence of craft

Crime fiction is a popular genre – the world's most popular genre among fiction sales – for multiple reasons. Those writers who consider the reader and the effect their work will have on them are also conceivably more likely to listen and trust others along the way. I will return to the more practical aspects of editing and the various approaches and responses to the revision and redrafting process later in this chapter. For now, and conceivably before we first hand on our manuscript to invested others (or to anyone willing to read our work), I'd like us to consider craft. We need to understand how the craft of writing crime fiction can affect our work, from the beginning to the end. The craft or writing is the bringing together of everything we know – all our resource and experience, and individuality – to make that manuscript as good as it can be. We employ our craft largely on our own, and before we seek advice, elsewhere.

Stav Sherez, cult author of among other works *The Intrusions* (winner of the 2018 Theakston Old Peculier Crime Novel of the Year) had this to say at the Noirwich Crime Writing Festival in 2017:

> We'll start by looking at the craft of writing a crime novel. Because that's exactly what it is: a craft. It's not hocus pocus or some innate skill that you're either born with or not. Sure, you need some basic writing skills, but writing a crime fiction is actually a craft that can be learnt with the right tools and a lot of hard work.

Craft and editing

I believe that work continues long after you first email off your manuscript. However, it is the work that you do, the craft that you employ, from the planning stage to typing the last sentence, that will determine everything. This is even more important if you don't yet have an agent and publishing team on board. And it is as important if you are going down the self-publishing and dissemination route (a world greatly enhanced and expanded by digitisation). That draft – the work that you believe to be finished to your best capabilities – is your calling card, your key to an audience. Hence the importance of getting it as right as you possibly can before moving it forward as a 'crime novel'. I began this section (and book) talking about crime fiction's popularity globally, as well as its extraordinary dynamism and ability to innovate. This book is, in the end, all about craft. Mine comes from my writing and teaching resources, my experience, and various interpretations and positions I've come to rely on. The essence of this chapter is to explain and explore how we can pull all this together to create effective, impactful crime fiction – and the sort of crime fiction we, individually, aim to write. Yet we also need to be mindful of what we mean by craft and whose craft we might be trying to employ.

Novelist and creative writing tutor Matthew Salesses in his key text *Craft in the Real World* argues that the dominance of one tradition of craft, serving a particular audience, is 'essentially literary imperialism'. 'We must be careful not to frame craft as prescription or even guidelines without first making clear where those guidelines come from and whom they benefit.'[3] He talks about rules: why we might rely on one set of rules and not another, for instance. He also makes the point that anything 'official' always has to do with 'power'. To Salesses, craft is cultural, and that learning aspects of craft is to learn aspects of certain cultural values.

> Craft is not innocent or neutral... Culture stands behind what makes many craft moves 'work' or not, and for whom they work. Writers need to understand their real-world relationship to craft in order to understand their real-world relationship to their audience and to their writing's place in the world.[4]

Here is the point, and in many ways the point of this book: know your writerly intentions, know the purpose of your fiction, and know who it's for. Yes, we, or many of us, want as large an audience as possible, and an international audience at that. But we can't be all things to everyone, and while trying to capture universal truths in our writing might be very noble, in essence we'd then only be trying to do that in a culturally specific way, which would be loaded with rules and tradition and conceivably privilege. Being widely informed of other perspectives and approaches can only help, while much reading pleasure comes from being immersed in other cultures and being introduced to other ways of doing things – other versions of the craft if you like. Indeed, it is not only worlds we are talking about but conceivably other solar systems, indeed universes. This is why individuality, openness and resource is so important. Experience and practice, nevertheless, will inevitably drive your fiction in certain directions. We can only ever do so much about the way we write, the stories and voices we strive to develop. Universality can come from specificity.

If we are too hard on ourselves, insisting on continually deconstructing and dismantling everything we know, while endeavouring to read and understand even a fraction of what is published around the world in our genre in any given month, the harder it can be to make sense of what we want to say creatively. Nobody can do all of it, all at once. We must step off at certain points, or attempt to slow the spinning world – in our minds at least – while we fashion a new novel, a new work. We need to trust ourselves in that moment, and rely on the inspiration, the energy – and what we do know – to see us through the manuscript. The 'literary' or creative exploration, if you like, will be an outpouring – for however many thousands of words, weeks or months (but not years, please) – rather than an ingesting. Yes, of course we continue to read and consider the world while writing, but we cannot continue to innovate and broaden any fictional worlds we are currently creating endlessly. Otherwise, they will never be finished, and certainly not with menace and motivation, pace and purpose. Coherence and consistency have to be considered. Another way to think of this is to regard each novel as a step on a lifelong journey (even within a series, or indeed, especially within a series). Steps should be solid, supportive suspensions in space and time. We can only do what we can do in a given moment, in spite of, or because of, our best intentions. It's impossible to do everything you might want to do in a single novel, or series, which is why we continue to search for new projects, new ways of saying things. Except, I believe it's best to finish one project before starting the next. Or at least realise when it's time to move on.

Mick Herron, award-winning author of the Slough House spy novels, said this about crafting a crime novel in the *Guardian*:

> Most ingredients are easily stated: characters, dialogue, prose and plot all need to be of a high quality. But to reach greatness rather than mere competence, a touch of alchemy is also required; the ability to put these things together in a way no one has managed before.[5]

Crafting crime fiction

Looking back on my own work I see the mistakes and unrealised potential – practical and thematic – before the magic! I would like to think each novel is incrementally better, as I became more resourced and experienced. But I know that is not necessarily the case. I can also see the novels' merits and am sometimes surprised by past flourishes and skill. What I do recognise, and what I am particularly pleased with, is the growing sense of genre purpose and intent. In many ways I feel the same about my teaching and pedagogical approaches. Obviously, you don't begin as a creative writing tutor knowing what you know years down the line. How you try to understand and enable other writers changes too, of course.

At this moment in time, those questions are bigger and more urgent than ever, as debates around culture and craft, power and decoloniality, echo through the once-staid corridors of publishing houses and academic institutions. Still, as individuals, we can but capture and express a fraction of the world, and use that fraction to suggest other fractions, while accepting we will never be able to depict the whole. This is my way of making sense of it all, now, which has changed in the past five years, and what I thought five years ago was different to how I encouraged and advised and discussed work ten years ago. I hope that both in my own fiction and in my teaching, my approaches have become more informed and pertinent over time. Yet, I can only be sure that at this moment, on this step, this is what I know about writing certain types of crime fiction, and what some audiences engage with and are entertained by. This is very far from exhaustive. Not least because you will never be able to read anything like as much as you wish. I've probably spent most of my life feeling guilty and inadequate about not reading enough, and I've read a serious amount. If I have any advice on this, it is to read as widely as possible. Be open, be prepared for surprises. Your sense of quality, of the worth of what you are reading will not only sharpen, but broaden.

Of course, you can spend time and money learning all there is to know about writing, but in the end, all education is limited to what is currently thought and taught. The creative urge doesn't care: much like good crime fiction, it seeks forward momentum and newness. Craft is an accumulation of skills that is honed over time, so by definition, it's made up of what has been, what was. However, as a set of tools, it is for you to choose how to use it, and can be a step, or steps, towards new territory. I have tried to be careful not to be too prescriptive, or include writing exercises in this book, as they can encourage sameness, and even, as Salesses might propose, a literary imperialism. All the same, I hope that the experience and advice I have shared with you might be helpful, and importantly spark different ways of thinking and creating. Frankly, I agree with Mick Herron, that craft is the essence of crime fiction.

John Banville, of course used to write crime under the pseudonym Benjamin Black, though has now dropped the pen name – perhaps in recognition of his true. For Banville, craft is certainly key. As he told me when I interviewed him for *The Times*:

> Just because a novel has a crime in it, doesn't mean it's a crime novel. It's down to craftsmanship and, particularly now, making the crimes life-like.[6]

I object to the gendered term 'craftsmanship', just as 'masterclass' is problematic (which is indicative of how words and terms, along with 'culture' are hugely dynamic, and often have the habit of wrong-footing you, or coming back to haunt you). But I understand where Banville's coming from, and also his deep involvement in the genre. After all, Banville (writing as Black) took on the mantle of Raymond Chandler with his Philip Marlowe novel, *The Black-Eyed Blonde*, sanctioned by the Chandler estate. How about these for Chandler-esq similes, from just the first three pages of the novel?

> An empty house has a way of swallowing sounds, like a dry creek sucking down water.

The old man was grinning at me, smug as a hen that's just laid an egg.

> Around here there are days in high summer when the sun works on you like a gorilla peeling a banana.[7]

At the Noirwich Crime Writing Festival 2018, Banville professed to reading very little crime fiction except works by Chandler and Georges Simenon. What a pair to learn from, you might think. Imitation (and limitation) was addressed in Chapter 3. We might now also consider how crime fiction can date, as well as innovate. Has Banville moved the genre forward? Has he, maybe more importantly, found his niche within it? Can we see where he has had some fun playing with the differences, and executing his take as Black, as Chandler, and now as Banville? This is very much a craft issue: knowing the sort of fiction you want to write and having some sort of idea about how to go about it. Craft, as Salesses suggests, is bound up with the past, with heritage and history, with all our resources as authors, including cultural knowledge. It takes time to shift perspectives and approaches, especially as we age and become more set in our ways and comfortable with what we might be writing, or how we might think we are finally beginning to get a handle on the genre. In order to write original and exciting crime fiction we need to innovate, to move the genre forward. At the same time, we need to sit still for a moment: that is, while we're writing a novel, and adhere to whichever step we might have landed upon. Otherwise, the constant drive to be new, to be different, could well shatter that step. Where would we then find ourselves? Quite possibly, swirling around in the vast, wildly unchecked terrain that is general or even literary fiction.

William Faulkner, who we know tried his hand at crime fiction following his immersion into Chandler-land, with his unsuccessful short-story collection *Knight's Gambit*, had this to say about craft: 'Let the writer take up surgery or bricklaying if he's interested in technique.'[8] Maybe he should have considered technique more. Though then we might not have had *Intruder in the Dust*, a novel with a crime in it, a murder, but arguably not a crime novel.[9] Finding your place as a crime writer, even if momentarily, can be profound. That comfort of slipping into a niche can have lasting impact on your relationship to your readers. In many ways it is just this comfort, these known quantities and attributes, that readers return to. Of course there are readers, like writers, who can never sit still and are forever searching for new work. The limits of genre, of crime fiction, are illusory. There are no limits, and there will always be writers ready to explore the furthest reaches. But other readers – as many in the more regimented and traditional areas of the publishing industry have long recognised – like nothing better than to stick to what they know and love. There is room in the market for innovators and niche-dwellers alike.

Certain writers and certain series are bound by sameness of intent. However, when done well, at their most effective, the elements of familiarity and repetition are strengths, tapping into reader expectation. The writer has struck gold, if you like (intentionally or otherwise), but at least they have come to recognise it, deploy it and hopefully tweak and enhance it. Meanwhile, the reader happily knows just where they are, even in a convoluted, twisty mystery. This is craft, fine-tuned. The literary critic Tim Parks writing in the *London Review of Books* had this to say about Georges Simenon:

> To read the breadth of Simenon's work is to be made aware of the unbridgeable gulf between genre fiction and serious fiction. The Maigret novels are immensely attractive. Simenon always creates a fine sense of place, simultaneously real and quaint; the characters are rapidly and effectively drawn, reassuringly recognisable, neatly arranged in relation to one another. Maigret's habits, his pipe, his beers, his brusque ways, his refusal to kowtow to authority and his generosity with the humbler classes are always comforting. But after reading five, six, seven Maigrets, one grows weary. Nothing new can happen in these books, however intriguingly the old pack is reshuffled.[10]

Parks was writing in response to Penguin Random House publishing new translations of all Simenon's 75 Maigret novels. As well as being a highly regarded critic, translator and literary novelist – author of *Europa* and *Destiny* among others – Parks also writes crime fiction. His novels *Cara Massimina* and *Mimi's Ghost* were after many years joined by another in the series, *Painting Death*, featuring amoral Morris Duckworth, who has quite a bit in common with Highsmith's Tom Ripley.[11] Parks, like Simenon, Banville, Highsmith, Chandler and so many others, has journeyed on the literary path as well as the genre path – with most (except, notably, Faulkner) invariably achieving greater commercial success with their crime fiction. The pull of parameters, of fixed points, solid steps, of a distilled

Craft and editing

craft, is also, for the writer of any genre, highly attractive, if not addictive. Parks says he wrote *Cara Massimina* and *Mimi's Ghost* 'as a kind of relaxation' between his 'serious' literary novels.[12] The joy Banville gets from writing his crime fiction as opposed to the terribly slow and hard process of his literary fiction, I've already mentioned. But to elaborate on this for a moment, we do need to consider what it means for your identity as a writer to be working within a genre, and how this relates to craft.

Authenticity

Can craft actually be learnt, as Stav Sherez proposes, with the right tools and a lot of hard work? There is no doubt in my mind that what can't be taught is 'authenticity'. To sound authentic, writers have fully to believe in what they are doing, why they are doing it, and who they are doing it for. Authenticity doesn't arrive by accident. This means that writing for a market, a genre, and within that market a sub-genre, can't all be about clever choices with only the book buyer in mind. What you seek to achieve and the tools you employ to achieve it must always tally with voice. The inbuilt mechanisms of 'literary' creativity (or artistic sensitivity, if you like) need to combine with all the aspects of craft to produce standout work. Yes, voice is distinct to the fiction, the novel, and there are very successful writers of wildly different series and genres and sub-genres. Walter Mosley, in *Elements of Fiction*, puts it like this: 'Because the novel is composed only of language, this living quality can be defined by Voice.'[13]

However, voice (as 'living quality') is also within the DNA of every sentence a writer writes – and the author's voice is not the same thing as the voice of a particular work. Another way of thinking about this is that if we all approached our writing prescriptively, with the same knowledge and experience of craft, and with the same thematic and structural aims, with exactly the same template, the work still would not be the same. This brings us back to Highsmith's key point. 'There is no secret of success in writing except individuality, or call it personality.'[14] The right tools are not just things you can pull from a box and use to fashion a beautiful work of art. However, without them you won't get very far, regardless of how impressive or unique the vision is.

There is another vital and determining question looming in the shadows here; and one which writers and tutors such as Matthew Salesses are questioning with some urgency now. This is: whose tools? What exactly are the right tools for us to learn to use, what can we happily, fruitfully reach for? We pick and mix, of course. And over time those tools might change as we become more focused, more adept, more experienced and even more wary. Is this another way of saying that we slowly, gradually know more about what we want to say and how we can say it, and frankly, just who we are to say it?

Craft tips

Over the years, I've tried to define and revise my approach and advice on writing crime fiction. I've compiled various lists of 'crime writing tips' to hand out in workshops and classes, both institutional and non-academic. My most comprehensive runs to 25 brief 'tips'. Looking at that list now – it's already a few years old – I stand by many of them, feeling they still represent my aims, my approaches, my understanding of the sort of crime fiction I like to read and try to write. Here they are (many borrowed and tweaked, as is the way with such writing advice,

Craft and editing

from others; predominantly those quoted and referenced in this work):

1. Let the writing dictate, not the action.
2. Think of the scene and the then the plot.
3. Suspense, as opposed to narrative drive, needs to control the pace.
4. Use violence sparingly and never gratuitously.
5. While a sense of place can be important, rounded characterisation is essential.
6. What people say says more about them than what they wear.
7. Interiority slackens momentum.
8. Literary depth comes from acute observation and emotional and intellectual insight, not just prose style or fancy research.
9. Authenticity (if something feels right) is more important than accuracy (something being factually correct) in relation to procedure.
10. Crime fiction should entertain before it informs.
11. Forget about polemics, but don't forget that what you write matters.
12. Everything you do write should be written with a sense of urgency and necessity, and pass the 'so what?' test.
13. A burning desire for justice, or revenge, can only harm the balance of a piece of fiction. Be inspired, but don't lose perspective.
14. Avoid occupying too many characters' perspectives. Intimacy comes from familiarity.
15. Don't avoid uncomfortable or awkward or distressing situations. The hardest thing to write about will very often be the most powerful.

16. Plan the structure of your work, but not to a hundred per cent. Have a good idea of the beginning, middle and end, but allow for deviation and surprise.
17. Constructing a piece of fiction chronologically will aid the narrative pull. Think of every sentence, every paragraph, scene and chapter leading to the next.
18. People like to laugh, but not all the time.
19. Death is a serious business. People get hurt, but not usually by serial killers.
20. Clichés are clichés for a reason – there's something true about them.
21. Not all detectives like beer or jazz.
22. Some of the best crime fiction doesn't involve detectives at all.
23. Decide whether you are more interested in solving a crime (as in classic detective fiction), or letting a crime(s) unfold (as in classic thriller fiction). Keep your intention clear.
24. Genres are forever dynamic.
25. Readers, not critics, are your most valuable source of criticism.

These lists, like Elmore Leonard's *Ten Rules of Writing*, should always be taken lightly (which is why I've tried to avoid them in this book until now). Such lists and rules have also always been strongly associated with crime fiction (detective fiction especially), notably from Ronald Knox's '10 Commandments of Detective Fiction',[15] to S. S. Van Dine's 'Twenty Rules for Writing Detective Stories'.[16] I believe that writers properly invested in the genre have spent the last century trying to disassociate themselves from those rules, and possibly rules altogether. However, the genre is a form in itself, and we necessarily continue to identify commonalities, as much as we try to deconstruct and then reconstruct our own versions of the form. We might even find ourselves fine-tuning our own 'rules' and tips. Again, in part this might have something to do with the comfort of repetition, parameters, boundaries, to a certain sort of form – both as readers, and as writers.

I reduced my list of 25 tips or points to what I called a '10-part guide to the theory and practice of crime fiction', which I delivered to *The Times / The Sunday Times* Crime Club in 2017:

1. Plot: begins and ends with character.
2. Character: defined by point of view and desire.
3. Events: get in the way.
4. Setting: a character too.
5. Structure: develops around a timeline.
6. Pace: where motivation meets descriptive economy.
7. Suspense: comes from questions, not answers.
8. Mystery: works better if the surprise has menace.
9. Entertainment: hangs on engagement.
10. Craft: pulls it all together.

So here we are then, having contemplated aspects of all of the above, trying to pull it together. While this book is an in-depth look at most of those 25 and then 10 points, it's also a fine-tune. We have nine topics or chapters, not ten. 'Events' has been replaced by 'Imitation and limitation', mainly because events, story points and developments should be covered elsewhere; primarily within plot, character, structure, suspense, even setting. Suspense and mystery have been joined in the same chapter because technically and theoretically they are so intrinsically linked. 'Editing' has been added to craft, because it's both a craft, and also it's what happens after all the various craft elements have been put to work, and the story has been 'pulled' together. I also like the number nine. As basic as it might be, I like all aspects of plot and structure to be divisible by three. Beginning, middle and end, the three-act structure. I am also not averse to bookending a novel with a prologue and/or an epilogue – as long as these elements are properly considered and invariably created after the main narrative has been written, and only then if they are enlightening and engaging, and add to the experience. That's why this work has a short introduction (rather obviously titled 'Beginnings') and conclusion ('Endings'). To me, symmetry and balance are as important as consistency and coherence. They are also incredibly useful in the construction and completion of a crime novel. Or perhaps that should be the sort of crime novel I aim to write, and enjoy reading: novels that display that great pulling together, that alchemy.

Lists and rules by their nature are there to be discounted, disrespected and variously ignored. That is, if some form of 'literary' freedom and 'originality' is being strived for. Lists also age. However, they can be useful, and especially in relation to form and genre: where to go, and where not to go. There are always fundamentals to consider and employ: ways of seeing and doing things that make the journey more fruitful, more enjoyable, more possible. Besides, without a solid grounding in key aspects of writing (the sort of writing that truly engages you), how can you begin to move forward, to do things differently?

This pulling together, and all such craft considerations amount to authorial control, and eventually, knowing when something works and doesn't work: when to cut, when to rewrite, when to add, when to take away and when to leave alone.

Craft and editing

Control

Effective editing requires extreme, detached control. This is why we rely on others. It can be a very difficult process to undertake alone, if you are not at a point where you have the luxury of passing a draft on to others. In a way, this is why understanding some fundamentals is so important. How do we know what to rewrite and edit, if we don't understand the sort of crime fiction we want to create?

'In my experience, an early novel draft looks nothing like its published form', says Matthew Salesses in *Craft in the Real World*.[17] Salesses goes on to discuss the importance of understanding a writer's process, ahead of a 'product', or the work itself. He also talks about how writers should not be confined by word count, but what length works for a particular fiction. He also recognises that deadlines are a fact of a published writer's life, even if somewhat arbitrary and distracting. For me, word counts and deadlines are part and parcel of control, or at least a feeling that you are in control and working towards a goal, an ending. Once you've reached that ending, you then need to go back to the beginning, to check all the key attributes of the crime fiction you are aiming for are in place. Invariably, they will not be.

The key aims of redrafting are focus and clarity. Is the text doing what you intend it to do? Am I bored reading a particular passage? Is such a line, paragraph or scene necessary, urgent even? Does it tackle the 'so what' factor? Obviously, your punctuation and grammar need to be correct and consistent. These are micro-considerations running alongside the more complicated or macro-issues of characterisation, plot, pace, mystery and suspense. Still, it's worth remembering that if the grammar and punctuation are flawed, an early reader's appreciation of a work might well be negatively influenced. Don't rely on others down the line, or the publishing process to fix the basics. Let's not follow the advice in Elmore Leonard's *Get Shorty*, where Chili Palmer questions low-rent mobster Catlett on the process:

> Chili opened the script again, flipped through a few pages looking at the format. 'You know how to write one of these?'
>
> 'You asking me,' Catlett said, 'do I know how to write down a words on a piece of paper? That's what you do, man, you put down one word after the other as it comes in your head. It isn't like having to learn how to play the piano, like you have to learn notes. You already learned in school how to write, didn't you? I *hope* so. You have the idea and you put down what you want to say. Then you get somebody to add in the commas and shit where they belong, if you aren't positive yourself. Maybe fix up the spelling where you have some tricky words. There [*sic*] people do that for you. Some, I've even seen scripts where I *know* words weren't spelled right and there was hardly any commas in it. So I don't think it's too important.[18]

Don't believe it! If you are not sure where to put the 'commas and shit', read a practical guide such as John Seely's *Oxford A–Z of Grammar & Punctuation*.[19] We all have blind spots, however. Over time, and rereading drafts, you will come to learn what they are and be on increasingly high alert for them. Repetition of words and phrases – by which I don't mean purposeful repetition for emphasis, but accidental or sloppy repetition – is another basic thing to be alert to. Keep on top of continuity as well, and make sure paragraph breaks don't jar.

My editing process is, in part, continuous during the writing of a first draft. If my planned novel is to be 80,000 words, at the 20,000-word point I'll stop writing and go back to the beginning to edit and remind myself of plot points, and so on.

Craft and editing

I'll then move on to the 40,000-word mark, or halfway point, and go back to the beginning again. At this stage the editing and rewriting can be quite time-consuming, as I tend to work at a pace of 10–15 pages a day. Once finished, I then move on to the 60,000-word or three-quarter point before going back to the beginning again and carefully going through all those 60,000 words, the first 20,000 for the third time. Once I've completed the manuscript, I go back to the beginning once more, and then through the whole thing again: the last 20,000 words for the first time. Once I've completed this, I'll then do at least one faster pass, trying to read the whole as a reader coming to the novel for the first time. At this stage in the process, I'll be especially alert to issues around pacing, suspense, plot and character development. The changes might be small: often cutting or rewriting phrases and sentences rather than anything more significant.

However, when these small changes, or tweaks, begin to mount up, the effect can be the difference between a work that appears patchy and rushed, and one that is convincing, coherent and 'professional'. Does this writer know what they are doing or not? As mentioned earlier, Mark Billingham likes to get to the point where his novels feel as 'taut as a drum' (as relayed to UEA Crime MA students in 2016). Certainly, anything superfluous, or unnecessary, anything that slows the pace and diverts from the overall purpose, needs attention, if not cutting. By this stage, any subplots and red herrings that might test a reader's patience too far need to be removed. Likewise, any complicated passages or convoluted articulations of mystery and suspense should be simplified, or cut.

Long before then, hopefully, flabby moments of over-description, introspection, rambling exposition, along with overly lengthy 'plot' explanations will have gone. Further and final checking of plot and character and situation set-ups, questions, developments, answers and reveals has to be done, and thoroughly. Are the surprises surprising enough? The twists, actually twisty? Are the pay-offs satisfying? What level of closure or openness remains? Are any loose ends there for a reason? Do they add to the effect aimed for? We live in a complicated, messy world. Do we want to reflect that, or add more comforting closure? This might lead us to consider, further, the aspects of entertainment and engagement we wish to enhance and exploit. Is the pitch, the register right and consistent overall? Are there any off-beats, moments that feel forced or out of tone? Fundamentally, is the characterisation as enhanced as possible? Do we believe in the characters? Are we wholly engaged by them? Is everything now in the right place?

In a way, editing is distillation. It's extreme control, for some writers coming after moments of much freer rein, where during the writing it might have felt as if the characters themselves were steering the direction(s) and narrative drive. Crime writers do not have to be literary perfectionists. But too much freedom early on can of course make a lot of work in the editing process. Andrew Cowan in *The Art of Writing Fiction* talks about 'automatic writing' being the work of the morning while editing is the work of the afternoon, 'or alternatively, automatic writing could be the work of this month and, editing the work of next month'.[20] While this could be inspiring and productive for some, I would suggest that considering all aspects of craft from the beginning could greatly cut down the editing time and burden later. Crime writers need to know what they are doing from as early in the process of writing a novel as possible.

Craft and editing

This might sound like an impossible ideal, and it might well be, but this is where our understanding and handling of all the craft issues becomes so impactful.

Certainly, by the redrafting and editing stage, you should feel that you are in charge of the plot, the characters, the setting, the structure, the pacing, the mystery and suspense. Besides, any sense of 'literary' freedom, of going with the flow, will likely have evaporated by then. Exhaustion and doubts will have crept in. Editing is actually a good way of rekindling that initial spark, and reminding yourself that there is some good work here, some good scenes and characterisation. Try to harness that as you rewrite. Editing equals improving, always. Cutting large or small passages might feel radical, even a personal slight, and you may fear losing something important, something you worked very hard on. Invariably, it will be more than worthwhile. It can take years to learn to be brutal with your work, but brutal you must often be. Nothing is that precious. They are just words, one after another … This is also why, I believe, when writing crime fiction, it pays to be swift, to not overly linger on a passage or sentence, as these might well be cut when going through a later draft. To create fast moving, pacy narratives, you never want to be too precious about your prose.

In *On Writing*, Stephen King talks about some writers, at the redrafting stage, being taker-outers and others being natural putter-inners. He was a 'putter-inner', until he received a comment from an editor (he sadly can't recall exactly who), following an unsolicited submission of a story.

Not bad, but PUFFY. You need to revise for length. Formula: 2nd Draft = 1st Draft − 10%. Good luck.[21]

Crafting crime fiction

He credits this 'Rewrite Formula' for largely turning his fortunes around. There are very successful writers, of course, such as Ian Rankin and James Ellroy, who are consummate 'putter-inners'. But I believe most crime writers are taker-outers, operating on both macro-and micro-levels. Even if you are removing an adverb, or an unnecessary speech tag, you should feel pleased with yourself. Economy and being succinct are not just syntactical skills, but attributes intrinsically linked to clarity, pace and purpose. My three Hotel Inspector novels are each just over 60,000 words. The last in the series was 67,200 words in first draft. The third draft came in at 63,241 words. A subsidiary character had disappeared, along with an overly complicated subplot, and many passages describing the weather at certain points of the day and during a storm.

However, my greatest self-editing achievements are reducing my novel-in-progress, *What You Should Not Miss*, all 33,000 words of it, to an 869-word short story 'The Wrong Goose', and turning the full-length manuscript (82,000 words) of *Run Free* into a 32,000-word novella, *Hot August Night* (forthcoming). Are these my greatest writing achievements, my best works? Arguably, no, because they required so much work to pull into shape. I should have planned more carefully before ploughing in and on. I should have known more of what I know now. Writing is learning, forever. Craft is a skill that can in part be learned to capture and enhance what talent you have. Editing is what you do with the craft and the talent.

Confidence is a different matter. Confidence comes from resource and experience, and perhaps recognition. Most importantly, however, it comes from believing in what you are doing. It's what keeps you going. For many, writing is a creative compulsion. But to turn that into some sort of a career – and

Craft and editing

everyone has ups and downs – you need commitment and self-belief. It also helps to enjoy what you are doing, that you find writing fun. We know where enjoyment leads: to entertaining and engaging work. This also means we need to know when to leave it alone, when to finish, when to stop torturing ourselves and to hand on the work to you, the reader.

CONCLUSION: ENDINGS

I'll try to be brief, and to the point. The very endings of crime novels are often quite unmemorable, the energy having dissipated over the last few pages as things are tied up, the pace now at a crawl while the author stabs around for poignancy. Commonly, we're left with emotions, a zooming out, and plenty of reflection and or introspection, rather than a final plot twist. Chandler said that the ideal mystery was one you could read even if the end was missing. For him, the scene outranked the plot anyway, and there are many critics who happily highlight his various loose ends, not least the chauffeur in *The Big Sleep*.[1] Series novels might point towards future unresolved plot issues, though these invariably are of a domestic nature. Gillian Flynn rightly gives Amy Elliott Dunne the last line in *Gone Girl*.

> I don't have anything else to add. I just wanted to make sure I had the last word. I think I've earned that.[2]

But *Gone Girl* is in part a consummate metafictional thriller, playing with both the genre and reader throughout.

Elmore Leonard is unsurprisingly spot on with the end of *Get Shorty*, and a line attributed to Chili Palmer.

Conclusion: endings

Fuckin' endings, man, they weren't as easy as they looked.[3]

The last line of my most recent novel reads:

Ben knew that life could also be far too short. Every minute of
every day counted.[4]

I acknowledge only too readily the sentimental edge. And
this is the point: endings of crime novels are as much about
the author tying things up in various ways (or purposefully
leaving those messy, realistic loose ends) as reflecting on what's
gone before (with possible hints of what might come next),
and also saying goodbye, to a clutch of characters and a self-
created world. Despite the redrafting and editing, the weeks
and months and sometimes years it can take to complete a
manuscript, it can be hard to say goodbye. Awkwardness can
slip in. We can say things we don't necessary mean, or at least
don't want aired. We might become muddled and flustered.
Yet, like beginnings, endings can have serious impacts and lasting effects.

One tendency is to rush them, and not to exploit every
potential plot point and dramatic turn. The last ten pages of a
novel should be as important as the first ten (Chandler aside).
Crime writers are in the business of attracting readers to their
work: pulling them in, and then, however many hundreds of
pages (though not too many, please) later, letting them go, satis-
fied but still wanting more. The novel, and especially the crime
novel, is such an extraordinarily flexible, powerful and accommodating form, the opportunities it gives writers are seemingly
endless. However, harnessing and controlling that form is a
two-way mean street. We are attempting to do things our way,
and perhaps make our mark, while also operating within a
genre, however broad and dynamic, which comes with not just

a history and a whole lot of baggage, but expectations. Yes, the horizons are vast and ever-changing, yet we've come to the genre looking for certain things: things that might shock and terrify us, that might enlighten us, but primarily things that engage and entertain us. We want to know where we are, and we don't want to know where we are. It's a very particular 'literary' conundrum.

As a writer there are myriad ways of approaching this. My hope is that this book has revealed some of them, via many of my favourite writers and a few critics and fellow academics. I began this book desperate not to use the term 'literary'; however, as it has progressed the term has crept in more and more – sometimes in single quotation marks (as if I'm still embarrassed to use it), and sometimes nakedly without. At the heart of writing is always this question of genre, of value, of audience. Genre should be inclusive. It is not by an elite for an elite. It is for everybody, which is just one of the reasons why crime fiction is so popular. To consider the other reasons would be to begin this book again, and seek out the brilliant new voices that continue to build and shape the genre with such flair and vitality. Don't stop reading, don't stop learning, don't stop writing. We're in this together, hopefully for the long haul, and to have some fun.

NOTES

Introduction

1   Raymond Chandler, *The Simple Art of Murder* (A Distributed Proofreaders Canada eBook, 2014, from the Howard Mifflin, New York, 1950 edition), 162.

2   www.newwriting.net/2020/05/lee-child-interviewed-by-henry-sutton

3   Henry Sutton, 'Why novelists are turning to Crime', *Sunday Times* (2011).

4   Patricia Highsmith, *Plotting and Writing Suspense Fiction* (London: Sphere, 2016), 65.

5   Henry Sutton, *Gorleston* (London: Sceptre, 1995).

6   https://noirwich.co.uk/attica-locke-the-noirwich-lecture-2020

Chapter 1

1   John le Carré, interviewed by George Plimpton, The Art of Fiction No. 149, *Paris Review* (1997).

2   Kurt Vonnegut, *Bagombo Snuff Box* (London: Vintage, 2000), 4.

3   https://crimereads.com/john-le-carre-offered-a-piece-of-advice-to-a-struggling-novelist-shell-never-forget-it

4   E. M. Forster, *Aspects of the Novel* (London: Penguin Classics, 2005), 87.

5   P. D. James, *Talking about Detective Fiction* (London: Faber, 2010), 12.

6   Margaret Atwood, Happy Endings, https://web.archive.org/web/20180114020928/https://www.galleybeggar.co.uk/y-short-story-prize-classics-atwood

Notes

7   P. D. James, *Talking about*, 90.
8   P. D. James, *Talking about*, 95.
9   Aristotle, *Poetics* (London: Penguin Classics, 1996).
10 Stephen King, *On Writing* (London: Hodder, 2012), 188.
11 Patricia Highsmith, *Plotting*, 38.
12 Patricia Highsmith, *Plotting*, 62.
13 Stephen King, *On Writing*, 190.
14 www.bu.edu/creativewriting/people/faculty/leslie-epstein-program-director
15 Stephen King, *On Writing*, 189.
16 Ruth Rendell, *A Judgement in Stone* (London: Arrow, 1978), 1.
17 Kurt Vonnegut, *Bagombo Snuff Box*, 4.
18 https://ideasimagination.columbia.edu/events/against-storytelling
19 E. M. Forster, *Aspects*, 40.
20 Patricia Highsmith, *Plotting*, viii.
21 Andrew Cowan, *The Art of Writing Fiction* (Harlow: Pearson Education, 2011), 3.
22 Walter Mosley, *Elements of Fiction* (New York: Grove Press, 2020), vi.
23 James M. Cain, *The Postman Always Rings Twice* (London: Orion, 2005), 1.
24 Oyinkan Braithwaite, *My Sister, The Serial Killer* (London: Atlantic Books, 2019), 2.
25 Patricia Highsmith, *The Talented Mr Ripley* (London: Vintage Books, 1999), 5.
26 Denise Mina, *The End of the Wasp Season* (London: Orion, 2012), 1.
27 Val McDermid, *The Mermaids Singing* (London: Harper, 2010), 1.
28 Henry Sutton, *Kids' Stuff* (London; Serpent's Tail, 2004), 1.
29 Stephen King, *On Writing*, 136.
30 James M. Cain, interviewed by David Zinsser, The Art of Fiction No. 69, *Paris Review* (1978).
31 Quoted in *Kids' Stuff*, 2005 edition
32 https://www.mulhollandbooks.com/books/the-dark-heart-of-noir/
33 Walter Mosley, *Elements*, 74.
34 Martin Amis, *Night Train* (London: Vintage, 1998), 1.
35 Andrea Camilleri, *Scent of the Night* (London: Picador, 2007), 3.
36 Elmore Leonard, *10 Rules of Writing* (London: Weidenfeld & Nicolson, 2010), 49.
37 https://languages.oup.com/dictionaries

Notes

Chapter 2

1   Walter Mosley, *Elements*, 75.
2   Elmore Leonard, *10 Rules*, 47.
3   Patricia Highsmith, *Plotting*, 48
4   Patricia Highsmith, *The Talented Mr Ripley* (London: Vintage, 1999), 91.
5   Patricia Highsmith, *Plotting*, 76, 77.
6   Patricia Highsmith, *Plotting*, 49.
7   Andrew Cowan, *The Art of*, 83.
8   Andrew Cowan, *The Art of*, 85, 86.
9   Elizabeth Bowen, *Notes on Writing A Novel*, www.narrativemagazine.com/issues/fall-2006/classics/notes-writing-novel-elizabeth-bowen
10 E. M. Forster, *Aspects*, 73.
11 Andrew Cowan, *The Art of*, 99
12 Andrew Cowan, *The Art of*, 98, 99.
13 Patricia Highsmith, *Plotting*, 20, 21.
14 Raymond Chandler, *The Simple Art*, 227.
15 https://mysteryreadersinc.blogspot.com/2009/10/val-mcdermid-place-of-execution.html
16 Val McDermid, *The Mermaids*, 1.
17 Thomas De Quincey, *On Murder Considered One of the Fine Arts* (London: Penguin, 2015).
18 Thomas Harris, *The Silence of the Lambs* (London: Arrow Books, 2013), 257.
19 James Wood, *How Fiction Works* (London: Jonathan Cape, 2008), 75.
20 Elmore Leonard, *10 Rules*, 15.
21 Tony Parsons, author endorsement, 2010.
22 *Guardian*, 2010.
23 www.valmcdermid.com/interview-the-perception-of-crime-fiction
24 Ruth Rendell interviewed by Alison Flood, *Guardian*, 1 March, 2013.
25 Patricia Highsmith, *Plotting*, 40.
26 Henry Sutton, *Get Me Out Of Here* (London: Harvill Secker, 2010), 26, 27.

Chapter 3

1   Arne Dahl, *The Blinded Man* (London: Vintage, 2012).
2   Belinda Bauer, *Exit* (London: Bantam, 2021).

Notes

3 Ruth Ware, *The Death of Mrs Westaway* (London: Vintage Digital, 2018).

4 November–December 2007 issue *World Literature Today* (University of Oklahoma), 39, 40.

5 www.newyorker.com/books/page-turner/t-s-eliot-was-wrong

6 https://quoteinvestigator.com/tag/w-h-davenport-adams

7 Jean Hanff Korelitz, *The Plot* (London: Faber, 2021), 64.

8 Jean Hanff Korelitz, *The Plot*, 227.

9 Derek Attridge, *The Singularity of Literature* (London: Routledge Classics, 2017), 150.

10 Andrew Cowan, *The Art of*, 180.

11 John Gardner, *On Becoming a Novelist* (New York: Norton, 2000), 5.

12 James M. Cain, *The Postman Always Rings Twice* (London: Orion, 2005 (1934)), 1.

13 Patricia Highsmith, *The Talented Mr Ripley* (London: Vintage, 1999 (1955)), 5.

14 Maj Sjöwall & Per Wahlöö, *Roseanna* (London: Harper Perennial, 2006 (1965)), 1.

15 Chester Himes, *A Rage in Harlem* (London: Penguin Classics, 2011 (1957)), 1.

16 Val McDermid, *The Mermaids Singing* (London: Harper, 2010 (1995)), 1.

17 Raymond Chandler, *The Big Sleep* (London: Penguin, 2005 (1939)), 1.

18 Ruth Rendell, *A Judgement in Stone* (London: Arrow Books, 1978 (1977)), 1.

19 Dorothy B. Hughes, *In A Lonely Place* (London: Penguin Classics, 2010 (1942)), 7.

20 Walter Mosley, *Devil in a Blue Dress* (London: Serpent's Tail, 2020 (1990)), 1.

21 Ted Lewis, *Get Carter* (London: Allison & Busby, 2013 (1970)), 7.

22 Denise Mina, *The End of the Wasp Season* (London: Orion, 2012 (2011)), 1.

23 Tom Benn, *Oxblood* (London: Bloomsbury, 2022 (2022)), 1.

24 Jane Harper, *The Dry* (London: Abacus, 2017 (2016)), 1.

25 Femi Kayode, *Light Seekers* (London: Raven Books, 2021 (2021)).

26 Oyinkan Braithwaite, *My Sister The Serial Killer* (London: Atlantic, 2019 (2017)), 1.

27 Leye Adenle, *When Trouble Sleeps* (London: Cassava Republic, 2018 (2018)), 1.

28 Attica Locke, *Black Water Rising* (London: Serpent's Tail, 2009 (2009)), 1.

29 Natsuo Kirino, *Grotesque* (London: Harvill Secker, 2007 (2003)), 3.

30 Nikki May, *Wahala* (London: Penguin, 2022), 1.

Notes

31 Fernanda Melchor, *Hurricane Season* (London: Fitzcarraldo Editions, 2020 (2017)), 7.

32 Ted Lewis, *Get Carter*, 7.

33 Ted Lewis, *Get Carter*, 31.

34 Cathi Unsworth, ed., *London Noir* (New York: Akashic, 2006).

35 Barry Forshaw, *Brit Noir* (Harpenden: Pocket Essentials, 2016).

36 Nick Triplow, *Getting Carter: Ted Lewis and the Birth of Brit Noir* (Harpenden: No Exit Press, 2017).

37 Graham Greene, *A Gun for Sale* (London: Vintage, 2009), 1.

38 Graham Greene, *A Gun for Sale*, ix.

39 Raymond Chandler, *The Big Sleep*, 1.

40 Raymond Chander, *Killer in the Rain* (London: Penguin, 1966), 13, 103.

41 Margaret Atwood, *Negotiating with the Dead: A Writer on Writing* (London: Virago, 2013), 43, 44.

42 Margaret Atwood, *Negotiating*, 45.

43 David Damrosch, Theo Haen & Louise Nilsson, eds, *Crime Fiction as World Literature* (London: Bloomsbury, 2017), 94.

44 Dorothy L. Sayers, 'Aristotle on Detective Fiction' (Oxford: *Journal of the English Association*, Vol 1, Issue 1, 1936) 24.

45 Jean Hanff Korelitz, *The Plot*, 231.

46 James Patterson, interviewed by Henry Sutton (*Independent on Sunday*, 14 September, 2008).

47 R. D. Wingfield, *Frost at Christmas* (London: Corgi, 1992), 11.

48 James Henry, *First Frost* (London: Bantam Press, 2011), 1.

Chapter 4

1   Ted Lewis, *Get Carter*, 7.

2   Raymond Chandler, *The Big Sleep*, 1.

3   Ian Rankin, *Let It Bleed* (London: Orion, 2008), 3.

4   Steph Cha, *Follow Her Home* (London: Faber, 2020), 1.

5   Henry Sutton, *My Criminal World* (London: Harvill Secker, 2013), 7.

6   Elmore Leonard, *10 Rules*, 5.

7   Elmore Leonard, *Get Shorty* (London: Phoenix, 2009), 1.

8   Elmore Leonard, *10 Rules*, 7.

9   David R. Slavitt, *Aspects of the Novel: A Novel* (North Haven, CT: Catbird Press, 2003).

10 Elmore Leonard, *Get Shorty*, 58.

Notes

11 Elmore Leonard, *Get Shorty*, 54.

12 Elmore Leonard, *Get Shorty*, 166.

13 Jim Thompson, *The Killer Inside Me* (London: Orion, 2010), 161.

14 Elmore Leonard, *10 Rules*, 55.

15 Margaret Atwood, *Good Bones* (London: Virago, 2010), 41, 42.

16 Sjöwall & Wahlöö, *Roseanna*, 50.

17 Sjöwall & Wahlöö, *Roseanna*, 12.

18 Sjöwall & Wahlöö, *Roseanna*, 44.

19 Val McDermid, Forensics: *The Anatomy of Crime* (London: Profile Books, 2014), ix.

20 www.valmcdermid.com/interview-the-perception-of-crime-fiction

21 Stuart Turton, *The Seven Deaths of Evelyn Hardcastle* (London: Raven, 2018).

22 Eleanor Catton, *The Luminaries* (London: Granta, 2013).

23 Abir Mukherjee, *A Rising Man* (London: Harvill Secker, 2017), 1.

24 Abir Mukherjee, *A Rising Man*, 3.

25 https://abirmukherjee.com/what-happened

26 Abir Mukherjee, *A Rising Man*, 1–2.

27 Isabel Ostrander, *Ashes to Ashes* (London: Forgotten Books, 2018) 1.

28 John Buchan, *The Thirty-Nine Steps* (London: Hodder & Stoughton, 2015), 1.

29 Agatha Christie, *The Secret Adversary* (London: HarperCollins, 2015), i.

30 Agatha Christies, *Secret*, 5

31 Abir Mukherjee, *A Rising Man*, 1.

32 Henry Sutton, *Bank Holiday Monday* (London: Sceptre, 1996).

33 Henry Sutton, *My Criminal World*, 7.

34 Henry Sutton, *My Criminal World*, 8.

35 https://mysteryreadersinc.blogspot.com/2009/10/val-mcdermid-place-of-execution.html

Chapter 5

1 www.uealive.com/features/people-and-paper

2 Heather Martin, *The Reacher Guy: The Authorised Biography of Lee Child* (London: Constable, 2020), 361.

3 Stephen King, *On Writing*, 188.

4 Patricia Highsmith, *Plotting*, 38.

5 Louise Doughty, *Apple Tree Yard* (London: Faber & Faber, 2014).

Notes

6 Heather Martin, *The Reacher Guy*, 212.

7 Heather Martin, *The Reacher Guy*, 212.

8 Heather Martin, *The Reacher Guy*, 208.

9 Lee Child, *61 Hours* (London: Transworld, 2010).

10 Patricia Highsmith, *Plotting*, 73.

11 Patricia Highsmith, *Plotting*, 75.

12 Aristotle, *Poetics* (London: Penguin Classics, 1996), 11.

13 John Yorke, *Into the Woods* (New York: Overlook Press, 2014), 24–44.

14 Heather Martin, *The Reacher Guy*, 405.

15 Charlotte Higgins, 'Fearless, Free and Feminist', *Guardian* (18/10/19).

16 Patricia Highsmith, *Plotting*, 42, 65.

17 Patricia Highsmith, *Plotting*, 63.

18 Linwood Barclay in *How To Write A Mystery*, ed. Lee Child with Laurie R. King (New York: Scribner, 2021), 39.

19 Raymond Chandler, *Trouble Is My Business and Other Stories* (New York: Ballantine Books, 1980), i–x.

20 Raymond Chandler, *Trouble*, viii–ix.

21 Raymond Chandler, in *Noir Film & Film: Diversions and Misdirections*, Lee Clark Mitchell (Oxford: Oxford University Press, 2021), 219.

22 Tom Hiney and Frank MacShane, eds, *The Raymond Chandler Papers: Selected Letters and Nonfiction, 1909–1959* (New York: Grove Press & Atlantic Monthly Press, 2002), 218.

23 Raymond Chandler, *Killer in the Rain* (London: Penguin, 1966), 13–59, 103–144.

24 Grace Paley, interviewed by Jonathan Dee, Barbara Jones and Larissa MacFarquhar, The Art of Fiction No. 131, *Paris Review* (1992).

25 https://theamericanscholar.org/every-story-is-two-stories

26 Eudora Welty, 'On Writing', *The Eye of the Story* (New York: Vintage International, 1990), 85.

27 Eudora Welty, 'On Writing', *The Eye of the Story*, 134.

28 Henry Sutton, 'The Wrong Goose', first published in *Norwich Resident*, December 2013.

29 Julie Myerson, *Nonfiction: A Novel* (London: Corsair, 2022), 60.

30 Julie Myerson, *Nonfiction*, 61.

31 Megan Abbott, *Dare Me* (London: Picador, 2012), 1–2.

32 Austin Wright, Tony & Susan (London: Atlantic Books, 2010).

33 Gillian Flynn, *Gone Girl* (London: Weidenfeld & Nicolson, 2013).

34 Val McDermid, *The Skelton Road* (London: Sphere, 2015).

35 Paula Hawkins, *Girl on the Train* (London: Doubleday, 2015).

Notes

36 Ian McEwan, *The Cement Garden* (London: Vintage, 1997 (1978)).
37 c/o Felicity Bryan Associates, literary agency.

Chapter 6

1 James Patterson, interviewed by Henry Sutton, *Independent on Sunday* (14 September 2008). (Some quotes from the full transcript of the taped interview were not printed in the article.)
2 James Patterson interview, *Independent on Sunday*.
3 James Patterson and Maxine Paetro, *22 Seconds* (London: Penguin, 2022), 8.
4 James Patterson and Maxine Paetro, *22 Seconds*, 13.
5 James Patterson, *The Thomas Berryman Number* (New York: Grand Central Publishing, 2006 (1976)).
6 William Strunk, Jr and E. B. White, *The Elements of Style* (4th edition) (New York: Pearson 2022 (1935)).
7 Stephen King, *On Writing*, 152.
8 Heather Martin, *The Reacher Guy*, 209.
9 Eleanor Catton, *The Luminaries*, 3.
10 James M. Cain, *Double Indemnity* (London: Orion, 2005), 1.
11 Patricia Highsmith, *Plotting*, 49.
12 Patricia Highsmith, *Plotting*, 50.
13 Sara Paretsky, *Breakdown* (London: Hodder & Stoughton, 2012), 1.
14 Denise Mina, *Wasp Season*, 339.
15 Densie Mina, *Wasp Season*, 35.
16 Denise Mina, *Wasp Season*, 387.
17 Denise Mina, *Wasp Season*, 1.
18 Denise Mina, *Wasp Season*, 44.
19 Denise Mina, *Wasp Season*, 44.
20 Iain Banks, *The Wasp Factory* (London: Abacus, 2013 (1984)).
21 E. M. Forster, *Aspects*, 134.
22 E. M. Forster, *Aspects*, 85–100.
23 David Chase, *The Sopranos*, HBO, 1999–2007.
24 Henry Sutton, *Gorleston* (London: Sceptre, 1995).
25 Harry Brett, *Time to Win* (London: Corsair, 2017).
26 Harry Brett, *Time to Win*, 1.
27 James Sallis, *Drive* (Harpenden: No Exit Press, 2011), 9.

Notes

Chapter 7

1   Mitchell, Clark Lee, *Noir Film & Film*, 219.
2   Patricia Highsmith, *Plotting*, 38.
3   Heather Martin, *The Reacher Guy*, 209.
4   E. M. Forster, *Aspects*, 88.
5   E. M. Forster, *Aspects*, 88.
6   David Lodge, *The Art of Fiction* (London: Vintage, 2011), 31.
7   Neil Nyren, 'The Rules and When to Break Them', *How To Write A Mystery*, 6.
8   Tzvetan Todorov, 'The Typology of Detective Fiction' in *Crime and Media*, ed. Chris Greer (London: Routledge, 2010), Ch. 22.
9   Leye Adenle, *When Trouble Sleeps* (Abuja, London: Cassava Republic Press, 2018), 133.
10 Leye Adenle, *Trouble*, 134.
11 David Lodge, *The Art of Fiction*, 72.
12 Andrew Cowan, *The Art of Writing Fiction*, 182.
13 Andrew Cowan, *The Art of Writing Fiction*, 179.
14 Leye Adenle, *Trouble*, 167–169.
15 David Lodge, *The Art of Fiction*, 31.
16 Anthony Trollope, *Autobiography* (1883): http://www.literaturepage.com/read/trollope-autobiography.html
17 As relayed by Louise Welsh, to a crime writing class held with Henry Sutton at Theakston's Old Peculier Crime Writing Festival, Harrogate, 2017.
18 Ruth Rendell, interviewed by Alison Flood, *Guardian* (1 March 2013).
19 Harry Brett, *Red Hot Front* (London: Corsair, 2018).
20 Harry Brett, *Good Dark Night* (London: Corsair, 2019).

Chapter 8

1   Natsuo Kirino, *Out* (London: Vintage, 2004), 1.
2   Paula Hawkins, *The Girl on the Train* (London: Doubleday, 2015) 7.
3   Natsuo Kirino, *Out*, 520.
4   Paula Hawkins, *The Girl on the Train*, 316.
5   Jo Nesbø, *The Leopard* (London: Vintage, 2011), 8.
6   Jeff Lindsay, *Darkly Dreaming Dexter* (London: Orion, 2005).
7   Luke Jennings, *Codename Villanelle* (London: John Murray, 2017).

Notes

8 As quote on the inside cover of the UK paperback, *Gone Girl* (London: Weidenfeld & Nicolson, 2013).

9 Also quote on the inside second page of the UK paperback, *Gone Girl*.

10 Gillian Flynn, *Gone Girl*, 356.

11 Clive Bloom in Christine Berberich's introduction to *The Bloomsbury Introduction to Popular Fiction*, ed. Christine Berberich (London: Bloomsbury Academic, 2015), 4.

12 Bran Nicol, 'The Hard-Boiled Detective: Dashiell Hammett', *The Bloomsbury Introduction to Popular Fiction*, 241.

13 Raymond Chandler, *Art of Murder*, 162.

14 Raymond Chandler, *Art of Murder*, 162.

15 Raymond Chandler, *Art of Murder*, 174.

16 Graham Greene, *Travels With My Aunt* (London: Vintage, 2020), 119.

17 Graham Greene, introduction, *Travels With My Aunt* (London: Vintage Classics, 1999), 6.

18 Carl Hiaasen, *Razor Girl* (New York: Vintage Crime, 2019), 3.

19 Carl Hiaasen, *Nature Girl* (London: Bantam Press, 2006), 3.

20 Carl Hiaasen, *Skinny Dip* (London: Bantam Press, 2004), 1.

21 Elmore Leonard, *Freaky Deaky* (London: Phoenix, 2009), 1.

22 Elmore Leonard, *Be Cool* (London: Phoenix, 2010), 1.

23 Oyinkan Braithwaite, *My Sister, The Serial Killer*, 9.

24 Oyinkan Braithwaite, *My Sister, The Serial Killer*, 9–12.

25 Kate Atkinson, *Case Histories* (London: Transworld Digital, 2010), 15.

26 Naomi Hirahara, 'Insider, Outside: The Amateur Sleuth', *How To Write A Mystery*, 23.

27 Henry Sutton, *Der Hotel-Inspektor Auf Mallorca* (Zurich: Kampa, 2021).

28 Henry Sutton, *Eine Aussicht Zum Sterben, Der Hotel-Insektor in New York* (Zurich: Kampa, 2022).

29 Henry Sutton, *Der Hotel-Inspektor, Massif de Mont Blanc* (Zurich: Kampa, 2023).

Chapter 9

1 Belinda Brett, *Mother* (London: Piatkus, 1998), her last novel.

2 Caroline Wood, Director, Felicity Bryan Associates.

3 Matthew Salesses, *Craft in the Real World* (New York: Catapult, 2021), 5.

4 Matthew Salesses, *Craft*, 14, 15.

5 Mick Herron, 'The Joy of Crime Fiction', *Guardian* (31 July 2022).

Notes

6 John Banville talking to Henry Sutton, 'Why novelists are turning to crime', *The Times*, 2012.

7 Benjamin Black, *The Black-Eyed Blonde* (London: Mantle, 2014), 1–3.

8 William Faulkner, interviewed by Jean Stein, The Art of Fiction No. 12, *Paris Review*, 1956.

9 William Faulkner, *Intruder in the Dust* (London: Vintage, 1996 (1948)).

10 Tim Parks, Quite A Show: Georges Simenon, *London Review of Books* (8 October 2014).

11 Tim Parks, *Painting Death* (London: Harvill Secker, 2014).

12 https://timparks.com/novels

13 Walter Mosley, *Elements*, 74.

14 Patricia Highsmith, *Plotting*, viii.

15 Ronald Knox, Ten Commandments or Decalogue, from his introduction to *The Best English Detective Stories of 1928* (New York: Horace Liveright, 1929). Variously available online: www.writingclasses.com/toolbox/tips-masters/ronald-knox-10-commandments-of-detective-fiction

16 S. S. Van Dine, 'Twenty Rules for Writing Detective Stories', *American Magazine* (New York: 1928). Variously available online: www.speedcitysistersincrime.org/ss-van-dine---twenty-rules-for-writing-detective-stories.html

17 Matthew Salesses, *Craft*, 169.

18 Elmore Leonard, *Get Shorty*, 134, 135.

19 John Seely, *Oxford A–Z of Grammar & Punctuation* (Oxford: Oxford University Press, 2013 (2004)).

20 Andrew Cowan, *The Art of Writing Fiction*, 44.

21 Stephen King, *On Writing*, 266.

Conclusion

1 Raymond Chandler: 'The technical basis of the *Black Mask* type of story on the other hand was that the scene outranked the plot, in the sense that a good plot was one which made good scenes. The ideal mystery was one you would read if the end was missing.' From The Simple Art of Murder, *Trouble is My Business*, 1950 version (London: Vintage Books, 1988).

2 Gillian Flynn, *Gone Girl*, 463.

3 Elmore Leonard, *Get Shorty*, 275.

4 Henry Sutton, *Der Hotel-Inspektor auf Mont Blanc de Massif* (Zurich: Kampa, 2023).

BIBLIOGRAPHY

Abbott, Megan, *Dare Me* (London: Picador, 2012).

Adenle, Leye, *When Trouble Sleeps* (London: Cassava Republic, 2018).

Amis, Martin, *Night Train* (London: Vintage, 1998 (1997)).

Aristotle, *Poetics* (London and New York: Penguin Classics, 1996).

Atkinson, Kate, *Case Histories* (London: Transworld Digital, 2010 (2004)).

Attridge, Derek, *The Singularity of Literature* (London: Routledge Classics, 2017).

Atwood, Margaret, *Good Bones* (London: Virago, 2010 (1993)).

Atwood, Margaret, *Negotiating with the Dead: A Writer on Writing* (London: Virago, 2013 (2003)).

Banks, Iain, *The Wasp Factory* (London: Abacus, 2013 (1984)).

Bauer, Belinda, *Exit* (London: Bantam, 2021 (2020)).

Benn, Tom, *Oxblood* (London: Bloomsbury, 2022 (2022)).

Berberich, Christine, ed., *The Bloomsbury Introduction to Popular Fiction* (London: Bloomsbury Academic, 2015).

Black, Benjamin, *The Black-Eyed Blonde* (London: Mantle, 2014).

Bloom, Clive, *Bestsellers: Popular Fiction Since 1900* (Basingstoke & New York: Palgrave Macmillan, 2002).

Braithwaite, Oyinkan, *My Sister, The Serial Killer* (London: Atlantic Books, 2019 (2017)).

Brett, Belinda, *Mother* (London: Piatkus, 1998).

Brett, Harry, *Good Dark Night* (London: Corsair, 2019).

Brett, Harry, *Red Hot Front* (London: Corsair, 2018).

Brett, Harry, *Time to Win* (London: Corsair, 2017).

Buchan, John, *The Thirty-Nine Steps* (London: Hodder & Stoughton, 2015 (1915)).

Bibliography

Cain, James M., *Double Indemnity* (London: Orion, 2005).

Cain, James M., *The Postman Always Rings Twice* (London: Orion, 2005 (1934)).

Camilleri, Andrea, *Scent of the Night* (London: Picador, 2007 (2000)).

Catton, Eleanor, *The Luminaries* (London: Granta, 2013).

Cha, Steph, *Follow Her Home* (London: Faber, 2020).

Chandler, Raymond, *Killer in the Rain* (London: Penguin, 1966 (1964)).

Chandler, Raymond, *The Big Sleep* (London: Penguin, 2005 (1939)).

Chandler, Raymond, *The Simple Art of Murder* (A Distributed Proofreaders Canada eBook, 2014, from the Howard Mifflin, New York, 1950, edition).

Chandler, Raymond, *Trouble Is My Business and Other Stories* (New York: Ballantine Books, 1980).

Child, Lee, *61 Hours* (London: Transworld, 2010).

Child, Lee, with Laurie R. King, *How To Write A Mystery* (New York: Scribner, 2021).

Christie, Agatha, *The Secret Adversary* (London: HarperCollins, 2015 (1922)).

Collins, Wilkie, *The Woman in White* (London: Collins Classics, 2011 (1859)).

Cowan, Andrew, *The Art of Writing Fiction* (Harlow: Pearson Education, 2011).

Dahl, Arne, *The Blinded Man* (London: Vintage, 2012).

Damrosch, David, Haen, Theo and Nilsson, Louise, eds, *Crime Fiction as World Literature* (London: Bloomsbury, 2017).

De Quincey, Thomas, *On Murder Considered One of the Fine Arts* (London: Penguin, 2015 (1827)).

Dick, Philip K., *Do Androids Dream Of Electric Sheep?* (London: Gollancz, 2007 (1968)).

Doughty, Louise, *Apple Tree Yard* (London: Faber & Faber, 2014).

Faulkner, William, *Intruder in the Dust* (London: Vintage, 1996 (1948)).

Flynn, Gillian, *Gone Girl* (London: Weidenfeld & Nicolson, 2013 (2012)).

Forshaw, Barry, *Brit Noir* (Harpenden: Pocket Essentials, 2016).

Forster, E. M., *Aspects of the Novel* (London: Penguin Classics, 2005 (1927)).

Gardner, John, *On Becoming a Novelist* (New York: Norton, 2000).

Greene, Graham, *A Gun for Sale* (London: Vintage, 2009 (1936)).

Greene, Graham, *Travels With My Aunt* (London: Vintage, 2020 (1969)).

Hanff Korelitz, Jean, *The Plot* (London: Faber, 2021 (2020)).

Harper, Jane, *The Dry* (London: Abacus, 2017 (2016)).

Harris, Thomas, *The Silence of the Lambs* (London: Arrow Books, 2013 (1989)).

Bibliography

Hawkins, Paula, *Girl on the Train* (London: Doubleday, 2015).

Henry, James, *First Frost* (London: Bantam Press, 2011).

Hiaasen, Carl, *Nature Girl* (London: Bantam Press, 2006).

Hiaasen, Carl, *Razor Girl* (New York: Vintage Crime, 2019).

Hiaasen, Carl, *Skinny Dip* (London: Bantam Press, 2004).

Highsmith, Patricia, *Plotting and Writing Suspense Fiction* (London: Sphere, 2016 (1983)).

Highsmith, Patricia, *The Talented Mr Ripley* (London: Vintage Books, 1999 (1955)).

Himes, Chester, *A Rage in Harlem* (London: Penguin Classics, 2011 (1957)).

Hiney, Tom and MacShane, Frank, eds, *The Raymond Chandler Papers: Selected Letters and Nonfiction, 1909–1959* (New York: Grove Press & Atlantic Monthly Press, 2002).

Hughes, Dorothy B. *In A Lonely Place* (London: Penguin Classics, 2010 (1942)).

James, P. D., *Talking about Detective Fiction* (London: Faber, 2010 (2009)).

Jennings, Luke, *Codename Villanelle* (London: John Murray, 2017 (2014–2016)).

Kirino, Natsuo, *Grotesque* (London: Harvill Secker, 2007 (2003)).

Kirino, Natsuo, *Out* (London: Vintage, 2004)

Kayode, Femi, *Light Seekers* (London: Raven Books, 2021 (2021)).

King, Stephen, *On Writing* (London: Hodder, 2012),

Lemon, Lee T., and Reis, Marion J., *Russian Formalist Criticism: Four Essays* (Lincoln: University of Nebraska Press, 1965).

Leonard, Elmore, *10 Rules of Writing* (London: Weidenfeld & Nicolson, 2010).

Leonard, Elmore, *Be Cool* (London: Phoenix, 2010 (1999)).

Leonard, Elmore, *Freaky Deaky* (London: Phoenix, 2009 (1988)).

Leonard, Elmore, *Get Shorty* (London: Phoenix, 2009 (1990)).

Lewis, Ted, *Get Carter* (London: Allison & Busby, 2013 (1970)).

Lindsay, Jeff, *Darkly Dreaming Dexter* (London: Orion, 2005 (2004)).

Locke, Attica, *Black Water Rising* (London: Serpent's Tail, 2009).

Lodge, David, *The Art of Fiction* (London: Vintage, 2011 (1992)).

May, Nikki, *Wahala* (London: Penguin, 2022).

Martin, Heather, *The Reacher Guy: The Authorised Biography of Lee Child* (London: Constable, 2020).

McDermid, Val, *Forensics: The Anatomy of Crime* (London: Profile Books, 2014).

McDermid, Val, *The Mermaids Singing* (London: Harper, 2010 (1995)).

Bibliography

McDermid, Val, *The Skelton Road* (London: Sphere, 2015 (2014)).

McEwan, Ian, *The Cement Garden* (London: Vintage, 1997 (1978)).

Melchor, Fernanda, *Hurricane Season* (London: Fitzcarraldo Editions, 2020 (2017)).

Miéville, China, *The City & the City* (London: Pan, 2011 (2009)).

Mina, Denise, *The End of the Wasp Season* (London: Orion, 2012 (2011)).

Mitchell, Clark Lee, *Noir Film & Film: Diversions and Misdirections* (Oxford: Oxford University Press, 2021).

Mosely, Walter, *Devil in a Blue Dress* (London: Serpent's Tail, 2020 (1990)).

Mosley, Walter, *Elements of Fiction* (New York: Grove Press, 2020 (2019)).

Mukherjee, Abir, *A Rising Man* (London: Harvill Secker, 2017).

Myerson, Julie, *Nonfiction: A Novel* (London: Corsair, 2022).

Nesbo, Jo, *The Leopard* (London: Vintage, 2011 (2009)).

Ostrander, Isabel, *Ashes to Ashes* (London: Forgotten Books, 2018 (1919)).

Paretsky, Sara, *Breakdown* (London: Hodder & Stoughton, 2012).

Parks, Tim, *Painting Death* (London: Harvill Secker, 2014).

Patterson, James, *The Thomas Berryman Number* (New York: Grand Central Publishing, 2006 (1976)).

Patterson, James, and Paetro, Maxine, *22 Seconds* (London: Penguin, 2022).

Pinborough, Sarah, *Behind Her Eyes* (London: HarperCollins, 2017).

Rankin, Ian, *Let It Bleed* (London: Orion, 2008 (1996)).

Rendell, Ruth, *A Judgement in Stone* (London: Arrow, 1978 (1977)).

Sallis, James, *Drive* (Harpenden: No Exit Press, 2011 (2006)).

Salesses, Matthew, *Craft in the Real World* (New York: Catapult, 2021).

Sayers, Dorothy, L. 'Aristotle on Detective Fiction' (Oxford: Journal of the English Association, Vol 1, Issue 1, 1936).

Seely, John, *Oxford A–Z of Grammar & Punctuation* (Oxford: Oxford University Press, 2013 (2004)).

Sjöwall, Maj, and Wahlöö, Per, *Roseanna* (London: Harper Perennial, 2006 (1965)).

Slavitt, David, R., *Aspects of the Novel: A Novel* (North Haven: Catbird Press, 2003).

Strunk, William, Jr, and White, E. B., *The Elements of Style* (4th edition) (New York: Pearson 2022 (1935).

Sutton, Henry, *Bank Holiday Monday* (London: Sceptre, 1996).

Sutton, Henry, *Der Hotel-Inspektor Auf Mallorca* (Zurich: Kampa, 2021).

Sutton, Henry, *Der Hotel-Inspektor, Massif de Mont Blanc* (Zurich: Kampa, 2023).

Bibliography

Sutton, Henry, *Eine Aussicht Zum Sterben, Der Hotel-Inspektor in New York* (Zurich: Kampa, 2022).

Sutton, Henry, *Get Me Out Of Here* (London: Harvill Secker, 2010).

Sutton, Henry, *Gorleston* (London: Sceptre, 1995).

Sutton, Henry, *Kids' Stuff* (London; Serpent's Tail, 2004).

Sutton, Henry, *My Criminal World* (London: Harvill Secker, 2013).

Thompson, Jim, *The Killer Inside Me* (London: Orion, 2010 (1952)).

Triplow, Nick, *Getting Carter: Ted Lewis and the Birth of Brit Noir* (Harpenden: No Exit Press, 2017).

Trollope, Anthony, *Autobiography* (1883).

Turton, Stuart, *The Seven Deaths of Evelyn Hardcastle* (London: Raven, 2018).

Unsworth, Cathi, ed., *London Noir* (New York: Akashic, 2006).

Vonnegut, Kurt, *Bagombo Snuff Box* (London: Vintage, 2000 (1999)).

Ware, Ruth, *The Death of Mrs Westaway* (London: Vintage Digital, 2018).

Waters, Sarah, *Fingersmith* (London: Virago, 2002).

Welty, Eudora, 'On Writing', *The Eye of the Story* (New York: Vintage International, 1990).

Wingfield, R. D., *Frost at Christmas* (London: Corgi, 1992 (1984)).

Wood, James, *How Fiction Works* (London: Jonathan Cape, 2008).

Wright, Austin, *Tony & Susan* (London: Atlantic Books, 2010 (1993)).

Yorke, John, *Into the Woods* (New York: Overlook Press, 2014).

INDEX

Index

Index

Index

Index

Index